GW01219598

The Illusion of Everything

Deirdre McMahon

Text Copyright © Deirdre McMahon
Deirdre McMahon has asserted her right in accordance with the Copyright Designs and Patents Act 1988 to be identified as the author of this work.

All rights reserved.

No part of this publication may be lent, resold, hired out or reproduced in any form or by any means without prior written permission from the author and publisher. All rights reserved.

Copyright © 3P Publishing
First published in 2021 in the UK

3P Publishing
C E C, London Road
Corby
NN17 5EU

A catalogue number for this book is available from the British Library

ISBN: 978-1-913740-19-1

Cover design: James Mossop

For my girls

Contents

Introduction	**1**
1. The Reunion	**6**
2. The Hypothesis	**27**
3. The Plan	**40**
4. The Illusion of Reality	**61**
5. The Illusion of Self	**78**
6. The Illusion of Form	**88**
7. The Illusion of Possibility	**106**
8. The Illusion of Sin	**122**
9. The Illusion of Evolution	**150**
10. The Illusion of Everything	**169**
11. Conclusion	**210**
About the Author	**225**

Introduction

'Science without religion is lame, religion without science is blind.' - Albert Einstein

Science and religion need each other. Religion needs science to weed out all of the dark and fearful nonsense that it has imposed on us throughout the ages, and science needs religion to make sense of its godless collection of elementary particles and fundamental forces. Many scientists would disagree with the latter and maintain that science does not need God at all, that science works very well without God, thank you very much. However, there is no denying the inherent longing that exists in all of us, scientists included, to find some meaning in our lives or some answers to some very difficult existential questions. Questions that lie outside of the realm of the very cold and complex scientific equations of the universe. Hard, head-wrecking questions, such as why are we here, what is it all about, why is it that we can inflict so much hurt on each other when we are capable of so much love, and why is it that I end up in the slowest-moving queues every time? These are questions that particle physics and quantum calculations struggle with or totally ignore, but are the questions that are probably the most important to us as humans. 'Reason' is what we search for in religion. While the job of science is to tell us 'how' it all works, religion endeavours to give us the great 'why' of it all. Religion, however, has a tendency to run away with itself and that is why we need science. Nothing divides us and unites us quite as extremely as our spiritual beliefs. Our different religious notions and ideologies, most of which seem to have been plucked out of thin air and handed down from generation to generation, have been as catastrophic as they have been beneficial to humanity. We ferociously cling to our acquired religious identities because they not only give us reason or solace in our most difficult times, but often, and much more importantly to our fickle human nature, they also make us 'right' and someone else 'wrong'. This is especially puzzling since most major religions agree on all the fundamental issues of love and unity.

That being said, religion has played puck with our ignorance and insecurities for as long as we have been here. If we really want to find the spiritual truth we crave so deeply, we need science. We need to use objective, scientific investigation instead of assumptions made through scholastic knowledge or even intellectuality. If we are to have any hope of figuring out what is really going on in this crazy existence, we need to line up what science is telling us about the nature of reality with its corresponding spiritual rationale. When we do, we might find that science and religion have more in common than either of them cares to admit.

As a nurse, I had always been in awe of the profound intelligence and utmost beauty in the biology and physiology of life. When you study the human body, it is impossible not to be impacted by the sheer genius of its condition. Physics, not so much. I had found it hard to be passionate about so many numbers, formulas and symbols and most of them went clean over my head in a steady stream of blah, blah, blahs. By some miracle I did manage to pass my biophysics exam all those years ago, but more recently I have found that physics doesn't have to be so impossibly difficult and it can be every bit as beautiful as the biology of life. After all, it is the science of physics that creates and coordinates all of the wonders that life and living affords us. So, if we want answers, we have to suck it up and get acquainted with a little bit of physics.

For my part, I got dragged back into its labyrinth of protons, neutrons and electrons by a crazy, grey horse that I did not want, so that I could be reminded of a fundamental truth that life in this realm had caused me to forget: that the same spirit that dwells in one dwells in all, regardless of the form we take. I also discovered that life is no more than an illusion of form and feeling where the only thing that is real is the experience and the only truth is its perspective.

To date, science has uncovered some fairly solid facts about the nature of reality, but plenty of uncertainties yet prevail. Religion is riddled with uncertainties, so both disciplines could benefit from a little collaboration. Sometimes, when we want to get to the truth of something, we have to be prepared to start anew, to suspend our biases and beliefs, to ask simple questions and to expect the unexpected. When I first started writing this book, I thought I was writing about an untamed rescue horse that had randomly arrived in my care. I had no idea that it would evolve into a mediation between religion and science but, as it progressed, I realised that our meeting had been no accident, for either of us. I realised that no meeting, for anyone, ever, is by accident. If we look closely enough, at the science and at the religion, we will find that meticulous planning is something they both can agree on. That the laws of physics and God's will or destiny are simply different names for the same phenomenon. Nothing is random or by chance. This horse was no fluke. Our serendipitous reunion on this physical plane had been scheduled since the beginning of time itself. And that was just for starters. It soon became apparent to me that so much more than our meeting had been divinely orchestrated. An undeniable connection with this challenging equine made me realise that I had never taken a 'wrong' turn or made a 'bad' decision and I had never ever missed an opportunity that was actually meant for me. With the help of a little science and a little maths, it became very clear to me that there has only and ever been one path I could take in this life. My story had already been written and I have been simply following script. A story where every life form incarnate, regardless of size, shape, form, texture or colour contains a unique perspective and experience and is a soul of equal magnitude to my own in nothing more than an elaborate earthy costume. We are all equal, just in different outfits and playing different roles. Our stories and our experiences are individual, but they are pre-planned, interconnected and combined as part of a larger, unfolding, geometrically accurate design and story.

   I have discovered that life is not a problem to be fixed. Life is about experiencing a path and a viewpoint that we had chosen before we got here, having already figured out the best possible outcomes for all involved in each and every circumstance. That we are served and we provide a service in every moment, in what we do or don't do. That we have nothing to feel bad or guilty about because we are doing exactly what we agreed and decided upon before we got here. We are infinite perfection in a temporary occupation and clever disguise.

A tranquil moment with Síon captured on camera

This book is the beginning of Síon's story and it is how I made peace with mine. Recent advances in science and technology have exposed the illusionary nature of our physical world. However, the fallacy extends well beyond all things tangible. The illusion is in everything; it is in our worst enemy, our greatest difficulty and our biggest fail, but most of all it is in the robes we wear. This horse has presented me with life's misconceptions in great detail. In doing so she dismantled a life built on regret, guilt and inadequacy. I have traded fear of the future for peace in the present and learned not how to forgive but that there is nothing to forgive; there never has been.

"To the Universe belongs the dancer."
"Amen."
"He who does not dance does not know what happens."
"Amen."
Jesus Christ, Gnostic Gospel of John

Chapter 1: The Reunion

I am her voice, she is my spirit. I am her human, she is my horse. - Source unknown

By any stretch of the imagination she was not destined for me. I did not want her. I was in no way qualified to have her. I did not visualise her, meditate on her or devote a single unit of energy, positive, negative or otherwise, consciously or unconsciously, to manifesting her. Yet here she was, in my field, munching grass and ploughing up the soft earth with her huge, thunderous gallop, much to the annoyance of my good husband. But I have come to realise that every choice I have made, every circumstance I have found myself in and every direction I have taken in my life has led me to this precise time and place so that we could reunite on this mortal plane and fulfil a role that we have meticulously planned, long before, from a place of eternal love and wisdom. As it is with every other encounter so far and to come.

Since the time I first laid eyes on her in a photograph, I have been more than a little suspicious that there is something other-worldly afoot. At that moment, the odds of our paths crossing were lower than hell's basement, but my soul recognised her instantly and I listened in complete bewilderment as my mouth gave voice to an excited spirit who would not be contained. In what I can only describe as an out-of-body experience, I heard myself say, 'There she is, that is the horse for me.' Except she wasn't for me and neither did I want her to be. I had felt my mouth move and heard the words out loud, but I was pretty sure I had not spoken them. The photo of her I was looking at was a Facebook post from a rescue centre that was announcing their delight to be delivering her to new owners the next day somewhere in Sligo, which is approximately an hour or so from where I live on the west coast of Ireland. That fact, of course, meant absolutely nothing to a scheming universe, which instead had other plans the next day to deposit her in my care.

For many reasons, she was a horse and a responsibility I did not want at the time. Though superficial but not least, was the fact she was grey. Grey is not a colour I have any fondness for. I live in the west of Ireland, and while it is a stunningly beautiful part of the world, we get far more than our fair share of the country's wet weather from a sky that struggles to hold up an abundance of grey clouds that can hang low and heavy for months on end. For me, grey spells gloom and I do not like it. I am, and always have been, a hard-core animal lover. Truth be known, I have always been much more comfortable around animals than humans, but my house and life was already filled with enough four-legged little darlings that occupied enough of my time and space. At that time, I had three dogs, two cats and two donkeys; it was time to draw the line. No, I did not want a horse, especially one that was fifty-shades of my least favourite colour. I was therefore a little baffled by my unintentional verbal outburst when I saw her picture on Facebook, but I reassured myself that I need not worry as she was mercifully promised to someone else. That someone else, however, found herself unable to accept her on arrival due to some unexpected family circumstances. Fate, it seemed, did not care that I did not want this horse and was determined to land her on me. Much to my amazement, the very next day that spirited grey mare, which was not meant for me, was kicking up a storm in my field and my life.

    I had become acquainted with the rescue centre a year or so previously when a few stray miniature ponies who had been wandering the roads found their way to my place. I had enquired locally as to who the owner was, but nobody seemed to know, so I needed to relocate them. I contacted the rescue centre, which was run by a very determined young woman called Suzanne, who promptly arrived less than a week later with her horse box in tow to take the ponies. Suzanne was confident she would be able to find good homes for them and I was relieved to be free of the responsibility. Talking with Suzanne, I was so impressed with her total commitment to animal rescue. She would drive to any corner of the country, day or night, to rescue any animal big or small. So, a year later, when my friend Yvonne needed her rescue services for a horse that she had inherited but could not look after, I had no qualms about contacting Suzanne again. I asked her if she could take my friend's horse and she happily agreed to come to Galway and pick him up. She had a horse to drop off in Sligo anyway, so she could swing round my way afterwards.

I was expecting Suzanne and her travelling companion to arrive sometime early in the afternoon. They had set off at around six in the morning from Kerry in the southwest of Ireland and headed to Sligo first, as planned. But the hours past and there was no sign of Suzanne. When I called her on her mobile phone, she explained there had been some little problem and would hopefully be with us within the hour. Finally, at about 6.30pm I heard the dogs barking as Suzanne's jeep pulled in. I ran out to greet our visitors and was surprised to hear movement and stomping in the horse box, which was supposed to be empty at this point. I enquired about the noisy occupant. It turned out that the Facebook horse that was to be delivered to her new owners never even got to be unloaded from the box. Upon arrival, Suzanne had found herself in the middle of a marital dispute about whether or not this horse was welcome as there was only one of them who thought it was. This was not the ideal situation in which to leave any animal, leaving Suzanne with no other choice than to return the horse to the sanctuary. I was disappointed for both the horse and for Suzanne, but when she asked if I would be interested in adopting the mare in the box, I promptly told her that if I was to do so, she would find herself in the middle of a second marital dispute that day.

I ushered the weary travellers inside for some dinner before it was cremated in my oven. During dinner, Suzanne explained how she had come in possession of the unfortunate mare that had now been in the horse box more than twelve hours. During the summer, the rescue centre had successfully raised sufficient cash with a sustained fundraising campaign to secure a bank loan for the purchase of an equestrian centre that was for sale at a bargain price because of the dramatic slump in the property market during the disastrous financial climate at the time. The owner had fallen victim to the death of the Celtic Tiger and the mare in the horse box outside was also a casualty of this downturn in fortunes. She was included in the property package that the rescue centre was acquiring or she would be sent to slaughter, like so many magnificent horses caught up in Ireland's shameful equestrian crisis brought on by misfortune, overbreeding and greed. As it happened, this five-year-old mare was the granddaughter of Cruising, who was a world-famous Irish sport horse stallion and international show jumper and considered to be one of the world's most significant sires of the twenty-first century. The stallion passed away in 2014 but was for many years the predominant choice for international breeders. Cruising has sired champion progeny that have achieved some of the highest accolades in elite equestrian sport, being the only stallion in Ireland to have a give-star rating for the performance of his offspring in both eventing and show jumping. He was indeed the champion of champions. At that time, I had never heard of Cruising or his offspring, but I later learned he was as well known for his determined character as he was for his sporting achievements.

On hearing this story, I thought of a nearby equestrian centre that may be interested in taking this horse from Suzanne, so that she would not have to make that long journey back to Kerry on some of the worst roads in the country, nay, the northern hemisphere. I called the equestrian centre, which was still open, and explained the situation. They said they would be happy to take a look at the horse if Suzanne could stop by on her way home. There would be somebody there until nine. I felt optimistic for her. There was no time to rest up after the dinner. It was dark by now and we needed first to pick up my friend's horse at a very remote location so that he could go back with Suzanne to the rescue. It was going to be a tight fit to make it to the equestrian centre with this Cruising mare before nine, especially since we didn't really know where we were going. The horse that Yvonne had inherited was being kept by a family friend who had land for grazing and horses of her own. Yvonne had never been to this place before, though, and all we had were the directions scribbled on a bit of scrap paper in order to find a horse that was loose in field, one of many identical fields, in the dark, in the back end of nowhere. I was not sure about our chances of locating this particular field in a part of the world that is little else but fields, each one framed with the same stone walls that also line a maze of identical little roads and by-roads that branch off in every direction and are enough to confuse a compass. I was a little anxious, but it didn't seem to faze Suzanne a bit. It was a normal enough day for anyone working in rescue. We all jumped in our own vehicles. I led the way, followed closely by my friend Yvonne in her car and Suzanne and her companion bringing up the rear with their Jeep and horse box, the Cruising mare included.

Predictably enough, we got lost; very lost. By the time our little convoy had circumnavigated the globe, our hopes for reaching the equestrian centre before nine were well dashed and I was feeling very responsible as I was the one leading the way with the 'map'. But at least the poor Cruising mare in the trailer would have company for the trip back home to the sanctuary when we finally managed to find the field and the horse, which we did. Loading him went smoothly enough once Yvonne had positively identified him in the dark field. Fortunately for us, he was an absolute gentleman to handle and box.

But I could not get this Cruising mare out of my head and for some reason, at this time, I felt compelled to phone my husband who was working up north at the time and ask him if he would be interested in temporarily fostering this horse that I was sure I did not want. I am still not sure why I thought this was a good idea, as I know very well how Brendan feels about all things equestrian. He's not a horse lover. But I said to myself that I would ask regardless, and if he said no, then I would be happy to let this mare head back to the rescue with Suzanne and her new horse friend. The phone call went exactly as I had anticipated with an outright 'no' from my husband. I was surprised that I was actually able to reach him, as he can be quite the elusive one when I am trying to contact him. I do remember feeling a sense of relief when he said no, as I knew I did not really want the responsibility or the inevitable aggro it would cause when I got attached to the animal and he got impatient with my reluctance to move it on. However, a couple of minutes later Brendan called back with a few of questions about her. I gave him all the information I had from Suzanne and to my amazement he said if I wanted to put her in the field beside the house until I could find her a good home. I wasn't sure if I was happy or not, but I told Suzanne that we would at least foster her for a bit until we could find a suitable home for her. Suzanne was delighted because she trusted that I would do the right thing for this mare and it was one fewer mouth to feed at a continuously struggling animal sanctuary. We said goodbye to Yvonne and she headed home. I then led the way for Suzanne back again to my house to offload the mare into the field where my two donkeys would be.

Her disembarking was neither simple nor straightforward, but I put it down to the length of time; now nearly eighteen hours she had been on the road, enough to rattle man or beast. However, I was a little suspicious that all was not average or ordinary with this horse when I heard Suzanne's companion mumble 'crazy mare' under his breath as he tried to offload her. I explained to myself that it was just his exhaustion and frustration as he struggled to reverse her out of the box. After all, it is not unusual for horses to battle with the process of loading and unloading. Eventually, we managed to get her out, but not cleanly.

So, after an eighteen-hour road trip she made her grand entrance into my life by bolting out of the trailer and galloping off into the dark field with her lead rope still attached and no immediate plans to return. Thankfully she wasn't running blind, as it was a clear night with a full moon and a prophetic eclipse. Horses also have better night vision than us humans, but the risk was that she could cause herself serious injury if she tripped on the long lead rope. We had to unload the horse that had been collected for rehoming and walk him into the field to entice her to return. The wonderful thing about horses is that they will rarely leave each other, and if you lead one the others will follow. Thankfully, she fell for the trap and followed us all into the cattle shed, where we were able to corner her and remove the rope. We then released her back into the dark field and Suzanne and her travelling companion made a swift exit with the other horse, back to the rescue centre. Their long journey home was just beginning at 11.30pm and I hoped they would arrive safely, as I was aware how much we need people like Suzanne and her team. I was left alone in the night's stillness watching the beautiful silhouette of a horse explore the length and breadth of her new home. Happy that she was out in a nice field, I was confident it would not take her long to locate the two donkeys, even though they were tucked away for the night at the far end of the field, under a bush, keeping very quiet and invisible during all the commotion. I would check on them first thing in the morning. The following day, after I had dropped my two young girls to school, I went out to check on my expanded little herd. When I entered the field Síon went on high alert. She cocked her ears and tail and went off for a gallop in the opposite direction, insisting the two donkeys join her. They were not at all impressed by this unaccustomed burst of activity, but were not going to argue with her, given her considerable size advantage. She was 16.4hh of power and grace combined and as her youthful curiosity grew stronger than her fear of me, she began to circle me in a sprightly trot, assessing me as much as I was assessing her.

I was more than a little surprised that a horse I did not want had managed to worm her way into my life, but I could not deny the air of providence she had about her. Chance had played no hand or part in this occasion. Destiny's child did not care about what I thought I did or did not want and she was not taking no for an answer. Her arrival was a shock to more than just me. Our two gentle donkeys, Kitty and her daughter Julie, were also a little taken aback by this huge, high-energy equid that had disrupted their easy pace and the status quo. They did, however, quickly form a very strong bond, even if she became a lot more bonded to them than they to her. They became a herd, with the donkeys being the perfect companions, providing a very stable and settling influence on her untamed and fearful streak. The donkeys themselves had been an unexpected addition to the family a year beforehand. Like this horse, they were a responsibility I did not particularly want at the time, but it was necessary to have them on the land in order for my husband to be able to claim the government farming grants. Life will have its way with us no matter how hard we resist. Turns out, theirs was a crucial role in the plot and they took up their position on the stage and in the storyline exactly as they were supposed to, in advance and in the background. They may appear to be just extras in this production, yet they are anything but.

I had no clue what was to be the outcome for this horse that had been placed in my care. It seemed life had been quite adamant that our paths should meet, so I decided that our crossing would only be a temporary one and I would do my part in this rescue case to find her a good home where she would be happy and realise all of her sporting potential. This was not a difficult task given her ancestry and breed. The Irish sport horse is a cross between the Irish draught horse and thoroughbred stock. Referring to temperament, this is a mix of the cool blood of the draught horse with the hot blood of the thoroughbred to produce the warm blood of the sport horse. The draught horse is known for its strength, calm disposition and its intelligence while the thoroughbred embodies speed and athletic ability. Put the two together and you have the power of the draught with the thoroughbred's pace and the agility to turn on a sixpence. Perfect for show jumping.

She was five years old, rising six, unregistered and unbroken, but I quickly found an ideal and willing taker in my donkey's farrier. She would be moving on as soon as I had her paperwork sorted. That, however, was not how the universe had written the story at all, and I was very gently but firmly redirected back to script. My plan to offload her was foiled at the eleventh hour by my dear father who always had an interest in the business of horse racing and sport. He suggested that I keep her and have her broken and trained, which would possibly make her a more valuable sale. He would give me the money to do so and she could be our little project. His proposal sat strangely well in my heart, because at this stage I had to confess I started to become a little uneasy with the thought of parting with her.

Within days of her being placed in the field beside the house, I began to notice something mysterious going out on. All three of them had access to about fifteen acres of grazing in three separate fields. Prior to her arrival, the donkeys would have spent most of their time in the farthest fields out of sight of the house where there is more shelter from the relentless wind and rain. Now this horse seemed to be holding her little herd in the near field next to the house and I had the distinct feeling I was being closely watched by her. My very routine comings and goings were being monitored and as soon as I emerged from the house I could feel her eyes on me, even from the furthest point of view. It was a strange feeling, more of being touched than being looked at. Many who have worked with horses believe them to be highly telepathic. I have found an occasional sense of telepathy in most of the animals I have owned over the years, but I had never had an experience quite like this. I do not have any expertise in horsemanship and my riding skills are basic at best, and I certainly did not have the courage to handle an unbroken, biting, kicking hot blood like her. I wanted to stay well away from her until she could be tamed and broken by a professional. This horse, however, had other plans, she had cast her line and she was reeling me in. As much as I tried to keep my distance from her, every day I found myself standing in my welly boots in the middle of her field, looking at her, not really sure how I got there or what I should be doing with her.

As the months passed my husband became increasingly impatient. He was not at all happy with the new addition to the family. He was a part-time farmer with a small holding of thirty-two acres, and animals on the land had to earn their keep or provide some financial return. The donkeys paid their way in that their presence helped qualify him for the government farming grants, but this horse was just a big white elephant, eating up resources and poaching the land. I had told him I was just helping out my friend from the rescue centre with emergency foster care when their rehoming plans had suddenly gone array. It was a temporary arrangement, I said, be grand, I said. When plans changed slightly it caused a little fireworks. I found myself fighting hard for something I thought I did not want. I started to worry that he might, as threatened, take it upon himself to relocate or dispose of her without my consent and I would lose her. This concern became the crux of my experience with her. If there really was some kind of divinely rooted objective for this horse to come into my life, then neither my irate husband nor anyone else for that matter would be able to interfere with it. On the contrary, they would be a part of it if they contributed any kind of involvement at all.

Of course, not knowing what that reason was made it seem as though there could be any number of possibilities for her presence. It may be that I would put her into training and she would prove her worth in the show jumping arena. It could be that I'd end up wasting a lot of money on a horse that had inherited no aptitude for the sport from her famous bloodline. It could also be that ours would be no more than a fleeting encounter and I'd be forced to rehome her in order that she end up changing someone else's life or direction. It could be any of the above or none. Or so it seemed. That was the illusion, that there were different possible outcomes. But I knew from the deepest place within me that our meeting was arranged before either of us got here and so, too, was our hereafter. I knew there was only one manuscript for our story. Just because we cannot see the path ahead does not mean it is not already paved. I decided to trust in this ready-made road afore, me and although it was poorly lit I had an inkling it was beautifully constructed, regardless of where it would take us. Even if what transpired seemed to be the worst-case scenario, I knew this would not really be the case. If it had reason and purpose in the greater scheme of things then it would be the correct path regardless. For I believe that that faith is not about believing that everything will turn out in as we would want it to, but rather, as it is *supposed* to. I decided to allow my husband to do what he felt guided to do and trust that he would be prevented from doing anything that was not part of the plot.

As it turned out, Brendan was directed to a man in a neighbouring village who could do the job of breaking her. It felt as though we had been given a stay of execution. I started to breathe a bit easier and I realised that believing everything would work out for the greater good did not mean I was going to be able to detach emotionally from the situation. I realised I was falling for her raw beauty and unbridled charms. My heart was emerging victorious from the ancient and honourable battle with its rational thinking nemesis, logic. Even so, I was apprehensive about having her broken. It is a process that relies largely on force and intimidation within a timeframe of one size fits all. She was fearful but feisty and I had an idea this might very well push a few of her buttons, the wrong ones. I reassured myself, however, that in the long run it was the best thing to do with her and for her. Once rideable, she would then have use or value in a world where she would otherwise be disposable.

With all the possibilities that appeared to lie ahead of this horse, it seemed likely that her fate was to follow in the footsteps of her famous show jumping lineage. She was bred to be a champion show jumper. Her pedigree was selected from the finest blood lines in world. To any qualified mind in the business, her future was set. Brendan had found somebody to break her and we would take it from there. Yes, that was the route I would pursue with her; it was surely the most probable. The universe, however, had other plans and after a year of repeated attempts by experienced professionals to break her, she was labelled crazy, dangerous and good for nothing. On top of that, she was a little less than ideal in size. She was short on the rein, short in her stride, pigeon-toed and had a sarcoid on the inside of her thigh. In all, she was mentally unstable and physically inadequate. She was, of course, none of the above, but it was necessary for her to present that way in order to be redirected towards her true purpose. She would not be a champion show jumper because her course had already been charted by a force far more benevolent and wise than the judgements and calculations of mere experts. Just as it is for all of us.

I had no real intentions of interacting with this crazy mare until she could be well tamed and broken by somebody else far braver or stupider than me. When it became clear this was not going to happen, I was devastated that my ambitious vision for her future would not be realised. When the last trainer eagerly returned her to me, he explained how this crazy mare had thrown his colleague twenty feet in the air and then, in temper, attempted to 'finish him off' as he lay on the ground. I was left standing in my yard, feeling completely hollow, as he took his money, spun his wheels and made a hasty exit from this crazy mare and her deluded owner. I had no clue how to proceed with a horse that seemed to have no worth or place in the ruthless, profit-driven world of horse dealing. If she could not be broken, she would be considered useless at a time when horses all over the country were being neglected, abandoned and dumped due to the downturn in the financial climate. Even as a broodmare, her future was uncertain, as Ireland was already awash with unwanted horses. The odds were stacked against her, not even including the ongoing battle with my less than sympathetic husband. But I had grown to love her. I felt connected to her. Again, I needed to fall back on that deep sense of knowing that we were travelling the right path. A glorious path and story where everything is planned and perfect even when it seems as though it is not.

Much happened between us in the following weeks. I began to view her a little differently. She was indeed beautiful. Her winter coat was a light, bright grey that lit up the bare and bleak surroundings. For now, it concealed her summer dapples that would emerge again in the summer sun. Her legs were three-quarters black, her mane was as dark as her eyes and her tail was blonde. Dotted on her body she had a few whorls. These are permanent birth marks where a patch of hair grows in the opposite direction to the surrounding hair. They are distinctive, like a fingerprint, and are used for identification and character evaluation. There is much folklore around these marks. The location, number and direction of the irregular hair growth is said to give an insight into the different aspects of a horse's personality, abilities and behavioural tendencies. For years people have relied on these markers to determine athletic potential, intelligence and soundness, among other things. Highly unusual whorls, meaning in odd places or odd shapes or lots of them, can indicate severe behavioural issues in an animal. Scientific studies done in Ireland and the US on this age-old method of horse assessment has shown that there may indeed be some credibility to the practice. As it happens, brain and skin formation are very closely intertwined during embryonic development. Hair swirl patterns form in the developing foetus at the same time as the brain is forming, both arising from the same layer of cells called the ectoderm, so it is not outside the realm of possibility that internal brain conditions could be reflected in an external dermal display. This horse had a perfect whorl in the middle of her forehead, which for those who believe in this phenomena, signifies great intelligence and soundness. However, she also had a few more irregular ones around her body, which made me think she might be a bit of a complicated character.

Regardless of whatever was going on in her head, she was a beautiful mover; she pranced around the field like a ballerina with head and tail high. She was the embodiment of grace and elegance except for the nervous snorting, growling and farting that was unashamedly directed at me. Her power and vulnerability on display like two sides of a precious coin. By now I was well baited and caught, she had me exactly where she wanted me. Looking back, I was an easy target and a soft catch.

It was now time to give her an identity. At this point she was still just a crazy grey mare. She had no name or papers that proved her prestigious heritage. My two daughters, Ciara and Cailin, who had gone to school on Inis Méain - which is one of the Irish speaking Aran Islands off the Galway coast - wanted to give her a fitting Irish name. Síon is Gaelic for wild wind or storm and Liath means the colour grey. So we called her Síon Liath, pronounced Sheon Leah or Grey Storm in English, because she was both. Now that we had a name for her, I was able to register her with Horse Sport Ireland and apply for her papers. Her cover certificate had been lodged with them when she was born, by her then owner, and now a DNA sample pulled from her mane made it official. She had her green passport and she was who she said she was, a Cruising. Of course, that did not mean a whole lot if all she was good for was looking pretty. The only option I had left with Síon was to try and work with her myself and I soon got the feeling that this had been her plan from the beginning. I had no illusions about being able to break and ride her, but I did think it might be possible to make some progress with her. It was obvious Síon had not been handled at all much in her five years, but she was clearly curious, intelligent and energetic. However, she was spooked by the slightest sound or touch and her time away in training did little to settle her. It did not help that one of her trainers had used a pressurised water hose in an attempt to desensitise her or as he phrased it, 'knock the nerves out of her'. Suffice to say that approach was not as effective in practice as it might sound in theory.

Síon still kept a safe distance from me when I was in the field with her. She threw me the odd glance as I groomed and fed the donkeys their apples and carrots, but she had plenty of lush green grass to munch on so she was not really tempted to risk coming any closer. I needed to figure out how to persuade her that I was not the enemy. At this stage I was informed enough about her and the Cruising blood line to know that force and intimidation was counterproductive, to say the least. I knew my only chance was to build a relationship of mutual respect and trust where she was comfortable in my company without restraint or confinement. She would not be bullied into submission, she had made that very clear. I started with some horse feed. Every day I went out, put some feed into the trough and stood beside it. The donkeys could not believe their luck as they had it all to themselves for a couple of days while she stood back trying to raise the courage to join us. It did not take long and after a few days the donkeys had to make room at the dinner table for her royal greyness. There was progress, slow but steady. Síon was happy to eat the meal beside me so long as there were no sudden movements or noise and absolutely no touchy-touchy.

After a few weeks I started to move about a bit and make a little bit of noise around her. Every time she startled and jumped away I calmly said, 'It's OK.' Síon very quickly learned to understand those two words and settled almost instantly when I said them. At the same time she learned the words 'All gone', which is what I said when she had eaten all her oats and was demanding more by banging the trough. As soon as I said this she stopped. I was now getting a good sense of how clever and willing Síon was as she was prepared to learn and accept my language to build a relationship with me. It did not seem like much, but small things often mean more than we give them credit for.

One typically wet and windy day I was standing beside the trough as usual while they were feeding when something curious happened. My beautiful daughter Cailin had joined me out in the field to keep me company. We were just having ordinary chat when Síon caught my attention. She was looking at me intensely with her left eye. For a moment I was frozen still. I felt as though my very essence was being sucked out and inhaled by hers. The experience lasted only a matter of seconds but paralysed me with a combination of excitement and fear. Thankfully, Cailin did not notice anything untoward and kept on chatting. I thought it best not to mention it to her at the time, as it is important for teenagers to believe that their parents are mentally stable. Immediately after this strange incident with Síon, she allowed me to touch her without jumping a foot in the air or galloping off like her tail was on fire.

I soon noticed that our little etheric episode seemed to have an odd effect on my thought process. My mind went into overdrive with very deep and meaningful thoughts as I tried to unravel the mysteries of life. I didn't take much notice at first, as I have a tendency to overthink most things anyway. It's a woman thing, I think. My predominant thought to begin with was that our little rendezvous was no accident. I began to piece together the many events that had long preceded and enabled our meeting. I was intrigued to find how each piece of the puzzle had been perfectly assembled a forehand and just how far back the plot extended. A meeting that on the surface appeared to be an in-the-moment, chance encounter was, on reflection, firmly rooted in an intelligence that went way back. There also came an intense feeling that there was some significant purpose for our union, though I had no idea what that might be. I was getting suspicious that she was far better briefed about the reason and the direction of it all than I was and that we were not the strangers that this life had made us out to be. The one thing that I was entirely certain about at that point was that there was much more than a horse beneath that equine robe and she knew a whole lot more than she was pretending.

It was nice to make a little progress with Síon but I had much to learn and do yet. She was now willing to give me a chance, but I needed to prove my worth. She was not going to make it easy for me, though. Where would be the fun in that? At this stage I had given up trying to guess or manipulate her future. I was getting wise to her. She had a plan of her own. Resistance was futile. She demanded the inevitable. Surrender seemed like it was the best course of action not just for me, but also for my husband, who had more or less resigned himself to the fact that he was fighting a losing battle in trying to get rid of her. Her fire and determination had ignited mine and I was territorial as a dog with a bone. I wasn't going to give her up. By way of compromise, I agreed to relocate the three of them to an unused plot of land some three miles from the house. This way, the sight of them every day would not be vexing my husband and I would not have to be continuously defending my decision to keep her. And although I really did not want her away from the house, their little place of exile turned out to be the perfect spot for them. They had roughly fifteen acres of grazing in bog land that grew as much rushes as it did grass. The rushes provided good fibre for their digestive health and the reduced grass content was a far healthier option for my two full-figured donkeys. So every morning, without fail, I drove up to our rugged sanctuary to find her waiting patiently at the gate, clearly excited to see me arrive.

    I wasn't quite sure how next to proceed with her, but decided to trust that I would be guided well by the unseen forces that had brought us together in the first place. I decided to abandon completely any personal objectives or expectations I had of this horse and just see what happened by simply spending time with her in the field. What we tend to overlook with horses is the fact that they are prey animals. This is why they can be so nervy and reactive; they are always on high alert for danger. Humans are predators by nature and the horse knows it. We move like predators, we communicate like predators and we behave like predators. We are always trying to catch them and force them into doing something completely alien to their instincts, such as corral them, separate them and get on their back. It doesn't matter that at times our intentions are good or that they are for the benefit of the horse, they don't read it that way. So if I had any chance of getting Síon to trust me, I had to pretend I was not a predator. I needed to move and posture as though I was not stalking her and appear to be completely indifferent to her in the field, so I made like she wasn't there at all. I turned my back to her at all times and fussed over the donkeys instead. It worked like a charm. Curiosity soon got the better of her and before long I could feel her breathing down my neck behind me. As much as I wanted to turn around, I needed to be sure she was really convinced of my lack of interest in her, so I brushed her off like a pesky fly every time she came too close. This really got her going. I kept my little act going for a few days or so until I had her right where I wanted her, head down, licking her lips and asking for parley. She wanted to discuss our relationship a bit more. I gave her a few rubs and scratches and walked away. She followed me. I had her. She was not viewing me as a predator. From then on Síon chose my company in the field above the donkeys' and was happy for me to start rubbing and even brushing her. Next, I wanted to see if she trusted me enough to lie in the grass with me. I started sitting small and quiet, relaxed and non-threatening in the grass near her. It was a little unnerving at first as she would tug at me or nudge me or stand almost right over me as though testing my nerve. All very fine until something spooked her and I get a hoof where I least wanted it, so I ignored her or shooed her away again. Thankfully there was no great drama, but it did take longer than I thought it would. I gave it over an hour every day, but even though she always came and stood with me, yawning her head off and wanting to lie down for a snooze, it took another few weeks before I would get that ultimate show of trust. When she did finally sit with me it was wonderful, even though she almost sat on top of me when she plonked herself down in the grass. There was a huge sense of achievement. I wanted to jump up and down in delight. It took all I had to remain calm and nonchalant. In the end I was glad that she had taken her time and made me earn my stripes. I realised that I had really enjoyed just being with her and the donkeys without feeling I should be doing something with her. It had been immensely therapeutic for all of us. Her energy was empowering and uplifting and I always came away with more than I brought. I was discovering the often-overlooked treasures of developing a relationship with a horse on the ground instead of on their back. So many horses are discarded if they have no great riding or breeding worth. Rarely do we recognise their value as an individual sentient soul, at their level, on their terms. They have so much more to offer than their back.

    As the months passed, Síon became more and more comfortable around me. Little by little she let down her guard and I was allowed to see a huge, vibrant personality that for a long time had been heavily concealed with fear. As she became more confident around me, she also began to test my character to see if I was somebody she really wanted in her private circle and if so, what position I should hold. At times she got cocky and pushy and I needed to be firm and determined with her. Every now and then she liked to remind me that I had no place being in a field with a one-tonne animal who could kill me in a second if I was timid or anxious. It is possible to be assertive without being cruel and I knew that was what Síon wanted of me. Creating boundaries was essential not only for safety reasons, but also because it gave her a sense of security in my presence, that I was someone she could respect and rely on. She demanded my courage and rewarded me well for it. Kitty, the mother donkey, was, however, the undisputed leader of the herd. She was the eldest, though not an old donkey judging by her teeth. Her unspoken, matriarchal position was acknowledged by us all, including and especially Síon, who yielded to her every nod or gesture. She was the sweetest, kindest, gentlest donkey in the world, who exuded a quiet authority that was hard to put into words but was so easily felt in her presence. Her daughter Julie was a bit more temperamental and cheeky than her mother and often reminded me of a moody teenager. As different as they all were, they had formed a strong bond together and I was aware that I was somewhat of an outsider, a strange, two-legged being who came and went every day. Even so, they accepted me into their fold, albeit for the carrots and scratches, the chat and the distraction that I provided.

After a year in the boggy land away from the house I brought them all home. Síon had slowly transformed from a feral, biting, kicking bundle of nerves to an intelligent, funny, curious and responsive companion. She is in the field beside the house and rarely takes her eyes off the house. I enjoy spending time with her every day even though she can be quite the handful, opening gates and getting up to mischief. Her energy is addictive and transformative. She has continued to learn more of my words and has become quite vocal in her own communication with me. She can be very loud when she wants to get my attention and sometimes gives me the softest, sweetest, high-pitched nickering sound that horses save for their nearest and dearest. She loves to do simple tricks for treats. She lifts her hoof, walks backwards, gives kisses and spins around on request. She will follow me anywhere and also allows me to lie on her back, but as yet I have not been brave enough to throw my leg over and sit up. I work with Síon without head collar or rope, and in her own field so that she always feels secure. She can walk away from me at any time, but chooses not to. She has made it very obvious that she enjoys learning something new. She locks her eyes and ears on me and picks up every cue until she figures out what I am asking her to do.

This doesn't usually take long at all and I often get the feeling that she knows from the outset what I want, but goes through the motions of pretending that she doesn't so that I can have the experience of teaching her. In this way she gives me a sense of achievement and value. This magnificent grey being knows exactly what she needs to do to allow me the illusion that my efforts towards her are for her benefit and development. The truth is that I have gained more from her than she has from me and I have taught her nothing that she doesn't already know. Yes, we have had our rows; she is a half thoroughbred, moody mare and she never lets me forget it. She is not a mushy or cuddly sort of a horse, much more of a high energy, 'let's go!' sort of a gal, but on occasion she can be as gentle and loving as a kitten.

Síon's entry into my life was quite a catalytic event. In the space of a very short time, it changed pretty much everything about how I viewed and responded to my world. Her presence, her behaviour and our connection initiated a cascade of revelations that brought profound peace and answered my toughest whys and wherefores about life. From the day I felt her pull my soul into hers, my head began to fill with thoughts that were, at first, unfamiliar, irrational and a little contrary to my Catholic schooling. It was like a slow download or drip feed of information from an invisible line that was connected from her heart to mine that at first led to a constant and head-splitting internal debate. I battled with and denied the thoughts as they came to me, but as I teased them out slowly and individually they started to make more and more sense. I realised that the reason I was so conflicted about the information I was receiving was because of the limitations and stipulations within my own thinking. From my limited awareness and a lifetime of mental conditioning, these thoughts were absurd, but I came to understand that this horse was sharing with me a perspective on love and life that had no earthly boundaries or conditions. They came from a place of infinite wisdom and love, where no such constraints exist.

In the west of Ireland, we do not get half enough fine days in the year, so when we do I do my very best to take full advantage by spending them outdoors in the field with my lovely ladies. One day as I sat beside them soaking up the warm rays, I dozed off for a few moments. I woke up with a fright when I heard a loud voice shouting, 'Write, write, write.' I looked up to see Síon standing over me doing her best impression of a clueless mare staring vacantly off into the distance, but at this stage I was wising up to the fact that she was something more than just a horse and I knew well it was her who had yelled at me. What she could not fake was her true nature, which was evident in the strong, authoritative sound of her voice that was not asking politely but was clearly giving an order. I would never have considered myself the most articulate, nor did I think I had any aptitude for writing, but by this time I had already felt a strong urge to write and had begun jotting down a few notes in what began as crude diary of my time and progress with Síon. However, every time I opened my iPad to document her activities, I found myself writing something completely different from what I had intended. The narrative became not so much about what I was doing with her and much more about why she had come to me in the first place. Science and spirituality took control of the written word and I realised that whatever it was that I was writing, it was a little more profound than a story about a horse and two donkeys in the west of Ireland. Feeling a little out of my depth with what was emerging in the text, I had put the task aside for a bit while I grappled with the thoughts in my head. But Síon was not going to let me give up on this and thought I needed an encouraging nudge to get me going again. I was a little startled by the abrupt and commanding tone of the voice I heard that day, but there was nothing vague about the message at least. I must write. I knew at that moment for sure why she had come into my life. I knew she was not going to be a show jumper or anything of the sort, but I knew she did have a plan and a purpose that she had ruthlessly roped me into. I was no longer confused as to why a horse I most certainly did not want had wormed her way into my world. I knew she had something to say and I was to be her voice. So I resumed my writing as instructed.

After a while, the opposing thoughts in my head had reached an armistice of sorts. The info was still incoming, but I was much more at ease with it and had fewer and fewer rebuttals to annoy myself with. Eventually I had no questions left to ask. All had been answered and my mind settled into a kind of universal understanding that brought an inner peace that I had not known before. My new perspective on life's great mysteries felt almost like an awakening or having blinkers removed and it was much more far-reaching than I could ever have anticipated. This was a little scary because I knew that what I had to write could sound a little 'out there' to say the least, and the ludicrous notion of a crazy horse giving spiritual counsel to her even crazier human was not lost on me either. To be clear, I don't want to give the impression that this horse and I were having regular, deep and meaningful conversations about the nature of existence in the English language; that would mean I really was crazy. The only time I experienced anything audible from her was when I heard the words 'Write, write, write'. After that, she was content to allow me to slowly process the barrage of thoughts in my head that she had initiated to begin with.

Writing was not an easy task for me, especially as I had no clear vision for how I would articulate or structure a spiritual understanding that seemed to be more at home in my heart than on the written page. For this I was thankful for my love of science and all the progress that has been made in both classical and quantum understanding to date, which I leaned on for some much needed support. This did not make my writing job any easier. Tackling the burning questions of our existence isn't as easy as you would think, especially when your co-author is a crazy horse. I should've known it wasn't going to be a simple case of horse tells human and human writes. True to her nature she made it a long and convoluted journey of self-discovery. Through every paragraph I battled large bouts of self-doubt, writer's block and just life in general, which on its own offered up a generous helping of personal challenges. My newfound spiritual enlightenment did not guarantee me a smooth sailing at all, but if I had learned anything from this horse, it was: where would be the fun in that?

Chapter 2: The Hypothesis

'God doesn't play dice with the universe.' - Albert Einstein

This is where the narrative changes and the focus is broadened. No longer a romantic story about a crazy horse and her floundering human who find solace in each other's shortcomings and differences; there is a bigger picture, a much, much bigger picture. This is where I came to understand that Síon's message was not to be about the course of her life or mine, but about the oneness and value of all life in this dimension, that all life, regardless of the form it takes, is having essentially the same experience of life, where our individual journeys are nothing more than a divinely crafted and meticulously calculated illusion of form and sensation. Every life is an adventure for spirit, but more than this, every life is a story already written in its entirety over which we have no more control than we have over the passage of time.

I understand that this hypothesis is totally counterintuitive to how we perceive our reality and indeed our importance as superior beings in this existence. The idea that we are not in control of our lives and that we are not as special as we think we are is ludicrous for sure. Or is it? This is where I am asking you suspend all of the superficial human conditioning that you have spent a lifetime acquiring and join me on journey into the fundamental truths of a reality that, as it turns out, is not everything it is pretending to be. Essentially, we will explore the eleven illusions of life, the paradox of the light and dark aspects of existence, and the constraints of destiny that enslave us all.

I had always believed in the notion of consciously creating our own reality and fulfilling wishes and goals though our own focus and effort. However, Síon's arrival made me question just how much of our life is shaped by us as we go and how much is orchestrated by an unseen wisdom, a destiny already mapped out in its finest detail before we ever embrace this physical form. Could there be a plan already drawn up before our entry into this mystifying and temporary incarnation? Moreover, an entire set of intertwining plans, lovingly crafted by a divine architect from which we pick one. Where we choose in advance exactly how our life will unfold and who will be a part of it. Where any attempt to stray off course is prevented by our own intuition which is wired directly to source wisdom. Failing that, God and his ever-ready team of celestial reinforcements will be on hand to sabotage lovingly any attempts to divert from said course, and it will be done with such discretion we will actually believe the choice was ours every time. Or are we creating everything in our reality by thought and action as we go? A reality where the outcome is an infinite number of possibilities based on our free will choices, level of awareness and/or gratitude or lack thereof. Where our present circumstances are a result of our past thought processes and our future self relies on the quality of our thinking in the present. This future reality will be as a result of conscious or unconscious creation depending on whether or not we are familiar with the law of attraction famously documented in the book, *The Secret,* which is well known in the New Age movement.

The idea that we can manifest anything we desire in our physical world by focus, affirmations, gratitude, action and dedication, etc, is a very popular concept that is supported by many anecdotal experiences based on the more than a little shaky concept of 'like attracts like'. According to this idea, we attract into our lives whatever it is we predominantly think about or focus on, good or bad. That we are, in every moment, creating our reality by the power of thought, whether we realise it or not. That our thoughts emit a frequency that attracts more of the same. That all the people, circumstances and events of our lives have manifested as a result of our thinking and that we have the power to change anything by altering our thoughts and focus. We have infinite possibilities and unlimited abundance available to us and we can attract anything we want if we just ask, believe and receive with a mindset of gratitude.

There are so many aspects of our lives that we do not actively seek, circumstances, events, people that are either a pleasant surprise or something we would never have chosen under any circumstances. Wittingly or unwittingly, we have all been touched by the unavoidable. There are many that claim to having transformed their lives using the principles of this law of attraction. But there are as many more that cannot seem to achieve the results they hoped for. This is often, nonsensically, explained away by perhaps not following the guidelines correctly. It is important, for example, when we are doing the asking that we be clear and precise about what it is we want. We mustn't confuse an infinitely wise universe with ambiguous intentions. I struggle to understand why an all-knowing intelligence, from which we have been created, might misinterpret our desires because we haven't phrased our request as well as we might. Also, we must have absolute faith that we will receive our hearts desire without being attached to any particular outcome as it may present itself very differently. In other words, we might not get what it is we wanted. Not because the universe couldn't give it to us, but because it might not be in our best interests or the interests of the collective. While it is not my intention to undermine anyone's personal truth, it has to be said that the whole concept is so obviously self-contradictory. Either way, we can ask for whatever we want, but we will only receive it if the unseen thinks it is a good idea in the first place. The will of God, it seems, oversees the law of attraction and has the last word on its discharge. The trouble with this reasoning is that it simply does not make any sense at all, because, if the law of attraction is going to use 'God's will' as an excuse as to why we are not achieving the desired results and outcomes in our lives, it is basically shooting itself in the foot. This is because God's will and the law of attraction are two totally conflicting ideologies and cannot exist in tandem. We cannot rationally believe in both the law of attraction and in God's will or destiny. If God is disallowing some things to manifest in our lives, by default it automatically follows that he is allowing other things to show up. This means that, either way, God is the one in control and we are not. So if we believe that such a thing as God's will exists in our lives then there are no half measures. God's will exists when we receive and when we are denied. So when we think we have acquired or created something ourselves it is only because it has been allowed or approved by God. It is often suggested that God just exerts his will here and there and for the most part we are in total control of our lives. That God steps in, on occasion, with a little intervening miracle to put things right when they go awry or get too far out of hand. Even if this is the case, it still remains that there are divine restrictions or guidelines on where it is all going. It means that there is not, as the law of attraction claims, an infinite number of creative possibilities at our disposal for the future we think we want. We do not have unlimited abundance available to us or unlimited anything if it is subject to God's say-so or dependent on certain criteria. If you believe in God's will, you can only have what you are allowed, good, bad or indifferent. If what we want shows up then it is only because we happen to have aligned our wishes with those of God. Aside from the fact that the law of attraction is so offensive to simple logic, there are a couple of scientific stumbling blocks that also get in the way. Proponents of the law of attraction often play the vibration card, claiming that because everything is energy pulsating at a certain frequency, like attracts like and energies of the same frequency are attracted to each other. It is our choice of these emotional frequencies that creates our reality and our future. If we choose to be joyful and optimistic, then our physical reality will be assembled in front of us with things people and circumstances that coincide with that frequency. Life will be peachy. But if we 'choose' to feel sad or pessimistic, then obviously we should expect to receive the exact opposite in our lives. However, contrary to the claims of many, there is no proof that this is so. There is no solid scientific evidence to support the idea that our thoughts can either construct our material world or manipulate our future.

In fact, science tells us something very different indeed about the forces that shape our physical reality. Let me explain. Everything in the world that we perceive around us and indeed the entire universe is made up of two things, tiny particles of matter called atoms, and the energy or forces that hold them together and make them move. Simple as that, for now. These microscopic atoms are banded together to make larger objects and systems that we can identify as our reality. Science identifies four fundamental forces that help organise these atoms into our material experience:

1. The gravitational force.
2. The weak nuclear force.
3. The strong nuclear force.
4. The electromagnetic force.

These forces govern how all objects or particles interact and how certain particles decay. They are behind every interaction experienced every second of every day from falling down to orbiting the sun. These forces have been assembling the arrangement and position of all the atoms in the physical world we see before us since the beginning of time. They have not needed our input to do their job for the last billions of years before humans arrived and they do not need it now. There is no force that we can identify as a law of attraction and our thoughts do not have any power over how these actual fundamental forces operate.

So the law of attraction cannot be validated using the vibrating forces or fields of the universe and neither can it rely on particle physics to give it any credibility, because at an atomic level like does not attract like, but rather opposites attract. This natural principle is axiomatic. The most obvious practical example is that the north pole of one magnet will repel the north pole of another. If you have ever tried putting them together you will know what a struggle it is. Atoms are made of teeny tiny particles called protons, neutrons and electrons. The charges on the proton and electron are exactly the same size but opposite. Since opposite charges attract, protons and electrons attract each other. Two electrons will tend to repel each other because both have a negative electrical charge. Two protons will also tend to repel each other because they both have a positive charge. In essence, like does not attract like.

Currently, there is no solid scientific proof that there is a connection between our thoughts and the formation of our reality. We have not a shred of proof that the atomic and subatomic particles of our tangible world in the future are amassed and assembled according to the energy of our thoughts, focus and efforts in the present. In fact, what we do know is very much at odds with this idea. What we do know is that the fundamental particles of our existence arrange themselves according to the laws of physics, not according to how we feel.

As stated, our world as we perceive it is made up atoms and the forces that mediate them. The crucial aspect to our reality is that, since the Big Bang, all the atoms in the universe and the forces that support them have been behaving in a very precisely calculated and mechanistic manner, according to some very defined laws of physics. What this means is that we occupy and experience a deterministic world where every particle in the universe is doing, has done and will do exactly what it is supposed to be doing according to some rigid behavioural rules. These fundamental components of all life in the universe (and that includes all the atoms that make up our bodies and their corresponding position in space and time) have organised themselves and shaped our world since the beginning of time using an unerring and mandatory set of laws that are totally independent and indifferent to our many and complex emotional states. In fact, these laws could not care less what we think about or desire. The forces of physics don't need our permission or our passion in order to operate and sentiment is not something that can be factored into the equations of the universe. The laws of physics have been dictating the position of every atom in creation from the very start and will continue to do so going forward. $E = mc^2$ whether you are happy about it or not.

What's more, these laws that have fashioned the past and the present are going to continue to do their thing well into the future, meaning that, just like our past, our future is a foregone conclusion that was set in motion from as far back as the Big Bang. Here's the shocker: our entire physical reality has evolved over time completely independent of our experience of it. So, the law of attraction is nowhere to be found either on an energetic or an atomic, physical level. This proposed force of attraction that supposedly determines our future has little more than anecdotal evidence to support it and also has just as much anecdotal evidence to discredit it. For something that is little more than a hunch it has been very successfully touted as a Universal Law.

The law of attraction has become widely accepted as fact by a great many people. Once it had been put out there by *The Secret*, this on the surface unsubstantiated observation took hold and spread like wildfire to become a formidable and comprehensive 'law' that has become almost paradigmatic in our lives. The rationale behind its existence has much less humble origins and actually began as an idea that grew out of the teachings of the American philosopher Phineas Quimby in the early nineteenth century. He never used the words 'law of attraction' and his postulation was based solely the area of health and psychosomatology, the mind-body connection and the view that disease is rooted in mental cause. Quimby was an exponent of healing the body with the power of the mind. His theories were popular and he has been credited as the overall intellectual father of New Thought. His ideas were picked up by subsequent authors and teachers and inflated to include all areas of our physical experience and circumstances. In the years that followed it was decided that not only could our thoughts influence our physical well-being being, but that they could also arrange and choreograph the atomic and subatomic structure of our environment to build the future of our dreams. To think was to create and we were doing it whether we knew it or not.

By the latter half of the twentieth century the idea had expanded, gathered momentum and grown a little more hair to become an ancient, sacred and vibrating law that began with the creation of the universe and holds us responsible and accountable for every aspect of our lives, within and without. For a theory that has no real scientific basis and very little solid logic, it has come a long way and made quite the impact. Incidentally, if the law of attraction doesn't seem to be working for you and your life is not turning out as well as you would like, it may be that you are unaware of its many complementary companion laws. There are about twelve or so, give or take, that have popped up in its wake that need to be adhered to, universal laws such as the law of action, the law of correspondence, the law of giving and receiving, the law of compensation etc, etc. Solid nonsense. The law of attraction has grown into a veritable encyclopaedia of dos and don'ts as it seems that creating the life of our dreams is not as simple as originally proclaimed by *The Secret*.

The law of attraction is often touted as a way of acquiring stuff, wealth or a suitable life partner. However, prosperity and abundance, like all of life, are perceptions, not reality. There are countless people who have much more than they think they need and still consider themselves lacking. Alternately there are those that have little in comparison but feel fortunate. Being happy or positive is not an essential requirement for attracting financial abundance or security, there are many highly 'successful' people who live in a cloud of negativity and darkness. There are many more living hand to mouth in the poorest of conditions that are beacons of joy and contentment.

Advocates of the law of attraction would say that Jesus himself was aware of its power and often quote his words from the Bible when he said, 'What things soever ye desire, when ye pray, believe that ye receive them, and ye shall have them.' (Mark 11: 24). The only problem with this logic is that I doubt very much that Jesus was referring to the 'things' that we are hoping to manifest in our lives. I doubt Jesus was talking about 'things' like a fancy car, fat bank account, big house or anything of the sort. Jesus had no interest in earthly possessions and his mission was spiritual rather than material so he could not have been giving us advice on how to create our world and fill it with stuff. I imagine the 'things' Jesus was talking about were the grace and strength we need to cope with the many challenges that we are presented with in this life. Jesus was just telling us how we can get help with difficulties as they are, rather than giving us the secret to changing our physical circumstances.

This truth is expressed beautifully in the words of the Indian poet, Rabindranath Tagore:

> Let me not pray to be sheltered from dangers
> but to be fearless in facing them.
> Let me not beg for the stilling of my pain
> but for the heart to conquer it.
> Let me not look for allies in life's battlefield
> but to my own strength.
> Let me not crave in anxious fear to be saved
> but hope for the patience to win my freedom.
> Grant that I may not be a coward,
> feeling Your mercy in my success alone;
> But let me find the grasp of Your hand in my failure.

The law of attraction encourages us always and only to think nice, positive thoughts or otherwise suffer the grave consequences of attracting their vibrational opposite. A bit unfair to all those who are not privy to the workings of this universal law and even worse for those who battle with any mental challenge or depressive condition. Bad enough to be struggling with the overpowering demons of dark thought without being punished for it as well. There was a time, in the heady days of *The Secret* when I was absolutely terrified not to be happy all the time. I imagined the terrible future fallout for me and my young family if I wasn't showing up with the correct vibrations of unbridled joy and gratitude. I soon found out that I was chasing an impossible dream and I also noticed how exhausting it was trying to feel something that I didn't. I am in no way against the promotion of joy and happiness or the utilisation of practices to relieve stress and encourage mental health, but it seems as though this global phenomenon of attraction has duped us into believing that no good can come of our lives unless we are perpetually positive. We judge and berate ourselves and others for having 'bad' or 'negative' emotions like sadness, anger, disappointment, frustration and even grief. These normal, natural, uncomfortable emotions have inherent value in our lives and are actually part of the whole experience of living. In addition, denying or bottling our true feelings in place of false positivity is never sustainable as internal pain always seems to make its way to the surface. Not only this, but pretending to be happy when we are not would also seem to work contrary to the law of attraction, as life has shown us that when emotions are pushed aside or ignored they just grow and fester until they erupt, often in a dazzling display of irrationalism. Denying difficult emotions in order to be cheerful and optimistic can ultimately make things worse. A healthier approach might be to acknowledge our emotions truthfully so that we are more able to determine their source or cause. This can then prompt us to take concrete and purposeful steps towards self-help in whatever area of our life we need to address. Emotions are often the sign posts to nudge us in the right direction as we navigate the journey of life. Labelling them either positive or negative is at best very short-sighted and at worst potentially damaging.

Never before has there been so much information and well-meaning guidance in the area of mental health, yet depression is one of the leading causes of disability in our supposedly advanced or civilised world. Simply thinking happy thoughts does not appear to be the cure-all we would like to believe it to be, and certainly not possible for someone suffering the tortures of depression. It has become increasingly obvious how counterproductive it is to deny our true feelings in any situation. Nor do we have the authority or insight to tell another how they should or should not be feeling about something that is their right alone. This law of attraction also implies that our emotions are largely a matter of personal choice. However, if we really did have a choice about how we feel, nobody, and I mean nobody, would choose to be miserable.

There is a huge variety of feelings for us to express in our lives and each has its own individual value and purpose. There is also perhaps a reason for all these emotions outside of our own individual experiences. Diversity puts the life into our world and it is not just what is outside of us, but it is what is inside us, too. How boring a world it would it be if everybody was happy all of the time. The childhood chronicles of Winnie the Pooh have much to teach us about this. All of the characters have different traits and talents to bring to the table and the marvellous thing about this eclectic group of friends is how their individual personalities, fears and strengths are integral to the story as they take us on the most wonderful of adventures. It is the diversity of their dispositions that makes their stories and their adventures most enjoyable for us, and even though Eeyore is obviously clinically depressed his friends never have a problem with it; they love, accept and involve him regardless. He is never expected to be any different. This is because, when writing the adventures, author A Milne understood the value of his condition and contribution to the overall experience and story. It just would not be the same without him, and as Eeyore would say himself, 'Thanks for noticing.'

Things aren't really adding up for the law of attraction from a scientific emotional and even a logical perspective. It does of course make for a very plausible theory because when we are happy the whole world and everything in it appears brighter and when we are miserable we find darkness in everything as though we are attracting it either way. However, in order for something to be considered a universal law, it must apply to all people, at all times, in all circumstances. This is clearly not the case with the law of attraction, because the fact is we don't always get what we think we want, no matter how much focus and energy we apply to it and bad things do happen to good people, positive people and happy people. Our reality is such that our life is neither good nor bad because of the circumstance but because of how we perceive it. If we alter our perception of something it is different even if nothing has physically changed. So yes, it is possible that we may be able to change how we perceive our lives with the principles of the law of attraction, but, as science indicates, we cannot use it to manipulate our physical reality.

Intuitively and understandably we assume that it is we, with our thoughts, emotions and actions who are controlling the circumstances and outcomes of our lives. However, there can often be a huge disconnect between how we feel and the conditions under which we live. Privilege and prosperity don't always guarantee happiness and nor do our aspirations for the future always manifest as we anticipate. Life doesn't always do right by us despite our very best efforts and all our good intentions. Even though we are emotionally invested in our lives, our thoughts and intentions are not as attached to our physical reality as it would have us believe. At an atomic level, our reality has a mind of its own, a reality that adheres to a very orderly and calculated set of physical rules that is not in the least bit obligated by what we are pondering or passionate about.

When Einstein said, 'God does not play dice with the universe,' he understood that nothing is by chance or accident. There is no gambling or uncertainty with the laws of physics, they are calculated and precise and they will have their way with us regardless of what we think about or the plans we make. The equations of the universe are the invisible language of the story of our lives that will play out exactly as God has written it.

Hopefully, these laws of physics that have been dictating the position and evolution of every atom in our perceivable world from the beginning have a plan for what is to come that is better than the way things have turned out so far. Because the idea that mankind might be in charge of the fate of the world is indeed a worrisome one. In the short time that we have occupied this planet we have inflicted an enormous amount of harm on each other and the living systems that sustain us. To date and on balance, man has been far more destructive than of benefit to life on earth and we are running out of time to reverse the damage. If man really is creating his own future and in charge of his own destiny, then I fear we may buckle up and prepare for the worst. On the other hand, despite what appears on the surface, things may not be as haphazard or as uncertain as they seem. I think we need to give God a little more credit than that and I strongly suspect that the surface illusion of chaos and disorder belies a much deeper composition of intelligence, love and purpose.

In truth, the law of attraction cannot sensibly be used to describe the nature of existence, so we must wash our hands of it and move on if we are to have any hope of finding out what is really going on. So far, as the laws of physics suggest, we are not creating our lives with thought or intention, but instead all of our bodily and cosmic atoms are caught up in an unbreakable chain of science's invisible maths calculations that have brought us thus far in the evolution of the universe and that will proceed to take us into a future that is yet unknown.

It appears that the pervasive, time-honoured theory that man is in control of his own destiny needs to be examined a bit more closely, because it doesn't seem to be what is really going on at all. I propose another hypothesis. I propose that the reason we cannot always manifest exactly what we think we want is because we have decided before we came here exactly how our story would unfold and what path we would tread. We knew who we would meet, where we would meet them and under what circumstances. That these details cannot be altered regardless of how much focus or energy is directed otherwise. Therefore, unless what it is we are trying to manifest here, is in line with what we had already planned before we arrived, it will not show up. That the reason we incarnated as we did was not so much to create our physical world but simply to experience a reality that we think we inhabit. I have no doubt that this horse and I had arranged to meet exactly when and where we did. Our meeting was no accident, nor was she the manifestation of any thought/emotion vibrational frequency in this infinitesimally short life. It was a destiny neither of us could have avoided. It was a reunion that had been scheduled since the beginning of time itself. This means that every event and circumstance in my life up to this had to be meticulously arranged in order to facilitate it. Not only that, but also the lives and movements of everybody else I met along the way would have to have been just as calculated as mine to accommodate it. Destiny is not a flexible noun and it cannot operate in a vacuum. Destiny's reach can extend far and wide through space and time and it will not be bargained with, ignored or threatened. Looking back on my life, it is easy to connect the pieces of a very impressive jigsaw puzzle of magnificently detailed, individual events that have fitted together beautifully.

Initially, the arrival of this horse brought with it many concerns and uncertainties. I was filled with doubt and worry for her future. She, of course, was completely unconcerned with the unknown; but then, why would she be concerned? She was just a horse. Animals appear to live in the present moment and trouble themselves not with what lies ahead. However, more than this, I had a deep sense that she knew exactly what she had to do; she knew there was a plan for us. My job was to figure it out.

A cunningly crafted plan had brought us together, a plan that was decidedly more coercive than what I thought were simply the gentle whispers of an intuitive mind or heart. A plan that had be drafted long, long ago by the finest architect and mathematician with subatomic detail and beauty. Well before our two equal and loving souls took up our earthly mantle and put on our earthly robes, Síon and I knew exactly how our journey would enfold, but for the sake of the story and the experience we needed to forget, or at least I did.

Chapter 3: The Plan

'A person often meets his destiny on the road he took to avoid it.' - Jean de La Fontaine

As a child in Catholic schools, religious education was deemed as important as the air we breathe. We were indoctrinated with the principles of Catholicism by an army of nuns for eleven or so years. Not a bad thing by any means. I am immensely grateful to all of them for their part and provision in my life's journey. They were indeed a colourful collection of characters despite the plain black habit of tunic and veil that failed miserably to hide their wonderful individuality beneath. This devout and disciplined sisterhood would teach me everything I needed to know in order to save my sinful soul from the horrors of eternal damnation.

In those green and gullible years, I was never sure what it was that I feared the most, the wrath of God or the fires of hell. I was haunted by the fact that my every move and word, even my deepest thoughts were being closely watched by a loving but formidable God, lest I succumb to the temptations or chicanery of the devil himself. My sins had nowhere to hide, I could be seen by the Almighty, anywhere and all of the time. I found it quite daunting in my early years, but religion did have its upside. The Bible had blockbuster stories to entertain us, like David and Goliath, Noah and the ark, and Moses and the Israelites. It had fun parables to decode, with their moral or spiritual lessons cleverly hidden in plain sight. And of course there were the divine mysteries to baffle us, in particular the unfathomable riddle of the Holy Trinity, the Father, Son and Holy Ghost. It was three people in one. How could that possibly be? Nobody knew, because our inferior human minds would never be able to comprehend such a holy complexity as this, so it must just be accepted as is. I was good with that; it was one less thing to trouble my little mind.

Apart from the unsettling lack of personal privacy that came with being a Catholic, I was content enough with the general philosophy. For me at least, religious education was not the worst way to pass an hour every day and it was indeed comforting to be of the religion that was in the right about everything, or so we were told. For the most part, I happily succumbed to a slow, subtle indoctrination from Genesis to Revelation, rarely questioning its content.

As compliant as I was in those early years, there were, however, a few small details in the Holy Writ that did unsettle me a little. In particular, there were important aspects in the story of Jesus that appeared to be either ignored, glossed over or conveniently interpreted to foster a sense of fear, shame and inadequacy in us. In truth, Jesus was practising and preaching something wholly different and as far as I could see, nothing Jesus said or did encouraged any such divisive and destructive feelings. It is, of course, not difficult to instil such corrosive sensitivities in new, spongy minds and young, delicate hearts, even though some of the most significant features of Jesus' life and death seemed to contradict the whole saint and sinner concept that was drummed into us every day in school and for an hour at Mass on Sunday. If we look a little closer we will find that Jesus gave us some very big clues and even some very direct answers to some of life's great mysteries that we are still struggling with today.

To begin with, Jesus' coming was predicated long before his actual arrival. Not only his coming, but also pretty much every detail of his ancestors, his life and his death, his preachings and his future impact had all been foretold with uncanny accuracy. It is estimated by some that there are more than 300 prophecies about Jesus in the Old Testament. Practically every last detail of Jesus' life was written before he arrived, so he had no control over anything in his life. Jesus knew this, he had no problem with it and he freely admitted it on multiple occasions. The multitude and precision of the prophecies that Jesus was bound by are such that the mathematical probability of him fulfilling even a handful of them, let alone all of them, is staggeringly improbable, if not impossible. But he did fulfil them, all of them. In a study conducted by Peter Stoner, Chairman of the Departments of Mathematics and Astronomy at Pasadena College and 600 students from the InterVarsity Christian Fellowship, they came to an astonishing conclusion when they examined just eight of these prophecies. It was found that the likelihood that anyone would satisfy just eight of those prophecies was one in 10^{17} or one in 100 quadrillion.

Peter Stoner describes it like this:

'Let us try to visualize this chance. If you mark one of ten tickets, and place all of the tickets in a hat, and thoroughly stir them, and then ask a blindfolded man to draw one, his chance of getting the right ticket is one in ten. Suppose that we take 10^{17} silver dollars and lay them on the face of Texas. They will cover all of the state two feet deep. Now mark one of these silver dollars and stir the whole mass thoroughly, all over the state. Blindfold a man and tell him that he can travel as far as he wishes, but he must pick up one silver dollar and say that this is the right one. What chance would he have of getting the right one? Just the same chance that the prophets would have had of writing these eight prophecies and having them all come true in any one man, from their day to the present time, providing they wrote using their own wisdom.'

So Jesus had it all to do in order to beat the unimaginable odds and fulfil only fraction of what was predicted for him. Still, Jesus, a true champion, came through for us, and not just eight times, but over 300 so that he could do everything that had to be done for God and for us. It is clear from these figures that the story of Jesus had been written well and truly in advance. Jesus had a specific role and purpose to fulfil and all of those predictions meant he certainly wasn't making it up as he went along. A precise and detailed account that was executed at that level of accuracy did not leave Jesus with much room to manoeuvre and it does little to demonstrate that infinite number of possibilities that should have been available to him according to what we believe life affords us. This was a chapter in our history where there was absolutely no potential for any other possible outcomes. Throughout his life, Jesus did exactly what he was supposed to do according to the will of God, and here is the hidden truth in this: so did everybody else.

The prophecies surrounding the life of Jesus were always freely discussed with us in religious education, but I feel that the significance of having such a volume of predictive information has largely been missed. What is not appreciated is the scale and consequence of this prewritten story of one man, because it is not just one man. What we often fail to recognise is that it also involves all those before, during and after his incarnation. Jesus could not have carried out his role with such accuracy without the predetermined participation of all the others. This determinism that dominated Jesus' life will include his ancestors, anyone he interacted with during his life and, as predicted, those who have been influenced by his words and actions thereafter and even those who have not. For the prophecies, that is a whole lot of people that had to be who they were and do exactly as they did, so that Jesus could be and do exactly as he was and did. That is a whole lot of people before and after Jesus whose lives were already mapped out for them and who were denied infinite, creative possibilities to choose from. Where was the law of attraction for them? Where was even free will?

Aside from the predictions of the Old Testament, Jesus himself made no secret of the fact that his life and the lives of all involved was a foregone conclusion. Evidence of this is provided in spades around the time of his death, in particular. At the last supper, Jesus announced that he would be betrayed that night by one of his beloved disciples. He knew it was Judas who would carry out the fateful act but refused to release his name, presumably because Judas would then surely be prevented from carrying out his sacred role by the other disciples. In addition, Jesus informed Simon Peter that he would deny Our Lord three times before the cock crowed. I remember as a child feeling such pity for Judas, who apparently had no choice but to do what he did, to someone he loved so dearly. Jesus knew what lay ahead of him, his destiny was already written. There was a plan that must be adhered to. So, for Judas, the dice was loaded from the start, he had no choice in the matter and there would be no getting out of it. He had to play his part so that Jesus could die by design. I always felt this was a bit unfair on poor Judas, who proceeded to hang himself with the torment of what he had done.

Jesus did not say that he 'might' be betrayed or denied that night. He did not mention that it was one of an infinite number of possibilities that might occur. Instead, Jesus knew his fate was sealed in a sacred plan that could not be altered. This knowledge did not lessen the pain and suffering that he would endure, but his awareness of the significance of his journey allowed him to accept it with grace and love. Not even Jesus' favourite, Peter, could avoid his part. Peter was Jesus' most loyal and trusted disciple, yet even when he was given notification in advance of how he would thrice reject his association to Jesus, he was unable to act to the contrary. Yes, Peter, too, had to fulfil his role. So from the disciple whom it was least expected, Jesus was denied three times as predicted. Jesus knew what lay ahead but chose to do nothing to avoid a destiny with torture and death even though it seemed like there were no shortage of opportunities to do so. Peter did not want to deny his association to Jesus but was unable to do otherwise, no matter how uncharacteristic it was of him. And clearly poor Judas had been chosen long before he was born to do the dirty deed of betrayal.

But Jesus, Judas and Peter were not the only ones playing their role and fulfilling their earthly assignment. In his conversation with Pontius Pilate, Jesus makes it clear that he, too, as well as many others, was merely following orders from a higher power. After his arrest in Jerusalem and prior to his dispensation by Pilate, Jesus faces a 'trial' by the Jewish judicial body, the Sanhedrin. Jesus is mocked and beaten during his hearing, but does not mount a defence and rarely responds to their accusations of blasphemy. Jesus understands that there is no point in arguing his case or resisting his fate. He is resolutely resigned to what is written for his life and his death and consequently is condemned by the Jewish authorities when he will not deny that he is the son of God. The Jewish court, however, cannot sentence anyone to death, so they take Jesus to the governor of Roman Judaea, Pontius Pilate and ask that he be tried for claiming to be the king of the Jews. To claim to be a king was a direct threat to Caesar and Rome and the Jewish authorities used this angle to petition for the death penalty. When placed in front of Pilate for questioning, Jesus is undaunted and maintains a staunch silence. Pilate then has to threaten him in order to get a response. Pilate points out that he holds the power to absolve or condemn Jesus, but Jesus is not at all affected by his proud boasts of authority. Jesus knows his fate is sealed but not by Pilate's mandate and brazenly reminds him of this fact when he says, 'Thou couldest have no power at all against me, except it were given thee from above.' (John 19: 11). Jesus knew that Pilate's position of authority was an illusion. He did not have any charge *at all* over Jesus' future as he thought. Pilate's sovereignty was subordinate to God's. Pilate, too, had to follow the script. He was acting under instruction from God who in his eternal wisdom had already determined his fate. God was the one who was really pulling the strings and it was a mistake to think otherwise. Pilate's supposed position of authority did not have the power to thwart God's plan at all and Jesus knew it.

Jesus is quite bold when confronting Pilate because, again he knew it would be pointless to argue his case as it was only going to end one way regardless. Jesus is wholly committed to what lies before him and does nothing to try and avoid the pain and torment of that eventuality, even though Pilate has no real desire to condemn Jesus to death, as, realistically, he can find no cause to do so. The high priests on the other hand and in particular, Caiaphas, had clear intent and definite motive to kill Jesus. There are, however, conflicting reports of what this motive was in the gospels. Whether they wanted to avoid the political unrest and subsequent wrath of the Romans that Jesus' huge following was threatening, or whether it was simply down to egos and incomes is unclear. Either way, Jesus ended up in front of Pilate and it was Caiaphas and his cronies who landed him there. Here, Jesus points out Pilate's error in believing he has some influence either way over the situation when he says, 'Thou couldest have no power *at all* against me, except it were given thee from above.' In the next half of his statement, Jesus says, 'Therefore he that delivered me unto thee hath the greater sin.' Jesus could not have been talking about sin in this statement if everybody was doing God's will. What Jesus is saying is that Caiaphas, who had delivered him to Pilate, was making a bigger mistake by thinking he was manipulating the situation for his own earthly ends, when in actual fact he too was an instrument of God's will. Though he secretly believed otherwise, it was God's will and agenda that Caiaphas was serving, not his own, with his underhanded efforts to dispose of Jesus using Pontius Pilate and Roman law. Caiaphas was acting out God's will, not outsmarting it as he thought. Caiaphas thought he was engineering the death of Jesus, Pilate thought he had the power to save him if he wanted, both were wrong. Both simply did exactly what they had to do in a story that was non-negotiable. What this chapter in Jesus' life tells us is that in the end, it is matter-less what we think we want or don't want because regardless of desire, motive or status. God's will will prevail. This is as true today as it was 2000 years ago.

During the life and death of Jesus there are numerous indicators that he was following a path, script or storyline. That God was in charge at all times and Jesus greatest desire was to fulfil that role and purpose, for God and for all of us. At no point in his arrest, trial, sentencing or murder does Jesus resist or object to his fate. Any rational person in that position would be pleading their case and begging for their lives but Jesus does nothing. Jesus is fully aware of what is in store for him but exercises total surrender to what he knows to be his destiny or God's will. In addition, as the son of God with the ability to perform miracles, Jesus could easily have called upon his divine power and authority to change the course of events but he did not.

Jesus was ready to die when he did. He never attempted to obstruct the course of events when the time came. There is no doubt he had the cosmic wherewithal to do so as he had already avoided being stoned by the Jews on an earlier occasion at the Feast of the Dedication, in Solomon's porch, when they tried to tempt him into an open and blasphemous declaration that he was God in the flesh. Such an admission could then be used as an accusation against him, punishable by death. Knowing this, Jesus fearlessly and without hesitation affirmed his Messianic identity to them and when they became violent and threatened to stone him, he made good his escape. Using his miraculous powers, we are told, Jesus concealed himself and passed through their midst. The text implied that Jesus had either magically made himself invisible or had altered his appearance to become unrecognisable to his would-be assassins. Either way, Jesus was not ready to die at this time or in this manner and used some form of celestial magic to sidestep the angry mob. It all made for enthralling reading in our religious education classes. Jesus was our version of Harry Potter with his invisibility cloak.

Jesus knew when and how he was going to die and had more opportunities than chances to be released from his obligation. Not only could Jesus have used his own extraordinary abilities to avoid his eventual fate, but he could also have called upon the power and resources of his father in heaven. When Simon Peter drew his sword against the soldiers and mob that had arrived to arrest Jesus in the Garden of Gethsemane, Jesus assured him that he did not want or need any protection or assistance: 'Thinkest thou that I cannot now pray to my Father, and he shall presently give me more than twelve legions of angels?' (Matthew 26: 53). Jesus had at his disposal all the might and muscle of the heavens, but when the time came to die, he handed himself over willingly to his captors in order for scriptures to be fulfilled. Jesus knew the time had come for him to die as planned. In his total compliance it could be said that, more than anyone else, the person responsible for the death of Jesus was Jesus himself. Jesus was sworn to live and to die as predicted and was never going to break that sacred covenant, just like everybody else in the story.

It was not only in the events surrounding his death did Jesus affirm that God is in charge of all things at all times. This truth is reiterated throughout Jesus' teachings with statements like:

'I can of My own self do nothing.' (John 5: 30).

'The word which ye hear is not mine.' (John 14: 24).

'I am come not to do Mine own will.' (John 6: 38).

'The words that I say, I speak not from Myself.' (John 14: 10).

Over and over again Jesus told us that nothing he either said or did was his own doing or will. Nothing. It could be said that the son of God was merely occupying an automated, pre-programmed physical body called Jesus that did and said everything that it was supposed to in exactly the right time and place. In his earthly incarnation therefore, Jesus did not have freedom of choice or the gift of infinite creative possibilities to manifest the future of his desires. The law of attraction did not apply to Jesus even though he was undoubtedly operating at an exceptionally high vibration of spiritual purity. It did not guarantee him a long and prosperous life. He did, however, live the life and the death that he desired not because of the law of attraction, but because the whys, wheres and whens were already determined and Jesus was happy to surrender totally to the Father's will down to the very last detail. It just so happened that unlike the rest of us, then and now, Jesus arrived with the knowledge of what that will was, the reason behind it and also the knowing that he had agreed to it long before he came among us. On the surface it would seem that, in this respect, Jesus had an unfair advantage over the rest of us, but the spiritual truth runs much deeper than that.

Every character involved in the story of Jesus made it possible. It was no accident that there was no room at the inn for a heavily pregnant Virgin Mary and her weary husband. Jesus needed to be born in a humble stable and all the people who arrived at the inn and checked in before them made that so. It was no accident that they ran out of wine at the wedding at Cana so Jesus could perform his first miracle. It was no accident that for the rest of his life there were very strategically placed sick people to be healed and sinners to be forgiven. It was no accident that in the end a baying crowd 'chose' an innocent Jesus for flogging and crucifixion over Barabbas who was a murderer and insurrectionist. Everybody played a blinder so that we could all, for ages to come, benefit from the most famous story in history.

It is strange how we can appreciate the fact that Jesus' life was a prewritten contract with God, but do not apply the same ideology for ourselves. All Catholics will recognise the fact that Jesus' life was the deliberate fulfilling of a prophecy written in the Hebrew Bible, but the broader ramifications for such a fact is very much lost on us. That is, that all the other characters in the story of Jesus are fulfilling their destiny with the exact same uncompromising accuracy as Jesus. The fact is that the wrongdoers as well as the righteous were under obligation to their fate and did not possess the freedom of choice we blame or exalt them for. That if there was a plan for the life of Jesus, there was also a plan for every other character in the story, too.

There is no doubt that Jesus' life and death was a meticulously planned, prewritten inevitability, which means that all the other players in the story had to be very precisely written in to accommodate it. It is impossible to pre-write and predict what one man will do for thirty-three years without doing the same for all the other people he interacted with. In addition, Jesus did not just appear out of nowhere, he had to have ancestors that accommodated his being, as everybody did. Every detail of Jesus' life was adhered to according to scripture, nothing was left to chance and nothing was amended or adjusted. Jesus knew the who, what and where of it all with absolute certainty. Jesus' life story was mapped out before he entered it, but he wasn't the only one. Every person involved in and every circumstance surrounding his story made it possible. This illuminating fact ripples out much farther than we are inclined to give it credit. Placing that number of people in a particular place, time and situation would take a serious amount of beforehand planning from every different direction in a plot that would have to go way back, to the very beginning of time. According to the laws of physics, it goes back to the Big Bang.

It is inconceivable to think that such a scrupulous degree of organisation surrounding the life and death of a man for thirty-three years is some kind of anomaly in space and time. That it was some kind of blip of order and accuracy in an otherwise random universe that is normally full of infinite possibilities for everyone else other than Jesus before and after. That this unique period of flawless structuring began with the birth of Jesus and came to an abrupt ending after his death when we all returned to living lives of indefinite futures and creative choices. I don't think so. On a physical level, every atom in the universe has behaved itself impeccably and evolved in time precisely to create our current reality since the beginning. On a spiritual level, too, things needed to be just as organised from the start so that all could work out as planned for Jesus. In order for destiny to be fulfilled, Jesus needed the sick and the sinners just as much as they needed him.

Jesus made no secret of the fact that his life was well and truly mapped out for him and he did also acknowledge the obligations of others in that same inevitability. Jesus knew that only some were destined to follow in his footsteps and some were not. If everybody that encountered Jesus, heard him speak or learned of his 'works' were favourably inspired to live with that same love and forgiveness then he would never have made it to the cross. He would not have been able to honour those long-written prophecies and God's wishes in his death because nobody would have wanted him to be crucified. In order for Jesus to fulfil his destiny it was essential for him to have people who were with him and people who were against him. For some it was their destiny to be persuaded by Jesus words, for some it was not. This is the reason that Jesus spoke in parables. Jesus was fully aware that his teachings would not resonate with or influence everybody in a positive way; only those who were chosen to follow him would do so. Jesus spoke plainly and frankly to his apostles, but for others he mainly spoke in parables so that only those destined to be swayed by his words and life could hear or see the hidden message. When he was alone, his apostles asked him about the parables, and he said to them, 'To you has been given the secret of the kingdom of God, but for those outside, everything comes in parables; in order that they may indeed look, but *not* perceive, and may indeed listen, but *not* understand; so they may *not* turn again and be forgiven.' (Mark 4:10–12). Read those words over again if you have to, because this is one of the most important insights into the nature of existence that Jesus reveals to us. He tells us that he is purposely speaking in riddles so that some people do not decipher the hidden messages and subsequently amend their wicked ways and be redeemed. Now why would Jesus be so unkind as to hide the secret to God's holy kingdom from some and not others? We have been led to believe that Jesus came here to save us all. Apparently, this not the case. The truth is that Jesus had no intention of saving everybody, because if he did, he would never have made it to the cross. His sheep would hear his word because they had been chosen by the Father to do so, this was not up for negotiation: 'and no man is able to pluck them out of my Father's hand.' (John 10: 27). Those who would not hear his message were not supposed to, because those who denied Jesus were as important to his destiny and God's will as those that followed him. Please let that fact sink in: that God's will exists in both the 'saint' and the 'sinner', because in order for Jesus to be crucified, God required the services of both the righteous and the irreverent. Jesus' extensive use of parables was not only important for sorting out his contemporaries into sheep and strays, but also instrumental in providing a huge platform of debate for future generations. Jesus' stories were purposefully open to interpretation so that we could find individual meaning, direction and, yes, even division for years to come.

In every parable that Jesus left us with it is possible to come up with various different interpretations and messages. Symbolism was rife in Jesus' lifetime and it is easy to use it to manipulate any of the stories to support any point of view. For example, in Mark 11:12–13, Jesus curses a fig tree to death because he was hungry and it did not have any fruit. On the surface, it looks like a simple case of low blood sugar making Jesus irritable and reactive. However, trees in the scriptures were often used to represent a mind or mindset, or way of thinking. Thus, when Jesus killed the fig tree, with its gnarled and twisted branches, he could have been making the point that he was putting an end to ignorance with his enlightened teachings. There are other interpretations also, one where it was reasoned that, while the tree had no fruit, it did have leaves, at a time of year when it shouldn't have and it could therefore be compared to someone promising to do good but not doing, and that is why Jesus cursed it. Interpretations range from the sublime to the ridiculous on just about any of Jesus' parables, and except for the times when Jesus speaks clearly and directly, everything is wide open for discussion. Whether you want to take the gospels literally or interpretively is up to you, but what is clear is that the scriptures were purposely written in code to hide the mysteries of life so that we can take what we are supposed to from it.

Indeed, it is not just Jesus' words and stories that are open for discussion, the entire content of the holy Bible is legitimately up for grabs to any curious and disputatious mind. There are lots of reasons why this is so, one being the translation problem. Originally the Bible was written in Hebrew and Aramaic. The New Testament however, was written in Ancient Greek which is one of the most difficult languages to translate. This is because it uses custom symbols that are not explicit but can mean many different things depending on the context of the text. The Bible was then translated into Latin and then English. It has been translated many times since then in many different languages. Translation can present problems that can interfere with the context of the text. Problems such as terminology, alternatives, grammar, syntax, rhetoric, cultural issues, comparison, metaphor, oxymoron, idiomatic phrases, sayings, irony, humour, sarcasm, not to mention personal bias. My point is that in the process of translation it is possible that the Bible gathered and or lost a little moss as it rolled through the different languages.

There is also the fact that Christianity and its teachings are very fragmented, with so many different perspectives and agendas it's hard to know what is sound and what is silly. Among others, Christianity today has persuasions such as Roman Catholics, Greek Orthodox, Southern Baptists, Methodists, Christian Scientists, right-wing Presbyterians and Pentecostalists. With each having its own take on the teachings and hidden meanings behind the words of Jesus, it is not unlike the Chinese Whisper that turns out to be a story barely recognisable from its original after a sequence of repetitions. The surface disunity of Christianity can be found to make its way right down to the gospels themselves. There were twelve disciples and more gospels written other than the four of Mathew, Mark, Luke and John, which were the only ones chosen to be included in the Bible, and even these four gospels contain their own amount of refractions and inconsistencies.

Christianity itself had a messy and divided start. It began with two alternative and antagonistic traditions, orthodox Christianity as we now know it and Gnosticism (from the Greek word, gnosis, meaning knowledge). The orthodox faction, which we are familiar with today, diligently nursed a strong political and theological agenda, while the Gnostics were chin deep in the search for the deeply hidden, esoteric truths of our existence. The Gnostics had their own set of gospels that depicted a different take on Jesus and his life. Gnosticism was much more of an experiential Christianity, with its emphasis on uncovering the hidden truths of reality and acknowledgment of individual divinity, rather than the sin and retribution theme of the orthodox camp. Gnosticism did not require forgiveness of sins or necessarily entail any type of physical sacrament, but was more concerned with acquiring secret knowledge, or gnosis. The Gnostics believed that our true divine nature is obscured by ignorance as well as religious conviction and fervour, a concept that was beyond offensive to the steadfast saint and sinner narrative of orthodox beliefs. As it transpired, orthodox Christianity seemed to attract the most mass appeal and won the people's choice award to become the accepted religion of the day. Gnosticism subsequently fell away into obscurity. Hell's fire and damnation won out at that time, but sure, who doesn't love a good crime and punishment story.

More recently, there is the intriguing theory that the whole story of Jesus is nothing more than a big fat fairy tale. That the Jesus of the New Testament is a mythical figure adapted from the ancient pagan myths of the dying and resurrecting godman Osiris-Dionysus, who as it turns out, was miraculously born on 25 December before three shepherds and went on to have a very similar life and death experience to that of Jesus Christ. Using modern scholarship, evidence of this is put forward in book, *The Jesus Mysteries*, by Timothy Freke and Peter Gandy.

We may never have definitive proof who is right and who is wrong (if there is such a thing) and the most anyone can do is find their own personal truth in whichever version or combination of versions resonates most with them. Individual interpretation and preference is, after all, what has been going on since the beginning and it is everyone's right to exercise those principles. That being said, this is where science can be extremely useful in sorting out all of the blarney that religion has cultivated out of spirit throughout the ages. Science and spirituality may not like each other very much these days, but when you align the evidence of modern science with its parallel spiritual truth, all of the shady and flimsy tenets of religion fall away very quickly. Because in science there is no personal perspective, there is no agenda, there are only facts. These facts are often highly counterintuitive but still remain, regardless.

As we have already established that our physical reality is not created according to how we are feeling, let us now move on to the issue of time and the natural assumption that the future does not yet exist for us. Intuitively, life would have us believe that, beyond the present moment, there is nothing. That we are intentionally or unintentionally creating our future by our choice of actions in the now. This is a very understandable assumption, given the enormous variety of occurrences and outcomes happening all around us for everybody else and when we cannot see what is coming for ourselves. The theory is that life is a work in progress. We live in the prison of a perpetual present that is rigidly wedged between memory and expectation. We are on a relentless journey towards a future that has not yet been created and is dependent on the free will choices we make in the here and now. We appear to be building our future with the bricks of today and considering the current, dire state of our planetary home, we desperately need everyone to make all the right decisions going forward. Because we are blind to the future we naturally assume that it has not yet been constructed, and that because it is so reliant on the conduct of so many it is therefore unpredictable, unstable and disposed to any eventuality good, bad or indifferent. At face value this is certainly how it would all appear, but in the perplexing complexities of our reality nothing really is as it seems.

For a start, neither the past, present nor the future has anything to do with the formation of our reality. Most of the laws of physics are symmetric with respect to time, meaning that it doesn't matter whether time moves forwards or backwards. If time ran in reverse, all the laws of physics would work the same. The pervasive belief that time only runs in one direction and that the future does not yet exist has no ultimate justification in the perfectly reversible laws of nature. Time and matter are not as dependent on each other as it would appear. The laws that govern the behaviour of the very fundamental particles of our existence are completely independent of time's direction. Yes, not only do these heartless laws of physics have no regard for our feelings, but also they thumb their nose at our experience of time. If you believe the laws of physics, there is just as much reality to the future as there is to the past and to the now.

We live in a world that is governed by time, where we chastise ourselves over past mistakes, fantasise over a potential future, and all the while trapped in an everlasting present moment. Practically every choice we make involves time at some level. Whether it is to do with our day's schedule, our age, our past decisions or our future plans, we cannot escape time. However, time is not as real as it pretends to be. The fact that we have to adjust our clocks to show the 'correct' time shows us that time is mutable. Time is not constant in the universe. Proven by several experiments, time is affected by motion and by gravity. A moving clock ticks slower than a stationary one and clocks in outer space tick faster than those close to the gravitational force of the earth's surface. If time is not a constant, how can it even exist? It was Einstein that first discovered that time itself was a perception rather than a reality. In a letter to the family of his deceased friend, Michele Besso, he states, 'For us believing physicists, the distinction between past, present and future is only a stubbornly persistent illusion.' The universal flow of time from a past that has happened to a future that has not makes perfect intuitive sense and is perhaps the most fundamental experience of our existence. Yet the perception of its flow does not correspond to the physical reality. Time doesn't flow, and past, present and future cannot sensibly be defined. Just because we cannot see what the future holds for us does not mean it does not actually exist outside of our abilities to perceive it. Our best theories suggest that time is not real and it is possible that the state of the universe as a whole doesn't evolve with time in any conventional way. In other words, the structure and behaviour of our reality has nothing to do with time.

    The difficulty in defining time is that, unlike atoms, it does not seem to have any fundamental properties that can be observed. Time is something that we perceive in much the same way as we perceive our physical reality through our senses of sight, hearing, touch, smell and taste, it is an experience and it is individual to each of us. Time appears linear to us, past, present and future, because our senses are programmed to perceive time in this way. Time is relative to the observer, it is individual and subjective and there is no such thing as absolute time. If time is a perception, then we cannot say that the future does not exist just because we cannot see it. There are lots of things around us that we cannot see. The future is by far not the only thing we have a blind spot to. There are many things that sit outside the range of our very restricted sensory perception. In fact, we are completely blind to 99% of all activity in this universe of ours and there are plants that see more than us humans. Not being able to see what life has in store for us in the future is not a good enough reason to assume that there is nothing there yet. In our efforts to define time scientifically, the future, even though we cannot see it, must be treated equally to the past and the present. We cannot separate the future from the past and the present and apply different laws to each. All are aspects of time. What this tells us is that if we do not have any control over the past, neither do we have control of the present or the future. If we cannot influence the past, we cannot influence the future. Time is time is time and must be subject to the same laws throughout, irrespective of our abilities or limitations to perceive it.

For science, determining the future is, in theory, not impossible, just very difficult. In physics, the 'state' of an object is a combination of its position and as its velocity. In the physical world that we perceive, there are things, systems and objects and each has a different state. They come in different arrangements and configurations, but the state of the system is basically everything you need to know to figure out what this thing is going to do next or has been doing previously. For example, with a tennis ball, if you know its position, its velocity and its orientation in space and the state of everything around it, you could use the equations of the universe to calculate where the tennis ball would be in the future and where it had been at any time in the past. By the same token, if we knew the precise state of every particle in the universe, we could work out the future as well as the past for everything. The movements of the greatest bodies in the universe, as well as that of the tiniest atom, could be calculated backwards and forwards from any given point in time. The future would be truly available to us and the past could be identified with an exactness more reliable than any subjective memory or biased history book.

Obviously, given the magnitude of the requirement (knowing the state of every particle in the universe), such information is a little out of our reach at the moment and the task is further aggravated by the Heisenberg Uncertainty Principle, which tells us that we can never know both the position and the velocity of any particle at the same time. This is because position and momentum are completely independent of each other. Crudely put, if something is in position it is not moving and if something is moving, it doesn't have a position. Poor scientists can't catch a break either way. However, the obstacles that prevent us from figuring out the future do not alter the fact that there is a determinate matter of fact at every moment about where everything is and what everything is doing and that the way everything evolves in time, too, is deterministic.

So far, according to science, all life as we know it is evolving independently of both time and thought, and not in a haphazard or random fashion. Life is progressing in an orderly and determined manner with an accuracy that dissolves into infinity.

It was not only Jesus that was subject to the laws of physics, but all of us have also been enslaved by them, not just on a surface or spiritual level but right down to the very atoms of our existence, too. The laws of physics have snared us in their plan for life, for the universe.

Our future therefore is not the open book or blank canvas we imagine it to be but is more like an inescapable destiny that sits beyond our perceptual abilities. This is where Jesus had the edge on us. Jesus had first-hand understanding of the uncompromising nature of his reality. Jesus knew that his future was already laid out for him and he knew what it was down to the very last detail of who, what, where and when. This information is not so available to the rest of us, but we are at least beginning to understand that life is not quite as uncertain as it would seem. Our lives, just like Jesus' life, are as orchestrated and organised as his was, down to the finest detail. Jesus also knew that his life was rigidly intertwined with everyone else's and remains so. To this day and just like Jesus, all our paths are set for a specific and sacred purpose. Just like Jesus our destiny, too, is unavoidable; it remains tied to his just as his is tied to ours, and to each other and to the continuing story. Jesus was not the only one of us with a destiny, but he was perhaps the only one who knew with absolute certainty what it was and why. I do not believe there would be a divine decree for the life of Jesus and his disciples and not for the rest of us. I do not believe such a thing is even possible. The story of Jesus continues and we are part of it. It began long before his birth with his ancestors and did not end when he died on the cross. We are all still part of that story, fulfilling our roles by design just as Jesus did. There is nothing accidental, indiscriminate or unplanned in our lives; uncertainty is an illusion of epic proportions.

When God created this world, in his infinite intelligence he did an excellent job at hiding the future from us. We cannot perceive it, we cannot calculate it and according to particle physics we cannot change it. But that doesn't mean it is not already there, and until science learns how to outsmart divine wisdom, we are blind to it. Until we find a way to locate every particle in the universe and then circumvent the Heisenberg Uncertainty Principle we must be content with fortune tellers or prophets, genuine or otherwise, who profit from our deepest insecurities about what lies ahead.

There has been a plan from the beginning of time. It is a story, already written from start to finish. It is the most incredible story ever told. It was written by the wisest, most loving and imaginative mind in the universe. Ours. It is a story that began with the creation of form and time from a place where there was neither. This spectacular new dimension was filled with colour, contour and diversity. It contains many worlds and is the setting for one huge, evolving story of innumerable individual experiences that are interconnected yet separate. These marvellously diverse experiences are made possible through the many different forms, perspectives, limitations, challenges and levels of awareness within each embodiment. Initially primitive and unsophisticated, the story slowly expands in form and complexity with increasing participation and awareness. Over time, new forms and experiences are added to the story while others are lost forever. It is a story that contains lots of white-knuckle rollercoaster rides of highs and lows, with many plot twists and turns and with magic and mystery where nothing at all is what it seems. Within this one epic tale there are countless individual stories of tragedy, sacrifice, love and romance, heroism, adventure and comedy that fit like jigsaw pieces in a sequence that builds into one glorious paradoxical pattern designed with all the mathematical precision and beauty of the finest architecture.

The author's name is love. Love is not a single being, but is composed of many beautiful, eternal entities or gods who wish to create and explore. So, love composed a story and constructed a stage so that the gods could all be a part of this marvellous narrative. In the story, these infinite, all-powerful, all-knowing gods can adopt a character and a role in order to experience things that are otherwise not possible from their place of being. Such things as time and form, growth and change, learning and service, diversity and adversity, as well as different emotions and states, but most of all they want to experience the challenges of limitation. These limitless beings wanted to experience different ways and levels of confinement because existing in an infinite state for an eternity can get a bit samey. So, these exuberant, curious and creative gods get to choose any character or form, because any and all of the splendid incarnations offer a unique and magnificent experience and perspective, as well as being a vital contribution to the storyline. They chose to abandon their sameness for a reality where they would have variety to stimulate them and limitations to challenge them. The gods fully understand that in their choice they will be required to forego temporarily who and what they really are or at least certain aspects of that. It is this limited awareness that will permit all of the illusions that make the reality of the role and experience possible.

To facilitate each experience and role, this new dimension will rely heavily on contrast. The absence of light will provide the dark, the absence of heat will give cold, the absence of joy will be despair. Their infinity will appear confined and their eternity will seem temporal. Even love will have a polar opposite and it will be called fear. Fear will be generated by the lack of awareness of who the gods really are and it will present itself in many different ways. All of this because in order to experience and/or demonstrate all of what they are, they will need to be exposed to all that they are not. In the wickedly, wonderful paradox of this new world, the infinite power of love will be illuminated by that which seems contrary, even in the extreme. They will all encounter these contradictions many times in their lives through their interactions with each other and their environment.

Within the confines of their earthly guise the gods will not remember who they really are, nor will they recognise all of their eternal soul mates around them masquerading in different costumes and roles. They will not realise that the challenges and difficulties they present to each other are firmly rooted in unconditional and unlimited love and devotion. Each incarnation will be an individual experience, but primarily each one is an undertaking of love and service to each other and the incredible story of a universe and its life forms. Some roles and journeys in this story will be longer or more challenging than others. There will be roles of privilege and prosperity, as well as tragedy and torture, and there will be everything in between. All characters will have a corresponding level of spiritual awareness to accommodate their role, which will be made available or withheld as required. Every part is sacred in this story. Every part crucial to the plot. Every entry, every exit, every thought, every word, every action, every form, every meeting, every cause and every consequence has reason and is a vital piece of a plan and an outcome that, once in, they will not see but we will be sworn to serve.

It is only from outside this wonderful new dimension and their unlimited place of being that the gods can see the story in its entirety. They can see the magnificence of its evolution in every detail from start to finish. They can see each role and path, its wonders, its difficulties, its value and its service. However, instead of observing it, they can, if they so choose, be a part of it. They can assume a role and a character at any point in the story, from its beginning to its end, for its individual experience and to contribute to its development and its animation. They can play any part or they can, if they wish, remain on set behind the scenes to observe and support. The gods do have free will, but only outside of the story. They can choose to participate in the story or not. That choice is theirs, but if they choose to take up the mantle and enter this new realm of experiencing, they must relinquish their will for the sake of the plot. In a story that was written a very long time ago, where everything has a precise and glorious purpose, they will be required to stick to script and follow the path that divine intelligence has already constructed. Ad-libbing is impossible in an already perfectly created illusion and story.

Chapter 4: The Illusion of Reality

'Reality is merely an illusion, albeit a persistent one.' - Albert Einstein

This is where things get a little abstract and mysterious, to say the least. This is where we leave common sense behind us for a bit and science shows us that everything we assume to be real about our reality is not. In essence, our everyday, intuitive understanding of our physical world and existence is nowhere near what is really going on. The catastrophic divide between what we perceive as our material world and the true nature of its constituent matter is nothing short of mind shattering. Nothing is really as it is seems, nothing is actually solid, nothing is liquid and nothing is really a gas; this is just how it all appears to us. Everything, including our own body, is nothing more than waves of energy. Everything is simply an illusion of sorts where our brains construct and convince us of the diverse forms and textures of everything we physically encounter during our time here. The fact is, the constitution of our physical world has much more in common with a dream than with materiality.

So far, science has had quite the journey in its quest to get a handle on the true character and composition of the reality that we see and touch all around us. A journey that began long before Newton's laws of physics has led into the magical and mysterious world of quantum mechanics and as it turns out, our tangible, observable world isn't as concrete as it might seem. Thanks to the wonders of current technologies, the study of the atomic and subatomic levels of our physical universe has exposed a very different structure, and disposition to a reality that we are not privy to, from the sophisticated but limited apparatus of the human form and physiology. Gone from our materiality are the fabrics of solid, liquid and gas that we were once certain of. Our universal substrate does not consist of or behave anything like what we humanly perceive it to be or do. In truth, our physical reality consists of some very shady goings-on between energy and matter. Fields of energy are what everything is really made of, particles are what we see, and the relationship between the two is cryptic to say the least, with matter's ability to dissolve into energy and back again depending on whether or not we are looking at it. Sound ridiculous? It gets worse.

In our ongoing quest to unravel the mysteries of the universe, so far we have managed to isolate what seem to be the two main components of our reality, waves of energy and tiny particles of matter. But things aren't really this simple at all. In fact, the true character of our reality is actually quite slippery. It is sometimes wave-like and sometimes particle-like and, as crazy as it sounds, it all depends on whether or not we are looking at it. Light is fundamentally ambiguous and the question of whether it is composed of particles or waves has been baffling scientists since the days of Einstein. Actually, light can behave both as a particle and a wave, but what is even more interesting is when it changes from one to the other. The transformation of wave energy into particles and vice versa was first noted in the famous and baffling double slit experiment, where it was found that light waves transformed into particles by the simple act of being observed by a measuring device. During this simple experiment, light mysteriously changes from waves of energy to particles when it is being examined. Light takes shape and form as it is being viewed and returns to energy when the focus is removed. It was first thought that it was only light that had the ability to behave as either a wave or a stream of particles, but subsequent experiments have demonstrated that all the quantum particles that make up material reality have this dual nature. What this quantum conundrum seems to suggest is that our physical reality only assembles itself when we are looking at it, but does not exist or mysteriously disappears when outside of our view. For example, the moon or anything else in this universe does not exist unless it has a pair of eyes on it.

Our reality, therefore, can be differentiated into two distinct but inseparable 'layers'. On the surface, a perceived materialistic and fatalistic occupation as outlined by Einstein's classical mechanics where atoms abide by an uncompromising code of conduct to construct a sure fated reality. This is the world we have been discussing already, the one we live in and are aware of. Hiding beneath the surface, at the smallest scales of energy levels of atoms and subatomic particles, is the wacky world of quantum queerness. Here there is no such thing as the state of individual things in the world, only a probability. Also known as the wave function of the universe, it is everything the world is. It is the invisible land of potential and possibilities that so flagrantly contradicts our experience of the world and has scientists scratching their heads in bewilderment. Here, the tennis ball that can be so accurately mapped out in Einstein's dimension is nowhere to be found, but could potentially be everywhere, even though there is no actual disconnect between the two worlds.

    The difficulty that this dual nature presents to science is how to interpret and define this unseen world of everything and nothing, which has given rise to a few different theories. The other problem is finding a solid scientific bridge or correspondence between these two worlds of atoms and energy to make sense of their separate but inseparable properties. There is also the glaring question that if atoms have the ability to transform into waves of pure potential and we are made of these self-same atoms why we can't do the same. Why can't we at least access this treasure chest of infinite possibilities in our daily lives? There are some that say we can, that because this field of energy and everything is our true nature, all we have to do is to tune into this source vibration emotionally and from there we can transform our lives with all of the possibilities that lie therein. Turns out that accessing this promised land of infinite potential isn't quite as simple as adjusting the feeling frequency a little.

    Here is the clincher, and this is important so you will need to pay attention. The difficulty with the quantum world is that it seems to be denied to us by the fact that we are alive. In our physical state we cannot access it. As already discussed, the double slit experiment shows us that the mere act of trying to observe this quantum world of waves of energy causes it to collapse and assemble itself into all the particles and form that we perceive in our physical world. We cannot yet definitively evaluate this mysterious waveform of the universe at the source of all that we are, because every time we do it turns into the particles of our material world. It is precisely that act looking at it that removes us from it. There is a dividing wall that keeps us from the everything and the nothing of our true nature; it is our life. As long as we are alive and awake in this realm we are continuously observing and appraising our reality, irrespective of any vibration we think we might be emitting. In this life we are incarcerated in a perceivable material existence where every particle in the universe is governed by the iron fist of the laws of physics. So, until we die, the infinite potential and possibilities that exist at the core of our being are withheld from us by the simple fact that we are aware of ourselves and our surroundings in this dimension. Even in sleep or meditation, we still have awareness, it is just directed elsewhere. It is that which disconnects us from our quantum self. It is our act of constant observation that keeps us here in this predetermined, precalculated prison of matter.

The hunt is ongoing in the world of physics to reconcile the unexplainable scientific differences and contradictions that arise between the matter/no matter aspects of our reality and there is a Nobel Prize waiting for the well-placed genius who figures it out. At the moment, quantum mechanics cannot be reconciled with classical physics and general relativity cannot explain quanta. As they search for some sort of sensible correspondence between the divide of matter and energy in our reality and Einstein's dream of a unified Theory of Everything, right now, it seems both worlds belong in Rudyard Kipling's *The Ballad of East and West*, where, 'East is East, and West is West, and never the twain shall meet.'

This perplexing dance between energy and matter is by far not the only peculiarity of our world. Not only is our physical reality not as real as we would like to believe, but it is also not even outside or around us. What appears in our outside world is entirely constructed within. We create our whole world inside our own heads. The physical world that we encounter and experience, including that of our own bodies, is a perception rather than a reality. Everything in our outside material world is constructed inside our brain. Everything we see, touch, hear, smell and taste is nothing more than an expertly manufactured manipulation of the facts inside our own heads. We are interpreting energy as matter. Each person's perception of their world is entirely unique to them. Nothing of what we experience in our life is external. This 'outside world' is fashioned by our physical senses supposedly picking up snippets of information from what we perceive to be an outside environment and then delivering it to our brain, which in turn assembles that data so that we can then piece together in our head what we think is an exterior world. For example, when we experience holding a flower, we see the colours, we see its shape, we smell its scent, and we feel its texture. It is our brain that interprets and binds all of these perceptions together into the concept of a flower. All that we see and feel about the flower is fashioned inside our heads. Everybody interprets their world differently from the workings of their own internal physiology. This explains why we often see things quite differently, we can smell and taste the same things in a different way. The interpretation of sound waves is also an internal activity and unique to each of us.

It is at brain level that we decode and translate all of the signals being collected from what we think to be outside and around us. Nobody's anatomy and physiology is completely identical to another's, so everybody is, quite literally, living in a world and in a reality of their own making. So what we accept as our world, its colours, shapes, sounds, tastes and feelings could in fact be nowhere near what is actually there, because if our brain was to change how it binds the information it receives from our senses, everything would then appear very different to us. Even when we say, 'I saw it with my own eyes,' it doesn't make it real, because our eyes don't see anything. All our eyes do is collect light and focus it on the back wall of the retina. Our eyes collect the information upside down and then our brains flips it back again and makes it into something we understand. Just like the double slit experiment where light takes shape by the act of observation, it is our brain that converts light into form, inside our heads.

While our senses are essential for collecting this 'external' information, our viewing is also restricted by them, as they are specialised to gather only certain aspects of what is seemingly around us. The senses are highly selective about what they pick up. What facilitates our perception of this reality also hinders our ability to identify anything else that could be out there. For example, the human eye can only process an incredibly small fraction of the electromagnetic spectrum. Less than 1% of all light that reaches us is in the visible spectrum. We cannot see cosmic rays, gamma rays, x-rays or ultraviolet. Nor can we see infrared, microwave, radar, radio or broadcast band waves. If we could see in all wavelengths, the night sky would be almost as bright as the daytime sky. It seems that we are missing out on quite a lot of the goings-on around us.

Our senses act as detectors to help us to figure out our position or situation, but they also act as filters, limiting information about where we really are and who or what we really are. In other words, the reality we perceive is very precisely tailored according to our ability or lack of, to pick up and piece together fragments of information that create a picture of our world that is unique to each of us and may not even remotely resemble what is actually there. It may be that there is much more than we have the ability to identify or it is possible what we are seeing is a very clever distortion of the facts. Irrespective of what is actually happening or not happening outside of us, our reality is generated within the confines of our senses and according to what is fabricated by our brains. Bottom line is that because human reason has to rely upon the partial and often deceptive data supplied by the limited instruments of our physical senses, our senses cannot be trusted to discern the truth of our reality. We are locked in a world that we make up in our own heads and fooled into believing in an outer reality that is not real at all, and that includes our own body.

On another level of artistry and genius in this dimension, nobody ever touches anything. We are never actually in direct contact with anything or anyone. This is because, on an atomic level, when electrons come to within a very small distance of each other, they begin to repel each other forming an unbridgeable gap between surfaces. For example, when we think we are sitting on a chair we are not. We are actually hovering over the chair, 10^{-8}cm over the chair to be exact, because when we get close enough to the chair the electrons of our bodies will repel the electrons of the chair. This will be true of anything we try to touch. We experience the pressure, impact and effect of touch where in fact there is none. We have never ever been in physical contact with anything or anyone. What we actually have is electricity creating the sensation of contact without the reality of it.

The other question that arises here is, is there really anything there to touch? Matter itself is still a bit of an enigma. Is it a wave or particle? Is it energy or solid? Science tells us that all matter possesses a wavelength. However, an object's wavelength is inversely proportional to its mass, so objects bigger than a molecule have a wavelength that is so tiny that it is considered negligible. But negligible does not mean absent, so matter could just be energy with a very, very small wavelength and still be energy and not matter in the solid sense that we perceive it to be. In other words, it doesn't matter how small the wavelength is, it remains that matter is just energy that we perceive to be solid. According to Einstein's famous equation, $E = mc^2$, energy is calculated by multiplying mass by the speed of light squared. If we jiggle the equation around in the way that Einstein fist presented the formula in his 1905 paper, we find that $m=E/c^2$. Not only does this maneuver tell us that mass and energy are interchangeable, it tells us that mass is the difference between energy and light. All well and good, but the question is, if neither light nor energy have mass, how can they make something with mass where there is none? It is like creating something out of nothing, where what we perceive as solid matter is made from the difference between two, not at all solid forces. Physics tells us that most of the mass in the universe is made possible through energy interactions, but there is something not adding up entirely.

Now, I know that Einstein's equation is not a simple as it appears; things get a little more complicated with motion. Yet this formula still tells us something very profound. If we think of c, the speed of light, as one light year per year, the conversion factor c^2 equals 1. That leaves us with $E = m$. Energy and mass are the same. If mass really is just energy then nothing is as solid as we perceive it to be and matter, like motion, time and gravity, could be an experience rather than a reality.

So far, nothing is really real, nothing is outside of us, time is an illusion and nobody is touching anything, and that is not the end of it. Nobody is even moving or going anywhere, it just feels like we are. Albeit, highly counterintuitive, under scrutiny, motion is nothing more than an illusion. Consider this: in order for motion to occur an object must change the position which it occupies. Using an arrow as an example, in any one instant of time an arrow is neither moving to where it is or where it is not. It cannot move to where it isn't because no time elapses for it to move. However, it can't move to where it is because it's already there. Simply put, if everything is truly motionless at every instant of time and time is composed of instants, then motion is an impossibility. This is the famous paradox proposed by the pre-Socratic Greek philosopher Zeno. There are those who say that Zeno was wrong because an object that occupies space, occupies a dense, infinite sequence of positions in time. Zeno must have got it wrong because he didn't have the conceptual wherewithal at the time for thinking about infinity. But, the curious thing is that if space and time do possess that infinite characteristic and cannot actually be reduced to a single unit, Zeno's paradox still stands. This is because if the arrow has an infinite number of positions to go through it will never actually reach its target. Either way, we have to seriously consider the possibility that motion might be a sensation rather than a reality.

There is also the obvious fact that if time is not real, then how can motion be real? When we describe motion, we do so as a function of time. For example, 100mph or 50km/s, etc. So the mathematical description of velocity is moot unless we can define time, which we can't.

Then there is the problem that motion can only be measured relative to other things. Any movement cannot be determined in relation to empty space alone, but is determined by the change in distance from something. That is, it has to be relative to something. For example, if a car is travelling at a speed of 90km/h, it is doing so in relation to the road it is on. If a second car overtakes that car at a speed of 60km/h, the first car would be moving at a speed of 30km/h in relation to the second car, but still travelling at 90km/h in relation to the road. As motion or speed is a relative concept with no absolutes and is the change in distance between two bodies, either one is assumed to be stationary.

Einstein's theory of relativity is based on the single principle of perspective, where the perspective of one reference frame is relative to another. Two observers, (or particles) moving relative to each other will not agree on three fundamental issues: one, how much time passes between events; two, how much space there is between things at any given moment; and three, the chronological order of events. However, each observer will measure things properly, meaning both are correct. In close proximity, these effects are minuscule and go completely unnoticed, but this does not alter the fact that if there is any disagreement on the sequence of events there is no universal division of events between past, present and future, where in the present moment someone's past is in someone else's future. All experimental evidence points to the fact that time and motion appear to be individual experiences rather than part of the nature of reality. This has some serious implications for the idea that our future does not yet exist and in turn challenges the whole concept of free will, which we will discuss later.

For now, even though, as all this suggests, motion is not real and we are stationary in every instant of time, the sensation of movement is not lost on us at all. We still get to experience the joy of motion, the stopping and the starting, the going and the coming, the effort of it and the rest from it. We get to feel energised and exhausted in it, we get to experience distances and speeds and be exited and frightened by it. Clearly God did an exceptionally good job at making the magic of motion feel so very real.

Then there is the issue with gravity. Einstein's later theory of gravity describes the presence of an invisible Lycra-type membrane called spacetime and how matter bends this conjoined fabric of space and time. It is analogous to putting a heavy bowling ball in the middle of a trampoline; the membrane will warp as the 'weight' of the ball pushes down on it. This is known as the curvature of spacetime. If you then place a golf ball on the same sheet, it will roll towards the bowling ball. This is gravity. It is a beautiful relationship between matter, space and time, where mass tells spacetime how to curve and then the curvature of spacetime tells mass what to move.

While Einstein's theory of gravity has stood the test of time and works exactly as he says it does, there are a few unexplainable problems with it. By right, Einstein's Theory of General Relativity should apply at every level of the universe, but while it correctly describes what we observe at the scale of the solar system, problems arise when you look at the universe at very small or very large scales.

Since 1929 physicists have known that the universe is expanding. In other words, stars and galaxies are moving away from each other. In recent years it has been shown that this expansion is speeding up. General relativity cannot account for this acceleration. It also runs into a problem on the small scale, as no quantum counterpart can be found for gravity and the tiniest particles of our perceivable world appear to be mediated by two much stronger forces, the strong nuclear force and the weak nuclear force. Gravity cannot be sensibly calculated on the quantum level. While electromagnetism is found to be consistent in both the quantum and in our larger observable world, gravity is a no show on the microscopic level. Electromagnetism can be identified at a quantum level as the forces of opposites attract and of like repel, which remains constant all the way up to our macroscopic experience with magnets. So if gravity is not a feature of the fundamental, then the three forces really influencing the quantum world of particles are electromagnetic, the strong nuclear force and the weak nuclear force.

And there's more! Gravity doesn't just affect the shape of space, it is also changes our experience of time. Because the gravity of a massive body, such as the earth, warps the spacetime around it, our experience of time speeds up or slows down depending on its distance from the mass. Time is theorised to slow down the closer one gets to the massive body. Using extremely accurate atomic clocks, physicists were able to detect a measurable difference in the passing of time between a clock on the surface of the earth and one at a higher elevation of only 33cm above it. Over a lifetime this difference would amount to approximately ninety billionths of a second, so it is not something we would be aware of in our day-to-day lives, but on planets with a greater gravitational mass, only an hour might pass by when several years may elapse here on earth.

This is the reason why Einstein said gravity is the curvature of spacetime, rather than just the curvature of space. Gravity and time are inextricably linked and if time is an illusion then I am not holding out much hope for gravity. In fact, all together, gravity, time, space and motion have a very tight relationship, so if one is an illusion chances are they all are. This is perhaps the reason why science has so far failed to come up with the holy grail of a unified theory of gravity, because it is an experience rather than a reality.

Matter, time, motion and gravity constitute the very bedrock of our perceivable reality, yet none is showing up as definitive or universally quantifiable. Not only this, but there also are a few dodgy details around the concept of space and separation. In 1997, physicist, Nicolas Gisin, at the University of Geneva, isolated a photon (the carrier particle of light) and split it in two. Then, in a way that only physicists could dream up and engineer, Gisin separated each half of the photon by nearly seven miles and made them spin. He demonstrated that a measurement carried out on one of the photons had an instantaneous effect on the other. The Photon behaved as though there was no distance between its two halves. This scientific curiosity is known as quantum entanglement or as Einstein called it, 'spooky action at a distance'.

Could it be that space is an illusion, too? It is certainly looking that way.

To sum things up so far, neither time nor feeling has any influence over the formation of our physical existence. That physical reality, or life as we know it, is not an external material anything, but instead is an internal mental fabrication of sights, tastes, smells, sounds and touch. Nobody is in direct contact with anything, space is suspect, motion is not happening and gravity can't hold down its own theory. Some seriously shady goings-on in this dimension and, worse still, it looks as though we are not in control of any of it. The laws of physics tell us that the atomic arrangement of our perceivable world exists independently and objectively of how we perceive it. In other words, we are not involved in the creation of our life, only in the observation and experience of it. The illusions of life are how we experience it through our five senses, as well as with time, motion, gravity and space. Like riding a roller coaster, we do not construct the route as we go, it is already there, so that we can experience the thrill of the ride.

So how can we explain the structural formation of the perceivable reality of our lives that seems to have been constructed before we arrived and without our mortal permission? In the block universe theory, our reality is described by science as a giant four-dimensional block of spacetime, containing all the things that have ever happened, are happening and will happen. The past, present and future all exist at the same time and everything happens together. The entire story of our lives is contained within this huge block dimension of space and time where every event, our births, deaths and everything in between simply coordinates within it. In this block universe, our sense of now is just reflecting where in the block we are at that instance, where our awareness shifts from one position to the next, the past being an earlier location and the future being a later one. The concept of time is an illusion made up of human memories and reality is just a complex network of events on to which we project sequences of past, present and future. From a physics point of view, the future exists just as does the past and the present. It is already constructed, it is structurally sound, mathematically accurate, iron-clad, insulated from and tamper-proofed against fool or genius alike; we just cannot see it. If we have nothing to create in a life story that has already been constructed. How can we create a future that already exists? We can't, but we can move into it and experience it as though we had.

The more we discover about the nature of our reality the more elusive and mysterious it becomes. The deepest feature of our experience is materialism, the presence of a tangible, exterior reality. Yet materialism is not the real nature of things and there is something beneath this physical perception that is far more real and that is the true nature of existence. Science examines the facts that appear to exist in an 'outside world', but actually, we and the world we live in are nothing more than a very elaborate thought. This hallucinatory characteristic of our physical universe is aptly summed up in the famous quote by Danish physicist Niels Bohr in the early 1900s: 'Everything we call real is made of things that cannot be regarded as real.' So, no matter how much we want to believe that there is a 'real' world out there with distinct, tangible properties, according to the information we have to date, it is little more than an internal mental construct. It has always been easy for us to appreciate the fact that our thoughts, feelings, intentions and awareness originate from somewhere deep inside of us, but now it seems so does everything else. Yes, all that is seen and unseen is happening from the inside and nothing really is outside.

In the words of the late, great John Wheeler, who worked with Einstein, 'There is no out there, out there.'

In this perplexing conglomerate of internal experiences it is possible that our lives are a sequence of snapshots played out in front of our awareness like a movie reel or a highly sophisticated virtual reality. A sequence of rapidly projected still pictures, giving the illusion of uninterrupted motion. A reality that is already written for us where we are wired into a fictional character, watching a train of events unfolding before our eyes. A very convincing simulation of happenings and circumstance that we have elected to participate in, experiencing everything that our chosen character endures. According to the laws of physics, the future already exists and as indicated by the rest of science, our reality is just an illusion that we are moving into and experiencing, one snapshot at a time. And just like watching a movie we cannot see what is coming next, only guess, hope or anticipate.

It is becoming increasingly clear that the only thing that is really real about our life is our experience of it. Just like the 3D experience that we have become familiar with in the cinema, our real-life movie is made up of those same dimensions of height, width and depth, along with all of the illusions that accommodate it. In fact, with the incredibly fast advancement of video game technology it is quite likely that we will soon be capable of creating a fully lifelike simulation of existence. According to Elon Musk, 'If you assume any rate of improvement at all, then games will become indistinguishable from reality.'

All things considered, there is mounting evidence that we are just characters living inside a simulation and as much as we would like to know what lies ahead there is a very good reason why we cannot. The not knowing is actually an integral part of our reality and how we perceive it. Crucially, if we knew what lay ahead of us, our experience of life would be very different indeed.

The fact that our physical reality is not quite as physical as it would appear is a fairly recent discovery by science, in the last century or so. However, many spiritual disciplines have had an inkling of this truth for thousands of years. In Sanskrit, the ancient Indo-European language, the word 'maya' is translated as magic, unreality, deception, fraud, trick, appearance, illusion.

It is a fundamental concept in Hindu philosophy, notably in the Advaita (Nondualist) school of Vedanta. Maya originally represented the magic power with which a god is able to make human beings believe in what turns out to be an illusion. By extension, it later came to mean the powerful force that creates the great cosmic illusion that this magnificent world is real.

Maya is thus that cosmic force that presents the infinite Brahman, the supreme being or God as the unreal and finite phenomenal world. The pretence of a physical world is by far not the only piece of trickery that we are duped by in the course of our lives. There are many other illusions on a spiritual level that we are continually confronted and fooled by in ourselves and in others through our own lack of awareness of who we really are and why we are here. On an individual and human level, the cosmic delusion of maya is manifest in two ways. Ajnana, is the lack of knowledge of the true divine nature of self and avidya is the lack of knowledge or the real nature of reality, its meanings and its context. Symbolised by darkness or poverty, it is this human ignorance and misunderstanding on both levels that creates the illusions of strife and discord and facilitate our lower, worldly existence. Enlightenment or the coming out of the darkness is the only thing that releases us from the physical and emotional constraints of our lives. Enlightenment does not guarantee a change in circumstances, only a change in how we perceive our position and purpose, on a journey where it is blatantly obvious that it is not our physical situation that determines our happiness, but our conceptual take on it that matters.

The concept of illusion is not confined to Hindu religion, but was a predominant fundament in the beginnings of Christianity, too. As already mentioned, in the early centuries after the death of Jesus, divisions arose among those who followed Christ teachings. The Gnostics, named from the Greek noun meaning knowledge or insight, were formed at the start of the Christian era alongside the orthodox teachings. In the early development of Christianity, the gospels of Matthew, Mark, Luke and John were not the only gospels doing the rounds. There were other writings attributed to Jesus and his disciples, writings such as the Gospel of Thomas, the Gospel of Philip and the Gospel of Truth, as well as other secret teachings, myths, and poems. The latter collection was popular with the Gnostic group, while the former four gospels of Mathew,

Mark, Luke and John were claimed by the orthodox group as they seemed to fit better with their social and political agendas.

The battle for religious supremacy was won by the orthodox contingent and the Gnostic gospels were somehow lost to us. That is, until a collection of texts called the Nag Hammadi Library was discovered by two brothers who dug them up in 1945 in the Egyptian town of the same name. Not realising their significance, some of these texts were inadvertently burned in the fire by their mother. According to the Gnostics, Jesus shared with some of the disciples the deeper, hidden meanings to life, which he instructed them to teach only in private to those deemed to have the maturity of mind and spirit to grasp such intellect. Even after his death, the Gnostics maintained that Jesus continued to appear to certain disciples revealing 'hidden mysteries' and 'secret wisdom'. These Gnostic gospels, a diverse collection of poems, chants, myths, gospels, pagan documents, and spiritual instructions, appear to hold a different view of Jesus, his teachings and his salvation. These texts explore a much deeper and more profound meaning to his life and words than the literal interpretation that came to dominate Christian thinking. The Gnostics tell of a 'living Jesus' who speaks of illusion and enlightenment, not of sin and repentance like the Jesus of the New Testament. Jesus is denoted as a spiritual being who comes not to save us from sin, but as a guide who helps us towards spiritual understanding.

Of the fifty-two texts unearthed in the Nag Hammadi, the best-known of these is probably the Gospel of Thomas, which contain the only complete text that survived. While it is estimated that the Gnostic gospels were probably written sometime between the first and fourth century according to Helmut Koester, it is quite possible that the Gospel of Thomas, or part of it, may have been written around the years 50 and 100 AD, that is, as early as or earlier than the gospels of Matthew, Mark, Luke and John. In one such text, Jesus compares our reduced sense of understanding and reasoning to being drunk. He tells Thomas, 'Because you have drunk, you have become drunk from the bubbling stream which I have measured out . . . He who will drink from my mouth will become as I am: I myself shall become he, and the things that are hidden will be revealed to him.' Here Jesus explains that in our earthly form we are 'drunk'. Our minds are therefore affected and we are unable to see the real truths of our existence. Being drunk, our 'vision' is impaired and our actions are uncharacteristic of our true selves. What is even more insightful in this statement by Jesus is that he reveals the fact that he is the one who spiked our drinks and served up this intoxicating, mind-bending, bubbling beverage to us after measuring it out precisely to achieve the desired delusionary effect. Every one of us has supped exactly the right 'measure' to diminish our awareness and accommodate our being, Jesus obviously hadn't drunk as much as the rest of us and therefore could see things much more clearly. It can't have been easy for Jesus, constantly surrounded by drunks. It must have been like being at a party when you are sober and all your friends are pie-eyed, talking nonsense and doing lots of stupid things. But nobody forced us from our eternal godly state and made us drink from the stream of this dodgy, bubbly stuff, it was our choice entirely. Make no mistake, we willingly accepted our chalice of contradiction and deception for the opportunity to experience this realm and partake in its story. We are all tipsy in this life and some of us are well pickled indeed, but we all come from the same divine source. It is that self-realisation that will bring sobriety and clarity.

Also in the Gospel of Thomas, Jesus discusses with the disciples man's incapacity to discern the truth about the 'Kingdom of God'. When they question Jesus about what it is and when it will come, Jesus implies that the kingdom of God is not a place, but instead a state of self-discovery or transformed consciousness: 'Rather, the Kingdom is inside of you, and it is outside of you.' Jesus says that 'the Kingdom of the Father is spread out upon the earth, and men do not see it . . . What you look forward to has already come, but you do not recognise it.' In the Gospel of Thomas, Jesus even ridicules those who thought of the 'Kingdom of God' in literal terms, as if it were a specific place or even a future event: 'If those who lead you say to you, "Look, the Kingdom is in the sky," then the birds will arrive there before you.' Jesus speaks of man's perceptual poverty or ignorance in his inability to see the spiritual and physical truths of his existence. 'When you come to know yourselves, then you will be known, and you will realise that you are the sons of the living Father. But if you will not know yourselves, then you dwell in poverty, and it is you who are that poverty.' Jesus knew that we are immersed in and consumed by the illusions of what we see and what we do not see. He came to teach us, not to change or condemn us. Jesus came to free us from our own ignorance. He came to free us from the darkness of ajnana and avidya. When Jesus said, 'I am the Light of the World. Whoever follows me will never walk in darkness but have the light of life' (John 8: 12), he was speaking about the enlightenment he offered through his life and words that would unmask the hidden truths about where we are and also of who we are, both shrouded under the veil of ignorance or the lack of awareness of our lives. Science has revealed that our hard and fast material world is not quite as legit as it would seem, but this is not the only misconception that we are entombed in. Our true self and divine status is expertly hidden well beneath a heavy cloak of deception. We are, by far, not who we think we are.

Chapter 5: The Illusion of Self

'There is God in you. Can you feel her dancing?' - Heather Keenan's Mamó

Being primordially flawed and shamefully sinful is every good Catholic's birth right. We hardly get a chance to draw breath in our new life before we are presented to the parish priest and doused in cold holy water to welcome us into the fold and free us from the original sin we are born with. Yes, we enter this complicated existence laden with a heavy load of sins before we even get started. Not to be taken personally, our sins are not our own; original sin isn't a personal sin of the unborn, but a sin of our forefathers, transmitted from generation to generation by birth. We are all born sinners, befouled from way back, and only baptism can wash it away. Unfortunately, most of us don't usually stay clean for very long and we fall off the wagon like an addict to his poison. Mercifully for the practising Catholic, we have the confessional where we can receive total absolution for just about any common indiscretion in return for three 'Hail Mary's' and one 'Our Father'.

Hammered into the Christian psyche down through the ages is the notion that Jesus was distinct from the rest of humanity, a superior being, an enigma to be worshipped and adored. He was better than us, he was the son of God. The rest of us are just unworthy, wretched sinners from birth and beforehand. Thanks to organised religion, generation after generation has accepted this goblet of shame and deficiency without question. What is most interesting about this divisive and wounding paradigm is that Jesus neither instigated nor encouraged this kind of thinking. Exactly the opposite. While Jesus wasn't completely without the odd human imperfection, for the most part he walked and talked equality and humility throughout his life. But despite his best efforts, his good deeds and compassion were misrepresented as an illumination of everyone else's inadequacies and shortcomings. Not the message that Jesus was going for at all.

Being anything other than a serial sinner is an understandably alien notion to the Catholic mindset. Being an actual God is utter lunacy for sure and quite averse to any rational assumptions that we may have about ourselves. We have always been told that God so loved the world that he gave his 'only' son in order to save us. Jesus may have been the only child of Joseph and Mary in his earthly role, but he never claimed to be the only son of God. In fact, throughout his life, Jesus did, in both word and deed, honour and appreciate the divinity in all of us. But it was in Solomon's porch at the Feast of the Dedication that Jesus tackles this issue head on. Solomon's porch in Jerusalem was a cloister on the eastern side of the temple of King Solomon of Israel and was no doubt a special place for Jesus. It was in such cloisters that the Levites resided and it was here that the doctors of the law met to hear and answer questions. By all accounts, it was a place of great beauty where Jesus taught, shared and visited with people. When Jesus was confronted by the Jews about the possible blasphemous claims that he was the actual son of God, not only did Jesus refuse to deny his own divine parentage, but he also challenged his disparagers to consider their origins by quoting their own laws in Psalm 82: 6, 'Has it not been written in your Law, 'I said, you are gods;' you are all sons of the Most High.' (John 10: 30–36). In general, Jesus had a very imaginative way with words and stories and was a hard man to get a straight answer from at the best of times. Most often, he liked to tease our thinking with parables and riddles that has left his messages open to individual interpretation throughout the ages. Not on this occasion, however. Jesus chooses to tell it as it is. Not wanting to be misunderstood on this fundamental issue, Jesus, uncharacteristically, makes a direct quote that could not be interpreted in any other way. 'You are gods,' is what he said, and while it might be a hard one to get the head around, it is true and Jesus knew it. This is such an understandably difficult notion for us humans to accept that many different interpretations and reasonings have been put forward in an attempt to twist its meaning and context as we struggle to reconcile our infallible divinity with our human inferiority.

The idea that we are all 'gods' is not as unusual as you would think. The belief in our divine identity is a commonality in all major religions. In Hinduism's *Bhagavad Gita*, there is the 'Krishna within'. The Buddhist scriptures speak of the Buddha within and the Sikh holy text tells us that 'the one God is all pervading and alone dwells in the mind. In the Koran, Allah is 'closer than your jugular vein'. When Jesus said, 'The kingdom of God does not come with observation; nor will they say, "See here!" or "See there!" For indeed, the kingdom of God is within you' (Luke 17: 20–21), again here, Jesus was straight talking, nothing else to interpret, no parable to decode, no hidden message. Jesus did not mince his words on the subject of who or what we are. Jesus was pointing out our fundamental divinity, the God within, our true identity and nature.

Jesus has been given many titles over the years to match his persona and his purpose. He has been called the Messiah, the Saviour, the son of God, the Ascended Master, among others. However, Jesus did not want fancy titles or personal recognition or reward for his efforts, then or now. While Jesus refused to deny his divinity, it was a truth he was fully prepared to die for. He was wholly aware of everyone else's divine heritage and this he freely and continuously acknowledged with his total and uncompromising humility. Jesus made many spectacularly obvious and purposeful efforts throughout his life to be anything other than superior, special or judgemental towards his fellow man. Instead, he went out of his way to communicate a spirit of equality and servitude, both in his preaching and in his actions. Jesus was born the son of a carpenter, on a bed of straw in a stable, surrounded by farm animals. His life began as an expression of humility and never did it waver from that. He owned no property or personal possessions. His entire life was one of servitude and submission to God and man. As he revealed in Matthew 20: 28, he came 'not to be served but to serve'. Throughout his life he sat with the worst and the best, without grandeur or judgement. One of his most enduring life lessons is that of humility, the entire circumstances of his life, his walk and talk is testimony to this. Regardless of religion or race, faults or failings, Jesus never considered himself to be better or more valuable than anyone else, not even his persecutors. He demonstrated the same respect and compassion for crook or cleric alike. His last act of love, before he was put to death, was a very deliberate demonstration of his humility and gratitude by doing the work of the lowliest of servants and getting on his knees to wash the feet of his beloved disciples, even the one who was about to betray him.

Jesus went to great lengths to drive home this particular point, that he was not better than or superior to anyone else. This was not a false modesty or a pity parade. Jesus was humble not because he was being patronising or because he was such a magnanimous fellow. Jesus' modesty was authentic. His humility was genuine because he knew that he was equal to all and superior to none. Jesus knew he was not alone in his divinity. Jesus knew the true identity of each and every person who contributed to the story of his life. He could see past all the complications of this realm and understood he was in the presence of gods no less eminent than himself. He knew who they really were and he knew the sacrifice and service everybody had undertaken to play their part and participate in the story. At all times Jesus knew what all the others had chosen to forget. That just like Jesus, we are all 'gods' and 'sons of the Most High,' who willingly choose to abandon our cosmic greatness in order to experience and serve a limited physical reality. We choose different roles, different paths and varying degrees of spiritual awareness, but our divine origins and motives are equal. We are all God's holy children. We are all as spiritually glorious and as magnificent as Jesus, in this life and in the next.

Not only are we gods, each and every one of us, individual, divine, flawless, magnificent beings of love and light, but we are also united as one, arising from the same wellspring of creation and intelligence. Central to all major religions and almost every spiritual path that humanity has ever pursued is the idea that everything is connected. Thanks to the wonders of science and technology now, our fundamental oneness of being is less of a religious or intuitive notion and more of a demonstrable fact. What was once just an eccentric suspicion is now explainable and acceptable on both a physical and a non-physical level.

On the surface we are individual characters on completely separate journeys in a magnificently crafted chronicle of experiences that are inextricably intertwined with each other and with the environment we occupy. Part of life's adventure is to experience separation and detachment, but even on an illusory physical level we cannot escape our infinite oneness. Our bodies appear as the recycling of the earth, the water and the air, a constant process of exchange with the perceived elements of our reality. The entire universe shows up in each and every life form. Every plant and animal holds the light from the sun and the moon, the rain from the cloud and all the air and earth elements within itself. If we remove any one of these elements from any form, that life will no longer be. The whole cosmos can be seen, can be identified, can be touched in a flower, in a butterfly and in each of us. In fact, we are the flower and the butterfly and everything else there is. We are everything that has gone before us, everything that is now and we are everything that is yet to be. There is no actual physical separation in a world that is presented as one large conglomeration of various, interactive molecular and energetic combinations, some we see, some we don't. We are each other, we are our environment. We are simply altering molecules and swapping atoms between us through space and time. We are the earth and we are the sky, we are Jesus and we are Judas, we are the universe, we are one.

The unified nature of life goes much deeper than all things physical. The non-physical and unseen connection that binds us is a little more complex and elusive, but is perhaps more real than anything we perceive in this dimension. Quantum physics has revealed empirically, theoretically and mathematically the presence of this 'invisible' field. The study of this invisible, pervasive and immutable connection to each other is part of the puzzle of life and journey to enlightenment. This gradual unveiling of our unified and inseparable oneness is progressively narrowing the divide between science and spirituality. The investigation of this mysterious waveform of everything at the core of our being that accommodates all of the particles that construct the universe and the forces that hold them together. An infinite, unified field of intelligence that creates and connects us all. It is the source of everything we are not just physically, but spiritually too. Good, bad and indifferent. It is the fundamental truth of our being at the basis of mind and matter. It is the truth beneath the illusion of life's diversity and chaos, it is the never-changing absolute that gives rise to all the mutability and mortality of our perceivable universe. But it is a truth we are excluded from by order of life in this dimension. Still, there is no 'other'. Separation is a trick of the senses. I am in you, you are in me, we are one, in the physical and the non-physical.

Jesus was not a quantum physicist, but he was fully aware of our cosmic connection and oneness. Throughout his life he made no secret of his true identity and universal nature. His refusal to deny his indissoluble unity with God became the most defining part of his mission and story. Jesus died on the cross defending this one truth. That he was God in the flesh, that we all are: 'In that day you will know that I am in my father, and you in me and I you.' (John 14: 20). This oneness with the father that Jesus spoke of must not be reduced to mere oneness in agreement or purpose, because if this was all Jesus was referring to he would not have been accused of blasphemy and subsequently sentenced to death. Jesus was indeed siting our divine source and status. Two thousand years later and we are just beginning to get the message that Jesus so willingly laid down his life for, that the Great Spirit resides in all of us.

There have been many very convincing scientific theories and experiments that could possibly demonstrate a correlation between this invisible field of oneness and consciousness itself and while we wait for science to prove this notion beyond reasonable doubt I am thinking it is fairly obvious we have located the divine. This omnipresent field of dynamism is the true essence of who and what we are cleverly hidden beneath its many and varied disguises of shape, size, colour and form. This of course means that our self, our inner being, is the intelligence that created the universe. We originate in and are spun from a common thread of pure existence, intelligence, creativity, joy, perfection and love. It comprises the very fabric of our being, it is in each one of us, it is who and what we are. We are gods and we are God.

God is not an old man with a big white beard who lives in the clouds and nonsensically gets angry or upset with us, despite his contradictory, unconditional love. He does not sit on a gold throne flanked by his most trusted angelic advisors to judge or punish us. We do not need to search for God. He is not in another dimension behind pearly gates and only available to those who have somehow managed to atone for the sins of their lifetime, as well as the sins of their fathers before them. God is not a he or a she or anything of the sort. God is not a separate being or entity from us. God is simply a name we have awarded to the ether or essence of who we are, which is love. God is a word for what we are made of, that which runs through us, comprises and connects us. God is the infinite, intelligent, indestructible thread of love that is you, that is me. God is you, God is me, God is the love that is you, that is me. So while churches, temples or holy sites may be ideal locations for refuge prayer or worship, they are not the only places to find or connect with God. In fact, we do not need to go anywhere else, either physically or spiritually, to reach or discover God. We are already there.

We are understandably inclined to think of ourselves only in terms of our human body and persona. Even after death most of us believe that we continue on in the afterlife as the immature and imperfect soul self, regretful and remorseful, to ponder on or be punished for the mistakes we made and the opportunities we missed in our lifetime. However, our earthly self bears no resemblance whatsoever to our true being and our temporary self is exactly that, temporary. After death, our mortal life form returns to the illusionary dust it was made from and our true self is liberated from its earthly shackles of physical restraint and limited thinking. We return again to the awareness of our infinity and perfection. Any notions of remorse, regret or retribution dissolve in the remembering and re-becoming of our true selves as we realise there is nothing to be sorry or vengeful for in a story we dreamed up and willingly participated in ourselves.

We are not who or what we think we are in this life and neither is anybody or anything else. Our earthly robes are but a temporary occupation that we leave behind at the end. Our true, eternal selves can wear any mask or robe within the story. This is the reason the disciples did not recognise Jesus after his resurrection, because Jesus appeared in the form of different people. For example, Mary Magdalene mourning for Jesus near his grave, sees a man she takes to be the gardener and only recognises him as Jesus when he speaks her name. (John 20: 11–18). He also appeared after his death to two disciples on the road to Emmaus as a fellow traveller.

(Luke 24: 13–21). Luke says that the disciples, deeply troubled about Jesus' death, talked with the stranger, apparently for several hours. They even invited him to eat with them and still did not know who he was until he sat down with them to bless the bread. Suddenly, then they recognised him as Jesus, at which point he vanished out of their sight. Jesus also appears to the disciples after his death in the form of a stranger on the shore of the Sea of Galilee who helps them land a huge catch of fish. (John 21: 1–13). In all of these cases, the disciples who saw the resurrected Jesus did not recognise him by his physical features, but by what he said and did. The physical bodies that we identify as ourselves and others are not at all who or what we are, not even close.

In the Acts of John, one of the most famous Gnostic texts, and one of the few discovered before the Nag Hammadi, Jesus is described not as human at all but as a spiritual being who adapted himself to human perception. The Acts tells how on one occasion John and James saw Jesus at the same time in completely different forms. From their boat James saw Jesus standing at the shore in the form of a child, but John saw him in the same moment as a fully grown man. 'When James pointed him out as a child, John said, "Which child?" And he answered me, "The one who is beckoning to us." And I said, "This is because of the long watch we have kept at sea. You are not seeing straight, brother James. Do you not see the man standing there who is handsome, fair and cheerful looking?" But he said to me, "I do not see that man, my brother."' Things got even more confusing when they reached the shore as John explains: 'He appeared to me again as rather bald-headed but with a thick flowing beard, but to James as a young man whose beard was just beginning.' The many different identities that Jesus presented with in his life and death were not the only oddity that John recorded in his gospels: 'I will tell you another glory, brethren; sometimes when I meant to touch him I encountered a material, solid body; but at other times again when I felt him, his substance was immaterial and incorporeal.' John also claims that he checked carefully for footprints, but Jesus never left any, nor did he ever blink his eye.

Both John and James are describing how they perceived Jesus in their own minds. They both recognised him in their own way, not at all alike and none of which was an actual depiction of his true self. We cannot know exactly how others see us; we cannot see what another sees. We just assume that it is the same as we see ourselves. This is never the case. The illusion of self is an individually held perception of form and persona. The person we think of as 'ourself' exists for us alone and there exist many, many different versions of ourselves in the minds of others. Every person we meet or have a relationship with or even make eye contact with in passing has a version of us in their mind. To each person we exist as a different perception. We are not the same person to our mother, father, daughter, son, brother, sister, friend, colleague, stranger, etc. We exist in this universe as a thousand different versions of ourselves and yet, even to ourselves, we aren't really a person at all, merely a perception of someone that we have concocted in our own minds.

The monumental fact that a person's real identity is ultimately God is rather a significant detail about ourselves that is understandably overlooked in the contradictions and arcaneness of our existence and it is certainly not given the attention it deserves in religious education. Jesus was conscious that he was living the divine life; we are not. That is the only difference between us and Him.

The truth is as Jesus says, we are all gods. End of. We are not actually the low-life sinners we have been led to believe by religion, each other and life in general. No, we are all gods, born of the most high, just like Jesus. More to the point, our divinity is not lost or absent in our limitations or our actions, but remains, just as with Judas, the will and love of God despite any surface illusion of right or wrong, good or evil. This is the eternal certainty that resides in all of us, but of course there is a twist, there always is.

Even though our true self is divine, perfect and limitless, we have chosen this journey to be human, flawed and confined. Even though as divine beings in another dimension we have the power to be, do or manifest anything we want, in this realm we do not. Here we cannot influence, change or create anything that we are not supposed to. Here we are to follow a perfectly crafted journey of experience and service. Here we are playing a character and have adopted a role of physical and spiritual limitations of varying degrees. We left behind a world of infinities to dwell temporarily in this materialistic and deterministic setting. Jesus knew this. He knew he was a God, but he also knew his limitations in this life. Granted, he was a lot less limited than the rest of us, but limited he was. If Jesus was not restricted or confined to script he could have done a whole lot more for God and man with his temporary existence. Had Jesus been free to utilise all of his endless almighty power his story could have been even more dramatic and far reaching. Jesus could have converted and saved every sinner he met, he could have been much more creative and prolific with his miracles and he could have convinced everyone of his and their divine origins. Most of all, however, he could have altered the course of his life and avoided such brutal and barbaric death. But that was not what he came here to do. Jesus came to do exactly what his story allowed him to do and only that. He said what he was supposed to say and did what he supposed to do, not just for the benefit of his contemporaries, but also for the generations thereafter. The question of whether Jesus could not or would not emend or revise his life story is irrelevant because he made it abundantly clear that he was committed by will and by want to stay on course and stick to the plan. It is the same for all of us.

From now on, for the sake of convenience when I use the word God I will be referring to all of us and our true nature of divine infinite love and wisdom.

Chapter 6: The Illusion of Form

'Know then that the body is merely a garment. Go seek the wearer, not the cloak.' – Rumi

Contrary to what we would like to believe, we humans are not the centre of the universe. Neither are we the most evolved, intelligent or superior beings in this brief existence. We are simply members of a whole, interdependent, mutually beneficial ensemble where each form and function plays a critical role for one another and for the aggregate. Each and every form, regardless of size, shape, colour or texture, has its own equal, inherent and irreplaceable value in this equation of life. Humanity is nothing more than a temporary adventure for an infinite soul in an alternative dimension and it is by far not the only one to choose from here. The fallacy of form and rank is the most pervasive and brilliant deception of our wonderful journey in this realm of experiencing.

It is ludicrous to think that the human form or experience is the only one we would want to occupy or undergo. Humanity does not have exclusive rights to magnificence, love, intelligence, importance, beauty, experience and service. Behind every set of eyes in every life form on earth there is a soul, a peer that we have known forever, perceiving, experiencing and serving a divinely crafted, bespoke course that we willingly chose to tread. Our short time here on earth is about experiencing life from a different vantage point of form and awareness, as well as providing the service that form takes. We provide for each other and the bigger picture all the different forms that make up this reality. The human vista and role is of no more value or service to an inquisitive eternal soul than any other species.

One of the most contentious existential questions hanging over mankind from the beginning is 'why' we are here. Religious, philosophical and individual theories abound and they are as deep as they are wide, but the reason may be a lot simpler than the ideas we have been debating for so long. What we do know is that we are all one. At the very core of our being we are a single, unified field of energy and intelligence out of which all of our different forms arise. Science has studied this field of energetic oneness at great length, but to date most of the research has focused on figuring out the structure and vibrations of this quantum energetic oneness. Believed by many to be consciousness itself, it is a field of energy that can be very precisely defined mathematically, but the difficulty in establishing it as consciousness is that there is no identifiable brain activity that indicates it. However, it might be more relevant and revealing to focus on its function instead of its structure, which as it turns out is a lot less complicated than its identity and its mathematical makeup. If we ask ourselves what we are conscious of, we will say everything to do with feeling. We can smell the flowers, taste the apple, we feel happy with the antics of a kitten or a child, we feel the pain of an injury or the anguish of grief, we feel uplifted by encouragement and devastated by negativity, we listen to the music of a bird's song and feel moved by its brilliance, we feel sad about a friend's misfortune: the list of how much we can feel is actually endless. We are also aware of our own self as real and reactive individuals; we see ourselves in the mirror and we are aware of our own thoughts, beliefs, and aspirations. Our awareness and our feelings are what being conscious is all about, it is what really matters to us as human beings and it may be that they are the only things that being conscious in this existence is about.

According to many studies carried out by Jesse Prinz, Professor of Philosophy and Director of the Committee for Interdisciplinary Science Studies at the Graduate Center of the City University of New York, 'Consciousness looks like it's largely about perception and emotion: it's not about thought or more higher human capacities.' In other words, consciousness or God or whatever is simply viewing and feeling. Meaning we are here, simply observing and experiencing our lives, nothing more. If this is the case, then there is nothing to suggest that all forms of life are having much the same undertaking that humans are.

All of the data that has been collected so far with regards to plant and animal life strongly suggests that all life on earth, regardless of the shape or form it takes, is experiencing its time here in much the same way as we humans do. In fact, when we examine life forms other than our own, we find that there is very little of life's experience that is unique to humans. Life and feeling runs through everything and is the very purpose of living. In other words, in every way that matters we are all the same.

In our world there is an intoxicating array of forms or species, each one exquisite in design and detail. There is not one more awe inspiring than the other. Animals are often thought of as lesser souls or lesser beings, regarded by many as no more than things, tools or commodities, resources for human consumption or entertainment. As sophisticated and intelligent as we think we are and with all the advancements we believe we have made, it is our disregard for the least of us that highlights more than anything the shortfall in our being. Life is life, regardless of the robe it wears. All animals are sentient beings, capable of feeling no different from us. We can herd them into species and categories to illustrate their differences on the outside, but each is no less an individual with its own characters and unique personality traits. Just because they embody a different shape, colour or texture than us does not make them any less of a soul. Every life form incarnate, regardless of its exterior appearance, contains a unique perspective and experience and is a soul of equal magnitude to our own in nothing more than an elaborate earthy costume. We are all equal, gods, just in different outfits, looking at the world from a different angle but experiencing the same things.

We think we are such a special and superior species, yet our very survival depends on the tiny bee, one of the smallest beings in our world that we are rapidly exterminating through ignorance, greed and apathy. We mass murder our own kind for all the same reasons. No other species is capable of the kind of widespread destruction that we are, yet we consider ourselves more intelligent or of greater importance. You can argue that we are superior in our ability to create and develop, but this is also debatable given the often extremely sophisticated social and survival abilities of many species. It is indeed a struggle to justify our self-appointed position of superiority at a time when our very survival on this planet is in jeopardy because the destruction we have inflicted on our environment and each other so far outweighs any of our advancements or contributions. What is it, I wonder, that makes us humans of a higher rank in this equation of life? Ability and success in any task is measured according to the goal or purpose. If the true objective of our existence is to plunder and pillage in the pursuit of every comfort, convenience and self-gratification then there is no doubt we are way ahead of any other species on the planet. However, if the real aim is to live in harmony with each other and our surroundings, then I fear we have a lot to learn from and are far less evolved than our furry, feathery and scaly friends. Each and every being and form conspires to make up our world and our reality and our story. Each one a vital piece of the sum total. In the equation of life as with any mathematical equation, each character is of equal importance. Some of the numbers in the equation may be bigger than others, some may add and some may subtract, but their contributory value is equal. Without any one of the numbers, big or small, the correct conclusion can never be reached. Similarly, any notions of superiority or inferiority in our place or being in this reality are nothing more than the illusions of a very selectively occluded perception. All souls are equal, just playing different roles and wearing different costumes in a mutually beneficial experience.

All animals are conscious and for the most part exhibit the same tendencies towards life and living that humans do. For those that appear not to it may only be that it is less obvious to us or we have not studied their behaviour closely enough. In science, just as with anything in life, lack of hard facts or experimental evidence does not equate to a negative conclusion. It is also entirely possible that there are other things outside of the human experience and psyche that we would like to observe, encounter and entertain. We are eternal souls with a limitless imagination and a lot of time on our hands and there are many other forms and roles in this dimension that are much more exciting, far less confining and decidedly more appealing than the human frame and journey.

For example, take the giants of the ocean, the sperm whales, whose brain physiology is not much different from our own except it is six times larger than ours. Their neocortex handles the same higher level functions as ours, such as conscious thought, future planning and language. Their brain also contains highly developed spindle cell structures that neurologists have associated with compassion, love, suffering and speech, not much different from humans, only bigger and better. Their language and communication skills are probably the most sophisticated of any species, using clicks that can be received by other sperm whales on the other side of the planet. By emitting these sound clicks, they can map everything inside and out by collecting the echoes under their jaw. These clicks can be so loud, about 236 decibels, they could vibrate a man to death and these mammals have been around for fifteen million years longer than we have. Now tell me again how special we humans are.

Our current understanding of marine life is still in its infancy, yet we are managing to destroy it faster than we can learn about it. We assume that fish do not feel pain, one, because we have not studied them enough and, two, they taste too good. However, anyone who thinks that fish don't feel pain, I'd say, is grossly mistaken. Just because we think fish do not express pain in the same way as we humans does not mean they do not feel it. In fact, fish have been observed responding to painful stimuli in much the same way as we do. For example, in 2003, scientists in Edinburgh, including lead scientist Dr Lynne Sneddon, injected bee venom on to the lips of trout. The fish were seen to rub their lips on the gravel in the same way as we would rub our skin when stung by a bee. They also demonstrated a rocking motion in response to painful stimuli, something we can all relate to. The same study identified fifty-eight receptors in the heads of rainbow trout that respond to electric and chemical shocks. And that's not all. According to Associate Professor Culum Brown of Macquarie University in Australia, fish are conscious enough to organise themselves into complex social communities where they keep track of individuals and can learn from one another. They also exhibit signs of Machiavellian intelligence that involve social manipulation, such as cooperation and reconciliation. They have very good memories and can even develop cultural traditions and can recognise themselves and others. Who knew?

It is taking us humans a long time to even begin to notice or appreciate the value of other beings in our midst much less identify the spirit within. Some animals such as the elephant make it quite obvious that there is very little difference in how we experience the world. Elephants are big and easy to observe. They quite clearly have been seen to demonstrate compassion, sympathy, social intelligence, self-awareness, learning abilities, basically all the same things that humans do. They are just doing it in a different anatomy from us, as it is with any animal we can or have observed to any degree. But who knew that on a much smaller scale, even ants have different behaviours that indicate personalities and individuality. It is believed that they even the ability to imagine! Ants can have certain personal specifications relating to where they would like to live. 'Some ants are picky, others are more liberal and will accept almost anything,' says Thomas O'Shea- Wheller at the Ant Lab of the University of Bristol, UK. 'Much like humans, not everyone wants to live in a mansion.' And some ants never seem happy, however nice a nest is. (I have a sister just like that.) 'They live there, but seem restless, and are more likely to scout. It means they are always searching for new things. They are the imagination of the colony,' says O'Shea- Wheller.

As it turns out, ants are also quite proficient farmers. Small ants bring home large seeds to eat, but no one knew how they broke through the seed's tough exterior. When studied by Walter Tschinkel at Florida State University in Tallahassee, it was found that Florida harvester ants actually plant the seeds and wait for them to germinate and then eat the soft spoils. Germination splits the tough husk, making the seed contents available as food for the ants and their larvae. There are at least eighteen genera of ants that harvest seeds, and colonies of some species can store more than 300,000 seeds in their underground granaries. That's impressive by any standards and relatively speaking they are probably much better at providing for themselves and each other than we have shown ourselves to be throughout our history. They have certainly got the skills of community, communication and cooperation down to a fine art, and who are we to say that they do not experience and enjoy all that it brings in an anatomy that is different from ours but no less functionally sophisticated and beautiful. If you don't think that insects are beautiful you should take a look at the work of Levon Biss, who has captured theses exquisite beings in microscopic photography that makes available to us images of jaw-dropping beauty that are otherwise denied by the limited human eye. It is no more than the restricted thinking of an egocentric mind that would assume that God would not want to experience life as an ant. Size and scale is matterless in the world of experiencing, which is quite evident when confronted with the scale of humans and even the earth to the rest of the universe. Humans are infinitesimally small on the vastness of the cosmic stage and our delusions of self-importance are just that, delusions. There is every possibility that even the tiniest ant is a beautiful, infinite being you have known forever that wants to experience that form and play its brief part in providing that aspect of your reality. When the earthly robes come off, we will understand and appreciate each other's guise and the significance of the role in the story and the outcome.

There are so many other forms and lives I would like to experience and perhaps I will or have done already. I imagine it must be incredible to surf the air currents as an eagle or any of the other beautiful creatures of flight. To view the world from above and navigate the earth's magnetic fields using my special magnetoreceptor protein Cry4 in the lens of my eye. I imagine it would be exhilarating also to explore the weightless wonders of the deepest seas, to slice through the ocean as a dolphin, racing a boat or leaping the waves. Dolphins have had larger and more complex brains than humans for the last twenty-five million years. They are wonderfully social, intelligent and joyful beings, often referred to as the humans of the sea. I would love to explore the world from their glorious perspective and at the same time be of help to a struggling human species of lesser intellectual ability. Any and all of the land, sky or sea life forms would be an exquisite adventure and/or service to participate in.

Animal forms play a vital role in our lives not just by providing us with an ecosystem to live in, but they are also major players in our reality and experience. For some their role is to make up the wild and the terrifying. Others provide us with comfort and company in a domestic setting. There are those that have much to teach us, those that are to be rescued, those that we think we need to feed us and those that have pledged to be instrumental in our exit from this reality. Each of us agreed to don a form that not only did we want to experience, but also we wanted that experience to be a crucial part of everyone else's journeys and the unfolding story. We must not underestimate the intelligence or devotion of our being to be able to honour ourselves and be of service to others, simultaneously, regardless of the shape we take or the challenges we present.

Man's anthropocentric view of the world is ironically what illuminates most his deficit in spiritual awareness. We need governments to pass laws in order to recognise animals legally as sentient beings, which some countries have accepted and others denied. To say that animals are sentient beings is to acknowledge that they can experience positive and negative emotions, including pain and distress. Of course you would be forgiven for wondering if insects or other 'lower' forms of life feel pain, as it is not immediately obvious; but other animals who actually scream in physical pain or emotional distress, really? We need to debate this issue? Really? Are we that stupid? I have no doubt that animals can experience more emotions than we can categorise into either positive or negative. Animals experience the same variety of emotions as humans do and I imagine that their life's journey and perspective is no less appealing to spirit than our own. Over the years I have seen every possible emotion in every pet that has joined me on this wonderful journey. I have seen, anger, fear, envy, shame, pity, trust, joy, sadness, grief, anticipation, disgust, but most of all love. In every species it is possible to participate in the love of parenting, the joy of youth, the benefits of community, as well as the challenges of life and living, not unlike our own. I expect they also have a sense of romance and attraction to each other. They will often demonstrate deep devotion and loyalty and many species, such as crows, swans and owls, choose a companion and mate for life. When an owl loses its mate, the grief is so great that it will turn its face into the tree and will itself to death, which takes about three days. Most animals experience their world with the same senses of sight, touch, smell, taste and hearing as we do. Some have extra or heightened senses and some have less according to their species requirements, but it remains that all experience the same life roles and challenges as us humans, just from a slightly different perspective and circumstance. All the things we came into this dimension to experience are pretty much the same regardless of our species. Different does not mean inferior. In the words of Charles Darwin, 'There is no fundamental difference between man and animals in their ability to feel pleasure and pain, happiness and misery.'

Furthermore, life experiences and journeys are not just restricted to human and animal. Most of us, not privy to the intelligence and sophistication of plant life, will disregard plants as senseless automata that exists solely for the benefit or pleasure of humanity. Nothing could be farther from the truth. Plant life is often looked upon as little more than a resource in man's quest to make life on earth more comfortable and convenient for himself. There are, however, a few botanical mavericks that between them have produced generous amounts of scientific evidence that suggests that we have been grossly underestimating our leafy companions. They have provided ample, irrefutable evidence that points to the fact that plants are conscious and intelligent beings that are able to perceive and react to what is happening in their environment at a level of sophistication often far superior to that of humans. Yes, that is correct; I said 'superior' to humans. Some plants have resources and capabilities that make us humans look like amoebas.

To begin with, plants were here long before us. They beautifully, intelligently and efficiently transformed an early world of rock and soil into an environment that sustains, nourishes and adorns our world. During a billion years of evolution, they have become masters of survival, capable of solving problems, learning from past experiences and adapting where necessary. Being able to sense and react to the environment is a basic evolutionary necessity, without which they would have perished long ago. However, plants can do so much more than just survive and adapt. Plants are Mother Nature's superstars.

The fact is that plants were the first beings to forge a life of service and experience on this planet and they developed an exquisite, physiology to help them do so. In addition to their ability to sense and respond to their environment, plants have also demonstrated incredibly sophisticated and dynamic forms of awareness and communication.

Just because plants do not appear to have sensory organs of a form similar to that of man does not mean they cannot see, hear, smell, taste and touch. Perchance, eyes and ears are not the only means by which it is possible to see or hear. Plants have fashioned themselves different sensory organs by which they can manage the same sensation and perception. Yes, plants have many ways of interpreting their environment, recent scientific research has shown precisely this, and so much more. The fact being, that plants exhibit perception above and beyond the varieties of the established five sensory preceptors of touch sight taste hearing and smell.

Without 'ears' and 'eyes', plants can hear and see as well as, if not better than, humans. Plants are able to distinguish between sounds inaudible to the human ear and colour wavelengths, such as infrared and ultraviolet, invisible to the human eye. In fact, more complex than human sight at the level of perception, plants see a much larger spectrum than we do. Plants see with their shoot tip, as shown by Charles Darwin and his son Francis, who successfully demonstrated rudimentary sight in plants back in the 1800s. Also using photo or light receptors in their leaves they can sense when they are being shaded by a neighbour, so that they grow away in another direction or taller to gain access to the light. For survival purposes, picking up light rays using photoreceptors is somewhat expected of a plant, but their optical abilities do extend a little more than that and far beyond our own range or capabilities. Remarkably, if a climbing plant is growing between obstructions that conceal a potential support on one side, it will unerringly grow towards the hidden support, avoiding the area where none exists. In other words, a plant can see through walls. We humans have not yet developed any such x-ray visionary skills and our 'third eye' still remains tightly shut. In the eye, most humans have three types of light-detecting cells, or photoreceptors, which are sensitive to red, green and blue light. But the *Arabidopsis thaliana*, a small weed that looks like wild mustard, has eleven kinds of photoreceptors. Yes, there is a weed that has better sight than us humans.

The auditory abilities of the plant kingdom are no less impressive than their optic. Without 'ears', plants are not lacking in their proficiency to detect an interpret sounds and as it turns out are extremely sensitive to vibrations above and below the ground. Plant roots have been shown to grow towards the sound of running water in plastic tubing when no other water was available. They knew it was there even if the only thing to detect was the sound of it flowing inside the pipe. In other studies, plants have been shown to react to the sounds of caterpillar chewing noises when presented with the recordings of the insects munching sounds, where the plants produced leaf volatiles to make their leaves less appetising to the non-existing insects. More evidence that plants can hear comes from the phenomenon of 'buzz pollination', in which a bee buzzing at a particular frequency has been shown to stimulate pollen release.

Sound is very important to a plant, though the scientific jury is still out on whether or not plants benefit from music. Some scientific studies have already concluded that the sounds of music are truly irrelevant to a plant. However, I think we need to keep digging on this one. While it is now generally accepted that plants do detect and respond to vibrational frequencies, many of the studies done on music that seem to demonstrate plants can grow better and faster when they are provided with particular musical stimulation have been largely dismissed as unreliable or pseudoscience. Music is not thought to be ecologically relevant for plants. The idea that plants do not benefit from music is, I believe, a premature, limited and hugely arrogant evaluation of non-human life. Forests reverberate with sounds and much of it is music. If plants have been shown to benefit from a bit of Beethoven or Bach, perhaps there is another facet to a bird's song that is well known in the plant kingdom but that we are overlooking or are unable to see. It may well be that the music of a forest is as essential in promoting health and stimulating growth as all the elements of air, water, soil and sun. It would certainly be in the best interests of the birds to encourage the healthy development of that from which they take shelter and draw nourishment. The plants flourish with the birdsong and the birds reap the benefits. Symbiosis at its very best.

Sound waves create vibrations that can easily be picked up by plants. These vibrations could be transmitted to the protoplasm, which is the translucent living matter of which all animals and plant cells are composed. It is not a huge deviation from the norm to consider that, just like us, these vibrations might impact the precise chemical reactions and processes at cellular level, thus influencing overall health and productivity. I expect plants have as much a capacity to 'enjoy' music as any other living organism. Just because a plant's response is not obvious to us or we do not have the wherewithal to measure it does not mean it is not there.

Humans enjoy the taste and smell of plants on a daily basis; at least, we should be doing as part of a healthy diet. But plants have their own sense of taste and smell. Both taste and smell are senses that are very intimately linked and in plants they are highly sensitive and communicate a great deal of information to the organism. Below ground, they taste and smell with their roots. Plants analyse substances that have been secreted by the roots of other plants to help them absorb nutrients. Based on what they taste or smell, they can make an assessment of another plant's proximity and vitality and decide whether or not to engage it in an underground skirmish for food and water. Nature doesn't make a habit of wasting energy unnecessarily and plants like to make informed decisions. Their senses help them do just that.

Plants communicate both chemically and electrically. They warn each other of approaching danger, such as foraging animals and insects. If a plant is being eaten, it secretes a substance that makes it much less appealing to its assailant. In addition to this, it also secretes other substances to alert other plants in the neighbourhood of impending danger so they can equip and ready themselves. Plants know exactly which insects are eating them because they recognise the differences in their saliva and pass that precise information on. Different repellents are produced in response to different insects. These plant volatiles can be secreted both above and below ground.

Plants also perceive tactile sensation, and some of them are actually more sensitive to touch than a human being. Plants feel direct contact, they know when they are being touched and they can differentiate between hot and cold. Some plants don't particularly 'like' to be touched; for example, as the *Mimosa pudica* is hypersensitive to touch and makes its thin leaves rapidly drop down at the slightest touch. Some plants rely on their sense of touch to feed and survive, such as the carnivorous Venus flytrap, which registers the touch of a fly on its leaf to trigger closing and subsequent digestion of its prey.

Plants also have the ability to store and recall biological information, indicating memory. Plant physiologist Mark Jaffe published one of the first reports of plant memory in 1977. Such capabilities in a plant seem impossible without the means to process and integrate information, i.e., a brain or nervous system. But it may be that we are wrong about that. The vast part, about 80%, of the plant organism lives underground in a secret world. At the very tip of each root apex there is a group of cells, thought to be a brain transition zone, that display the same change in electrical potential that the neurones of our brain use to exchange information. There may only be a few hundred of these cells in each apex, but consider the enormous amount of root apexes per plant. Relatively speaking, the common decorative house plant may have a bigger brain than the average human who is watering it. Every single root apex is able to detect and monitor concurrently and continuously at least fifteen different chemical and physical parameters. The plant keeps its brain in the safety of the underground just as we keep ours beneath the hard bone of the skull, and while it may be structurally different from ours, its basic operating system is the same.

In addition, the parallels between plant and human biology are not as distant as you would imagine. All the characteristic responses exhibited by animal tissue are also to be found in plants. On a genetic level plants are more complex than many animals. Genes in plants have been identified that are also part of human DNA. The human genome, on the other hand, contains several genes known to be involved in plant development. The wild tobacco plant in Utah has a genome that contains a multitude more genes involved in environmental perception than most animals.

So far we are not looking altogether too dissimilar from the fern and foliage that surrounds us, if not a tad inferior. Carl Linnaeus, the Swedish botanist, also known as the grandfather of botany said plants differ from humans only in their lack of movement.

However, he might have been underestimating the capabilities of our vegetative occupants in this regard, as this misconception was corrected by Charles Darwin and his son Francis in 1880 in the publication *The Power of Movement in Plants*, showing that every tendril has the power of independent movement. Raoul Francé, Viennese biologist, said plants move their bodies as freely, easily and gracefully as the most skilled animal or human, just at a much slower pace. Plants live in a much more expanded timeframe than we do. An appreciation of plant movement requires technology such as time lapse photography, where young plant shoots can be observed playfully pushing and shoving like any other young child or animal. Without technology, we humans are oblivious to this facet of plant life, but just because we cannot appreciate it with the human eye does not mean it is not there.

On one hand, we cannot equate human behaviour to the way plants function in their world, but on the other hand, yes, we can. Plants have a very dynamic existence. They engage, communicate and cooperate with their environment and have a social life. Plants have been shown to exhibit self-awareness. If you block their ability to hear themselves they go a little crazy by producing more flower and leaf volatiles, the chemical equivalent of a scream. Relatives identify each other through chemical signals in their roots. A kinship study by Dr Susan Dudley, Plant Evolutionary Ecologist at McMaster University, Ontario, on sea rocket showed siblings politely restrained their root growth in contrast to those planted with strangers. Plants have individual habits, characteristics and dispositions; they can be infallibly accurate, intuitive, creative, have endless cunning and can even be deceptive. They react to the attitude with which they are nurtured, they have sex and like to sleep when it gets dark. They are masters of construction. They have structures of tremendous resistance that support fantastic weights against the forces of nature, using fibres wrapped in spirals that far exceed any human engineering achievement.

In the rain forests of Columbia, the Douglas fir trees live 1000 years and grow up to 300ft. In a beautifully organised and complex system, trees have been shown to provide for and nurture their young and other species by sending them excess carbon, above and below ground, and even reducing their root space to make more room for their kids. They recognise family members, possess empathy and communicate with friend and foe. They live interdependently with fungi, trading carbon-based sugars for other nutrients in a vast underground network of biological pathways that connect to each other and allow an entire forest to behave as one symbiotic unit. An injured or dying tree will release carbon and messages of wisdom regarding defence to the next generation of seedlings. Trees talk to each other constantly and understand their strength as a unit rather than as an individual. In the documentary *Intelligent Trees*, German forester, author and tree expert Peter Wohlleben, along with Suzanne Simard, an ecologist from the University of British Columbia, examined the sophisticated and sensuous existence of forest life where it is claimed by Wohlleben that trees 'can form bonds like an old couple, where one looks after the other. Trees have feelings,' and, 'Trees like to stand close together and cuddle. They love company. They can feel pain, and have emotions, such as fear.'

Scientifically, we have but scratched the surface on the dynamism of plant life, how much it is engaged in the experience of life and the critical role it plays in ours. Science is slowly demonstrating what indigenous people instinctively knew long ago, that plants not only have a life of their own, but also make available a multitude of healing properties for those who nurture and respect them. Every forest is a veritable medicine cabinet for its inhabitants and a simple walk through its trees will provide more health benefits than a small hospital. Trees produce aerosols that reduce blood pressure and improve circulation, they act as anti-cancer shields and have antibiotic, antifungal and anti-rheumatic effects, as well as reducing stress hormones. These aerosols are taken in through the lungs and absorbed through the skin, some will go directly to the brain, others will go straight to the major organs of the body. The trees of a forest understand the importance of supporting the health of its inhabitants that in turn play their role in the balance and experience of life. Plants are living, breathing, communicating creatures, they are sensitive to and emit energy forces and natural biochemicals that are beneficial to each other and to man. The Native Americans knew this; when they felt their energy fading they would go into the forest and put their back to a tree to replenish themselves.

Plants are sentient to orientation and also to the future. The species of sunflower *Silphium laciniatum* leaves accurately indicate the points of the compass. The Indian liquorice plant has a keen sensitivity to all forms of electrical and magnetic influences and has been used to predict the weather. It appears that plants have a more primary or fundamental sense of perception than humans and are constantly observing and recording events and phenomena to which man it totally oblivious.

It is understandable that it would take humans so long to notice or consider the hidden abilities and sophistication of plants, as our rudimentary senses are not fine enough to understand or appreciate them fully. Our senses are so very primitive that we have had to develop technologies in order to observe and understand them better. Because of our own sensory limitations, our ability to examine and understand all of the capabilities of plant life is reliant on the current sophistication of our equipment to measure and evaluate it. At this stage, what is still not visible to us is likely to be far greater than we can ever imagine.

Plants have been around a lot longer than us humans and while we might be heedless to them, they are not to us. Throughout the ages, plants have supported, us, fed us, sheltered us and provided us with an ecological panorama that is uplifting and awe inspiring. Humanity has been decidedly less intelligent and gracious towards them over the years. It is becoming increasingly obvious that humans are not so special after all. We are the last species to arrive on earth and compared to many others we are basic, ignorant and self-destructive. We do not naturally possess any of the superpowers that we fantasise about, such as the power of flight, x-ray vision, telepathy, or the ability to breathe underwater like some other animal or plant species. All things considered, one could easily conclude that humans are the least aware and least evolved variety on the planet.

Most of us would have great difficulty in accepting the idea that the little potted flowering plant in their living room is a living, seeing and feeling organism not much different from ourselves. That, just like us, it is having an experience of life and responding to the world around it. However, it seems that is exactly what it is. It is our own lack of awareness and sensory limitations that keep us from this truth.

If, as Professor Jesse Prinz, believes, life in this dimension is all about the experience, then, for my next life I am coming back as a catfish. Not joking. Probably the most finely tuned creatures on earth, they have about 75,000 more taste buds than us. With sensory organs both inside and outside of their body, they can taste with their whiskers, belly, back, fins, sides and even their tail. Imagine how much they must enjoy their mealtimes. If you were a catfish, you could taste all your favourite foods just by rubbing up against them. And that is, by far, not the extent of their astounding sensory abilities. Their sense of smell is equally as impressive. According to Dr John Caprio of Louisiana State University, 'Catfish can smell some compounds at one part to ten billion parts of water.' They also have a heightened sense of touch so sensitive to vibrations they are thought to be able to detect earthquakes days in advance. Catfish also have an excellent sense of sight and hearing, says Caprio. 'The eye of the channel catfish is used in many medical centres for research in vision.' The absence of ears does not make a catfish deaf; its body is the same density as water, so sound waves travelling through water go right through a catfish, as well. To top it all, catfish have a sense of electroreception, just like sharks, where they can find their prey by detecting the electrical fields of living organisms. That's a whole lot of feeling packed into one little life form. Sounds like an ideal way for any curious soul to pass away a little lifetime in the great expanse of infinity and eternity.

At the most fundamental level of our existence there is no distinction of form or species. Everything we know and see in this life, all of the diversity of the natural world, is made of the same elementary particles, just with slightly different arrangements repeated over and over. Every living being that we encounter, regardless of species, is having the same experiences of life that we are. The robe that it wears is a surface illusion that does not exist at an atomic level. Beneath the innumerable variety of colours, shapes and textures that this life presents resides the exact same spirit that dwells in us all. The idea that one form is of greater value or superior to another is one of the illusions that makes up our reality. We are all one great spirit, experiencing itself from different perspectives. We all have a different role and purpose, spiritually; none is of greater value than another.

The exquisite physiology of the natural world, plant and animal, allows it to survive, grow, adapt and even experience its environment, just like our own, often in spite of man's destructiveness. We are not distinct from the natural world, we are one with it, on both a fundamental and a surface level, and we are totally dependent on it. In the most literal sense, what we do to each other and to the environment we do to ourselves. Science has done much to expose this oneness, intelligence and interdependence that is present in all life forms that forces humanity to come down from its lofty perch of superiority and admit that we are not the centre of the universe as we would like to believe. Nor are we the most magnificent or cherished of all God's creation. God has been experiencing itself for billions of years from the innumerable perspectives afforded by animal and plant life; humans are simply another variety of form and feeling for an adventurous spirit. Different does not mean better, and since we are all one, we have nothing to be better than.

There are many different ways to have an experience of life, there are many different ways to be born, different mechanisms by which to interpret and respond to our surroundings, different ways and things to see, hear, feel, taste and smell, different challenges to face and fight, all wrapped up in a different but no less magnificent form. Humanity is but one way that God gets to explore the delights of his creation and it is by far not the most superior or advanced. Animals and plants are spirit, just the same as we are. They provide the colours of our reality and the opportunities to experience the many different facets of our lives. I am grateful to them all, to all the souls, just like me, that dwell within their exquisite forms.

Chapter 7: The Illusion of Possibility

'Free will is the ability to do gladly that which I must do.' - Carl Jung

The idea that our lives are a limited and inevitable occupation of matter arising out of an otherwise free and open state of endless energy forces us to tackle the issue of free will, as well as the availability of infinite potential and possibilities. If everything is plotted and planned well in advance and all of our stories exist already from start to finish, where then is our free will? It would seem there is none. This is surely an absurd notion, because if there is a plan then we are not free agents and do not possess that infinite potential to transform our lives as we wish and evolve into ever better versions of ourselves, or not, if we so desire. The laws of physics suggest we are at the mercy of an invisible force over which we have absolutely no control. By the same token, it also means that we are not responsible for our actions, good or bad, and cannot therefore be punished for our wrongdoings or praised for our acts of kindness or our achievements. The issue of whether or not we possess free will has been debated from the perspective of many disciplines, philosophers, theologians, physicists all have their own take on it.

Our perception of life and our religious beliefs give us impression that we have free will. If this truly is the case, then God would not intervene at any time or under any circumstance in our lives. However, the Bible is just bursting with stories of God sticking his nose into people's business and telling them what they must do, even when they didn't want it. And we can all relate to life not panning out according to the specifications of our meticulously constructed dream board, through no fault of our own. I, for one, did not envisage ending up, knee deep, in a muddy field with a crazy horse in the wet and windy west of Ireland. I had other plans for my life. Personally, I think it is becoming increasingly obvious that free will is nothing more than a very clever illusion, but in the name of good discussion we need to rationally examine the 'for' and 'against' arguments on the issue.

It is easy to understand why we would so easily be under the impression that in every moment we are creating our own reality with our moment to moment free will choices. There is an overriding, visceral feeling that we are ever in the process of examining our situation and making decisions for our immediate and future self. It also seems as though any number of alternative actions or choices are available to us in the present and could have been made at any time in our past and so therefore we have the power or ability to create our own future or influence the world in different ways. This automatic assumption is emboldened by the fact that we are unable to see beyond the immediate present and there appear to be so many options available for everything in each and every moment. Free will is an intuitive deduction based on feelings and appearances, but unfortunately that is the extent of the argument in favour of free will so far and is certainly not enough to prove we possess it. There is actually a whole lot more evidence to suggest that we do *not* have free will than that we do.

Despite a very clear sensation that we have power and control over each and every moment, on an atomic level the laws governing the behaviour of the fundamental particles of the universe tell a different story. The physical world is bound by its physical laws, which give rise to cause and effect where no physical event can occur without having been caused by a previous physical event. This is known as event causation and from this we can concede that the physical world is deterministic and has evolved in a controlled and calculated way since the first atoms began interacting with each other after the Big Bang. This means that everything that has happened, is happening or will happen can be attributed to a mechanical process initiated by events that took place long before we ever were even born.

At odds with this idea is the notion that the mind of a person or agent is independent of the laws of physics and can therefore start a whole chain of causality that wasn't caused by anything else. This is known as agent causation. Three problems with this. First, this conclusion is based on the idea that our thoughts are non-physical and therefore not bound by the physical laws of the universe. However, this view is not exactly bulletproof, as thoughts can actually be reduced to the physical state. All biological systems are actually complex chemical processes that obey the laws of physics. If we consider that our mental state stems from our brain state, which is a biological state arising from a physical state, which is indeed subject to those laws, then even our thoughts are deterministic. Second, if we are not biologically creating our own thoughts, how can we be in control of them, and consequently, our actions? Third, if an event is not a cause of a prior event, but is instead random or without reason, it is by definition not under the control of a free will.

We are all familiar with the notion that thoughts become things. That everything in our physical world is the end product of what was once just a thought in someone's head. We think up an idea, act upon it and consequently create our world. On the surface this would certainly seem to be the case, that we are actively creating a reality and a future with an infinite number of possibilities depending on what were are thinking about or where we are directing our efforts. If we take one step back from the concept of conscious creating to point out the simple fact that, despite all our progress and increased understanding of brain function and neuroscience, no one really knows where a thought comes from or how it is made, which begs the question of whether human beings are really thinking for themselves or are instead receiving information and direction from an invisible source or intelligence. A source that is possibly withholding and releasing information, thoughts or ideas at its own behest. Perhaps our brain is just receiving and sorting our thoughts or perhaps it has nothing to do with thought the process at all. Just because we constantly discuss our thoughts in our head does not mean that our thoughts are actually generated there. In a nutshell, if our thoughts originate in our brain from our own biological processes, then they obey the laws of physics and are deterministic, and if our thoughts exist independently of us, then they cannot be regarded as 'free'. Either way it is not looking good for free will so far.

It can also be argued that our behaviours, too, are events occurring along an actional pathway and are a consequence of prior conditions. And again, as with thoughts, adding random factors to behaviour would not confer free will. In fact, adding randomness decreases freedom rather than increasing it. Random behaviour is not free will. So, the cause and effect modus operandi of life is not just operational on an atomic level, but can also be identified as governing our thoughts and actions. This means that if everything that has happened in the past is a consequence of a previous event, we had no power over what took place in the past and there is only one unique outcome possible for the future. Which raises the question, how can we have control over the future?

Truth be told, our thoughts do not always line up with what we are doing. Oftentimes, our best laid plans, clearest of intentions and most deliberate of actions take us somewhere else entirely and to do something other than we had intended, even in the short term. Just because our thoughts appear to revolve around what we are doing or plan to do doesn't necessarily mean that the thought came first or that it initiated the action. This is the surprising discovery that was made by the late Benjamin Libet, neurophysiologist, at the University of California, San Francisco, in the 1980s, which demonstrated that we make our decisions to act before we are even consciously aware of them. Libet showed that specific brain activities leading to a voluntary act begin approximately half a second before the conscious will to act, meaning that what we become aware of has already happened about half a second earlier. The brain has already decided on an action that we later become aware of. So conscious free will isn't generating the decision to act and it isn't generating the action because Libet's research showed that the brain activity bringing about the movement started before the individual willed anything to happen.

Half a second delay is a very long time in brain activity, long enough to be extremely significant but also short enough for us not to notice the time lapse. Clever! Further investigative studies have revealed that the tardiness between action and awareness could be even longer. Studies done by John-Dylan Haynes, a neuroscientist at the Max Planck Institute for Human Cognitive and Brain Sciences in Leipzig, Germany, suggest there may be a difference of about ten seconds. Using fourteen volunteers, Haynes imaged their brains during some decision-making tasks. The area of the brain examined was the frontopolar cortex, at the front of the brain, immediately behind the forehead.

When the data was analysed, it showed that brain activity to act began seven seconds before the volunteers reported having made their decision. Given the delay of a few seconds in the imaging meant that the brain could have initiated the act as much as ten seconds beforehand. Haynes results were published online in *Nature Neuroscience*. This study alone paints quite a damning picture of the notion of free will and when combined with all the other scientific evidence makes for quite the talking point. Such evidence also rubbishes the whole notion that it is our thoughts that create our physical reality as we have been led to believe by many life coaches and the law of attraction. As it turns out, our physical reality is way ahead of our thoughts and it is more likely that the reverse is true. Evidence seems to suggest that our thoughts do not precede our actions and may only be creating the emotional and intellectual response to our physical one.

Not only is our conscious awareness in a permanent state of catch-up with our actions and our reality, but also, according to numerous studies carried out by cognitive neuroscientists, we are only conscious of what is going on about 5% of the time. This means that most of our decisions and behaviours, even our emotions, are generated in an unconscious manner, meaning that a staggering 95% of brain activity goes on beyond our conscious awareness. Some scientists estimate this percentage to be as high a 99%. The primary function of consciousness in the nervous system is still a bit of a mystery to science, but what is clear is that it isn't in as much control as we often assume. Such was the conclusion demonstrated in a study carried out by associate professor of psychology Ezequiel Morsella and his team of researchers at San Francisco University. In a statement accompanying the paper published in the journal *Behavioral and Brain Sciences*, Morsella says, 'The information we perceive in our consciousness is not created by conscious thought. Nor is it reacted to by conscious processes. Consciousness is the middleman and it doesn't do as much work as you think.'

It would seem that the conscious mind isn't as productive or as responsible as we have always believed. It is more about awareness than action and it doesn't do a very good job with that, as it rarely shows up for life's adventures and when it does it is always late for the party. That part of our brain that makes us conscious has been taking the credit for our highest achievements and the blame for our most dastardly deeds, but with data like that it is hard to imagine how we could possibly be responsible for anything, good or bad. The evidence suggests that we are more likely watching events unfold rather than being the cause of them, which, as it happens, fits in nicely with our simulated reality theory.

There are some who will argue that free will exists because our true identity arises from the quantum world, which is non-deterministic, with events occurring randomly and where there is no reason or cause for an atom to decay at one time and not at another. This doesn't work either, because random does not equate to free. As we can appreciate from the double slit experiment, we cannot apply this non-deterministic characteristic to our lives because we do not live in the quantum world. We may have come from there, but we do not live there now.

In this reality, we occupy a perceptual material world where there is an already constructed, mathematically sound block universe through which our awareness moves one frame at a time. From the neurological research collected on the delay between the intention to act and action itself, we can assume that our awareness on the block universe is lagging slightly behind its position by anywhere between half a second and ten seconds. Not an error on God's part, there is of course a very good reason for this asymmetry in the otherwise infinitely accurate, architecture of existence, which we will discuss later.

For now, let us take a closer look at this block universe superstructure that we are encased in for the duration of our lives. What is it made of? Understandably, you might assume that the basic building blocks of the universe are the atoms. However, there is something much more fundamental than the atom. It is numbers. Yes, the entire universe, including ourselves, cannot only be described by mathematics, but also it is mathematics. We are not really the blood, bone and tissue that we think we are, we are actually made of numbers and equations and expressions. Put it this way. Molecules are atoms put together in a certain way. Atoms are made of even smaller particles called quarks and electrons, the properties of these tiniest pieces of matter are purely mathematical. At a microscopic level, everything can be reduced to a list of numbers and that includes us. All of the fundamental particles of which we are comprised can be expressed numerically. We are all just self-aware parts of a giant mathematical object and there is no evidence right now that there's anything at all in our universe that is not mathematical in nature. Mankind did not invent numbers or mathematics, we discovered it, because no matter where you look in the universe one plus one equals two.

Maths is a little different from science in that the ultimate determiner of correctness is proof rather than empirical evidence. Mathematics can therefore prove or disprove its own hypothesis. Unlike science theories, which have been wrong many times, maths can never be wrong. Science uses maths to verify its theories. So the numbers and formulas of the microscopic laws of physics underpinning our very existence are is the invisible precision that permeates and pilots our being. The core of our physical world is as calculated and as deterministic as it gets. Life, despite its complications and bewilderments, is ordered and precise beyond our wildest dreams. Although you would be forgiven for thinking otherwise, given the surface impression of discord and disorder.

This perceived, surface chaos is all thanks to the Second Law of Thermodynamics, which states that over time, everything moves from an ordered state to a disordered state or at the very least remains constant and is the only law of physics that can't go backwards. It implies time and gives it a direction. It is the reason that you cannot un-whisk your egg back into an intact shell or un-stir the milk from your cappuccino. Our universe has been in a fairly constant state of expansion since the Big Bang, ominously headed towards a final state of maximum entropy, when our individual molecules will be lost in oneness as they are diluted and homogenised by the irreversible Second Law of Thermodynamics. Entropy is everywhere; it plays a huge role in the nature of life. From the micro to the macro, entropy is at work. On a microscopic level, our cells are constantly degrading. If we scale up, we have a few more grey hairs and wrinkles than we did yesterday; further out, relationships are dying and businesses are collapsing, there's a little more to social unrest and upheaval. Keep expanding outwards and you will find the entire universe collapsing. On the other side of the coin, life as we know it would not be possible without entropy. Everything would appear static, no would never get sick or age, nothing would decay or break and my house would always be clean and tidy. I like the sound of it, but then it would be a very boring life for consciousness to navigate. Everything would be perfect and we wouldn't need to experience things like learning, progress, work, goals, creativity and innovation, etc. Entropy keeps life in motion and makes it interesting.

So, entropy may not be as chaotic as it would seem. From a physics perspective it is not chaotic at all. For a start, because we live in a permanent present, the state of everything is just a particular arrangement of atoms in that particular instant of time. At every single moment, it is what it is. It is neither order nor disorder. In addition, every arrangement of atoms in every moment in time has been organised very precisely by mathematics. So, entropy is extreme order, very cleverly disguised as extreme disorder. Entropy is the illusion of disorder that arises from the bedrock of unparalleled order and accuracy that really steers us.

It is a mistake to think that the definitiveness and exactness exhibited by the laws of physics lies only in the unseen, microscopic layer of our experience. Accuracy and order is abundantly visible to us as it bubbles to the surface with exquisite displays of mathematical perfection in our natural world. Entropy and disorder are quite the deception in a mathematically calculated dimension. Mother Nature is just bursting with the precision of numbers. The mathematical wonders of the Golden Ratio, pi, fractals and the Fibonacci sequence can be located just about anywhere we look, all of which can be related to each other in one way or another.

Surface mathematics is everywhere we look, but we are often oblivious to it. First, the Golden Ratio is an intriguing mathematical ratio present in many different natural objects. It is the irrational number 1.618..., a number that continues to infinity and is found when a length of line is divided in one very special and unique way. Dividing a line into two parts gives you three measurements: A is the length of the line before it was divided. B is the longer part of the line when divided and C is the shorter part of the divided line. The Golden Number arises at one particular point of division on the line and nowhere else. It results in the ratio between the length of A and B being the same as the ratio between the length of B and C. At this point the Golden Ratio of both is 1.618 to 1, or phi.

This proportion is interesting because it appears throughout creation and extensively in the human face and body, as well as many other animals. It is also found in geometry, in architecture and design, even in the Bible and our DNA.

Next, the Fibonacci sequence is a series of numbers where the next number is found by adding up the two numbers before it. Simple. So the sequence goes 0, 1, 1, 2, 3, 5, 8, 13, 21, 34, 55... on and on and on. The relationship between the Fibonacci sequence and the Golden Ratio is a surprising one, two seemingly unrelated topics producing the same exact number. For example, if we divide each number by the previous number we get $1/1 = 1$, $2/1 = 2$, $3/2 = 1.5$, and so on up to $144/89 = 1.6179...$. The sequence looks like this: 1, 2, 1.5, 1.666..., 1.6, 1.625, 1.615..., 1.619..., 1.6176..., 1.6181...,

1.6179...where the numbers hover around and get tantalisingly closer and closer to 1.618, which is the value of phi: the Golden Ratio! And if we put the Golden Ratio and the Fibonacci sequence together, something absolutely beautiful happens.

The Golden Ratio can be applied to shapes to create a golden rectangle. A Fibonacci spiral can be created if we take a perfect or golden rectangle and break it down into smaller squares based on the Fibonacci sequence. By adding an arch in each square, we end up with the diagram of the Golden or Fibonacci Spiral. You will have seen these spirals many times in your life, but perhaps not recognised them. Accurate to the point of infinity, these spirals manifest themselves in biological settings from seashells to hurricanes to galaxies. In the sunflower, the display of its florets are in perfect spirals of the Fibonacci sequence 55, 34 and 21. The fruitlets of the pineapple create this same spiral, as does the pine cone. The curve of the ocean wave can be plotted diagrammatically at the points 1, 1, 2, 3, 5, 8, 13, 21, 34, and 55. Petals on a flower, the body of a starfish and in particular the nautilus shell are formed with this exact same blueprint. Even the spiral of the galaxies above us are formed with the exact design that a tiny shell is formed.

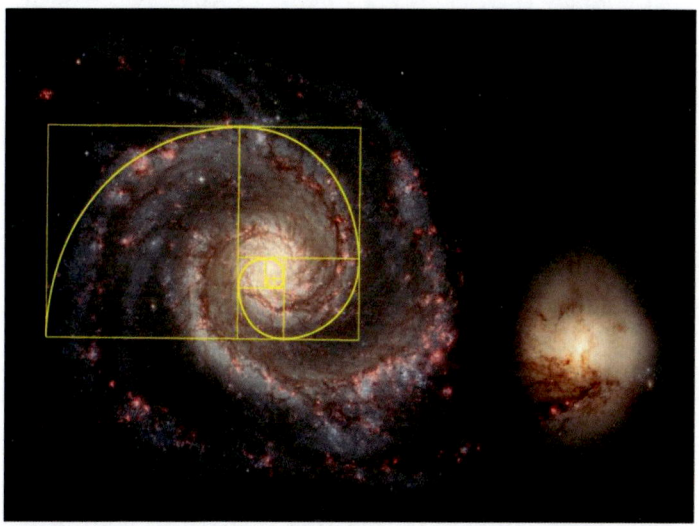

Source: NASA, ESA, S. Beckwith (STScI), and The Hubble Heritage Team (STScI/AURA)

Of course, not everything in nature is created according to the Golden Ratio and the Fibonacci numbers. Nature can sometimes appear rough and irregular, especially if we are to compare it to standard geometry. For example, mountains and clouds do not display perfect symmetry, but they are mathematically sound formations known as fractals. Fractals are nature's geometry that disguises an infinite order in the supposed chaotic shapes and processes of life. A fractal is a never-ending pattern where similar patterns recur at progressively smaller scales. If you take a small extract of the shape it will look the same as the entire shape and if you zoom into a fractal, the patterns and shapes will continue repeating forever.

Source: Deirdre McMahon

Fractals form exquisite structures in nature. Nature is full of fractals, hiding in plain sight all around us. One of the most obvious fractals is the fern plant. The entire fern is mostly built up from the same basic shape repeated over and over again at ever smaller scales. The leaves are shaped like little copies of the branches and the entire fern is mostly built up from the same basic shape repeated over and over again at ever smaller scales. Other examples of fractals include trees, river networks, coastlines, clouds, mountains, blood vessels and lightning bolts. Abstract fractals such as the Mandelbrot Set can be generated by a computer calculating a simple equation over and over, feeding the answer back to the start. These fractals are infinitely complex meaning we can zoom in forever.

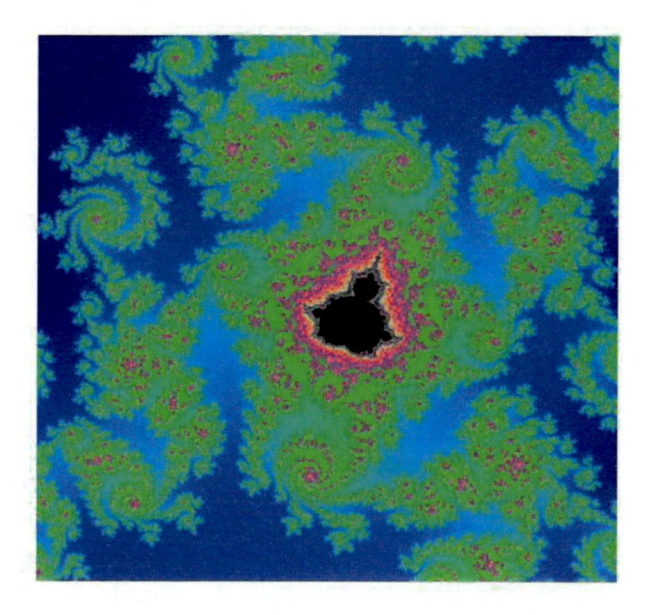

Then there is the illustrious pi, defined as the ratio of a circle's circumference to its diameter. Regardless of the size of the circle the ratio is always the same. So for any circle, dividing its circumference by its diameter will give you the exact same number, 3.14... So pi is rife in mathematics, but it also abundant in nature as it appears everywhere there is a circle, in the disc of the sun, the sunflower, tree rings, the pupil of the eye, even in the spiral of the DNA double helix. Surprisingly, pi also emerges in the shapes of rivers. Its 'meandering ratio' arises when we divide the river's actual convoluted length with its distance from source to mouth as the crow flies. This is known as the sinuosity of a river. Some rivers such as, Dublin's Liffey, like to take the scenic route and do a lot of twisting and turning along the way, and therefore have a high sinuosity, while other rivers, such as the Sacramento in California, do a lot less dillydallying and thus have a lower sinuosity. But, turns out, the average meandering ratio of rivers around the world is roughly pi.

The result was first published in *Science*, dated 22 March 1996. In a paper titled 'River meandering as a self-organization process', Hans-Henrik Stølum used empirical data and simulation to study the chaotic behaviour of a river's form over time, noting that the value of sinuosity tended to oscillate between a low value of 2.7 and a high value of 3.5, but with an average sinuosity of 3.14.

Possibly my personal favourite display of nature's perfection is the humble dandelion. It's mathematical and ecological wonders are so often overlooked or underestimated, as it is regarded as no more than a nuisance weed that should be eradicated, particularly by farmers and gardeners in their pursuit of greener fields and perfect lawns. The simple dandelion is the epitome of mathematical precision and beauty and possess an unparalleled tenacity and a ferocious will to survive and serve the natural world from which it emerges. There is nothing at all humble about the dandelion. From root to tip at various stages in its lifecycle, all of the above mathematical concepts can be found. The downy dandelion seed head displays fractal symmetry and in if we look at it from above we can see clearly that it spirals according to the Golden Ratio and Fibonacci sequence. And of course, it forms a circle in the arrangement of its bright yellow petals that gives us – you guessed it – pi.

As structurally impressive as the dandelion is from a maths perspective, it must be noted that nature's accuracy is not isolated only to the shapes it presents us with. Precision and perfection can also be found in the placement and purpose of individual species. Aside from its mathematical complexity and precision, the totally unassuming dandelion plays a unique and specific environmental and ecological role. Many insects rely on the dandelion as a food source for themselves and for their larvae. The bright yellow flowers provide bountiful stores of nectar for butterflies and moths, while the seed heads are also a valuable food source of food for seed-eating birds. Dandelions are crucial for the development of a healthy ecosystem; they can help transform waste ground by stabilising soil conditions and enriching the environment attracting other plant species.

Its long taproot is particularly effective at drawing nutrients from deep down in the soil. Its leaves are packed with these valuable nutrients, making them beneficial to human and animal alike. The curative power of dandelions has been well known for some time in treating a variety of ailments from liver complaints to haemorrhoids, from eczema to warts, the list is endless. They are a source of fibre and vitamins A, C and K, as well as many other micronutrients. Young leaves make an excellent addition to any salad, the flowers can be made into a wine tonic and the dried roots can be dried and roasted to make a coffee substitute. Not forgetting its beautiful aesthetic, a flush of dandelion growth in the summer can make the world look like a painting by Monet and many a child's wish has been carried to heaven with an earnest blow of the fluffy ball of seeds. Sometimes referred to in Ireland as 'the little flame of God', dandelions may not be as flash and alluring as other plants and flowers, but they sure do pack a heavenly punch and are the very definition of perfection in pattern, in placement and in purpose. As is everything in the universe.

Accuracy and determinism is all around us. It is just as solid in the macroscopic as it is in the microscopic. Emerging from the invisible unerring laws of physics, our larger observable world makes no mistakes. Nothing, absolutely nothing, is left to chance. The natural world, including ourselves, is crafted with the same accuracy and order as its underlying equations and it goes to great lengths to show us. At a fundamental level we are all just a collection of cold, hard, indifferent numbers operating under and obeying some very strict laws of physics. Everything outside of the precisely calculated nature of our being is merely human baggage and perspective. So relax, because just like the dandelion, you are doing exactly what you are supposed to be doing, exactly when and where you are supposed to be doing it, despite any surface illusion of chaos and disorder, good or bad, right or wrong.

It sometimes hard to believe that the variety of forms we experience in our physical world, with all their colours and charms, are nothing more than an assortment of numbers. Yes, God is a mathematician, a very good one at that, because he has calculated everything and everybody's, form and journey from the beginning of time all the way to the end, whatever that may be.

Italian astronomer and physicist Galileo Galilei is attributed with the quote, 'Mathematics is the alphabet in which God has written the universe.' This does appear to be the case. In order to be considered a language, mathematics must satisfy certain criteria. In order to be qualify as a system of communication, it must have vocabulary, grammar, syntax, and people who use and understand it. Mathematics meets this definition of a language. What's more, maths is a universal language. It is not subject to the same divisions and misinterpretations we experience with verbal or written communication. The symbols and organisation to form equations are the same in every country of the world. The story of the universe was written in the book of the block universe and it was written in the universal language of mathematics.

Uncertainty, chaos and disorder, there is none. As much as it would seem otherwise, humans are not disconnected from the cosmic tapestry. We are made up of these mathematical particles that comprise the universe and we cannot live outside of the laws of physics. We are not separate or autonomous. Nor do we hold some divine dispensation to be random, chaotic or even free, no matter how strongly we feel that we are. We are all an integral part of this physical reality and governed by these same laws. Whether we call them the laws of physics, destiny or the will of God, we cannot escape them. We are bound by them and are acting according to them at the most fundamental level our being. It is nothing personal, it is just maths.

Scientifically, it is much harder to prove the existence of free will than its absence. It would seem that free will is more of an assumption than a fact in a reality that we are very easily fooled by. Yes, there is free will, but not in this realm. Free will and infinite potential exists only in spiritual form or quanta that we left behind for the opportunity to experience our story of limitations, confinement, differences and learning. We had a choice to enter into the story or not; we had a choice of roles and forms to experience, to live in a world that seems uncertain and imperfect, where it would appear that things often go wildly wrong because of all of the possibilities that seem to be available to us. Our future is a mystery that we mistakenly believe is being crafted by a combination of personal choice and chance. The illusion of possibility is generated by our inability to see what lies ahead and also by the immensity and diversity of all our different paths and the multitude of different outcomes and occurrences that are playing out all around us now, as well as all that has transpired historically. It makes for a very clever illusion whereby just about anything can happen and often does. However, there is nothing haphazard about life in this dimension. This is just another aspect of the grand illusion that we are participating in. In truth, everything is perfect and all is assured. In truth, there is nothing being left to chance and nothing has ever gone wrong, ever. There is not a single atom out of place or misbehaving in this space-time continuum. To think otherwise is a serious underestimation of the infinite power, intelligence and devotion of our source. Every single life, death, path, outcome and event is being piloted by the mind and heart of a God that lives and breathes in each one of us. God has not lost control no matter how it may appear. God is in charge at all times and God doesn't make mistakes. God only deals in perfection. In fact 'God's will' will be done, is being done and has been done ever since it all began.

Chapter 8: The Illusion of Sin

'The novelist does not long to see the lion eat the grass. He realises that one and the same God created the wolf and the lamb, then smiled, "seeing that his work was good".'
- Andre Gide

This is the big one. The question of moral responsibility, one of the grandest philosophical puzzles man has had to grapple with throughout the ages. Sin. It is fair to say that from the beginning mankind has been the source of much grief, frustration and annoyance for our almighty creator. Initially, God was quite pleased with his work. According to Genesis 1: 31, 'God saw all that he had made, and it was very good.' But the form and life that he created with so much love and in his own likeness has gone seriously rogue. We have gone to town on our 'gift' of 'free will' and taken it to the absolute limits of human and divine endurance. In fits of exasperation and temper, God periodically lashes out with catastrophic events such as floods, tornadoes and earthquakes. Granted, if I had as many children as God has I would have a job keeping it together, but his vengeance has killed many millions of often innocent and undeserving individuals, so much so that you would be forgiven for thinking that our supposedly unconditionally loving creator is as unstable as we are.

But some things are just not adding up for the rational thinker. Man incarnates into ignorance, with no memory of anything before him, who he is or the reason for his being. He is often born into difficult and even dire circumstances through no fault of his own, but of the doings of generations before him. The idea that God would allow an innocent child to be placed at such a disadvantage, spiritually, physically and mentally, and then punish it for making some very understandably 'bad' decisions does not make any sense, especially when the punishment is an eternity in the fires of hell. A bit harsh, to say the least. This God that we have dreamed up resembles more of a sadistically cruel and insensitive despot, rather than the unconditionally loving father that Jesus tells us he is.

According to the Bible, God has poured out his wrath on many occasions where good, innocent, men, women and even children we decimated along with the bad and guilty. The floods of Noah, the destruction of Sodom and Gomorrah, and the ten plagues of Egypt are three biblical events attributed to God losing his temper with us. If killing is wrong, how is OK for God to do it?

It must be said that since this God created everything, he is ultimately responsible for the unpleasant fallout that has ensued, because he created the possibility for evil in the first place when there had to have been other options. God had to have known where he was going with all of this, as he could just as easily have given us this supposed free will where we could choose one of many different alternatives where no one got hurt or offended. But no, God created his children ignorant and helpless and then let us off into the unknown, feral and unattended, to figure it out for ourselves. Sounds like one of the worst fathers in the history of fathers. People have gone to prison for less. To be fair, he sent us a few enlightened individuals such as Jesus, Buddha and Mohammed to give us some guidance, but much too late for primitive man and clearly not enough for modern man. Either God is really struggling with this parenting stuff or there has to be a very good reason for his parental neglect and excessive violence towards us.

What exactly is sin? According to the Cambridge Dictionary, sin is 'the offence of breaking, or the breaking of, a religious or moral law.' For us Christians, that moral law would be the Ten Commandments that God trusted to Moses after he had liberated his 'chosen' people from slavery in Egypt. (It seems God has his favourites among his children. Not cool.)

Anyway, with these laws, it meant that we could do what we like with our free will so long as we didn't. Hmm. Being given the freedom to do what you want with a set of conditions and consequences isn't being given the freedom to do what you want. The other problem with these laws is that it is absolutely impossible to be a living, breathing human without breaking one or more of them. If you are not familiar with the Ten Commandments here is a list. They vary slightly in wording and order depending on which religious denomination you are affiliated with, but are essentially the same.

1. I am the Lord thy God and thou shalt not have strange gods before me. (Tough break for all those pre-Christian, nature-loving pagans that didn't get the memo on time.)
2. Thou shalt not take the name of the Lord thy God in vain. (As the phrase, 'Ah Jaysus' is an indispensable part of the Irish vernacular, that's every Irish person ever, gone or going to hell.)
3. Remember to keep holy the Lord's Day. (Shift workers and farmers are doomed.)
4. Honour thy Father and Mother. (All well and good if you are lucky enough to get responsible and loving parents, many do not.)
5. Thou shalt not kill. (A bit of a double standard from a God who ordered the brutal death of his only son! Who does that?)
6. Thou shalt not commit adultery. (That would be a common enough slip up.)
7. Thou shalt not steal. (Even more common.)
8. Thou shalt not bear false witness against thy neighbour. (Fair enough.)
9. Thou shalt not covet thy neighbour's wife. (Apparently it is OK to covet thy neighbour's husband.)
10. Thou shalt not covet thy neighbour's goods. (We must not desire what someone else has. Really! Has God met us humans?)

I am not for a minute saying that God did not actually give Moses the Ten Commandments, and nor am I trying to belittle what was an epic journey for freedom for a tortured and enslaved nation of people. The Ten Commandments have certainly stood the test of time and are not a bad set of values to strive to uphold in our daily lives. My point is simply that our beliefs around a free will that has restrictions and unconditional love that has conditions just don't make any sense. Unconditional love is exactly that, without condition. It is a bit like infinity in that there is no room for anything else. God cannot love us unconditionally, but only on condition that we make all the 'right' decisions. If God's love is unconditional, then we are loved and forgiven no matter what.

In addition, Jesus said we are one with the Father and I believe him, because science tells us the same. Christianity is founded on the false belief in the permanence of self, the individual self, but Jesus and science both concede that at the essential level of existence we are all one. Since all is one, the concept of the self as a permanent, separate, is an illusion. The spiritual dilemmas that we struggle with are generated by the illusion of free will, sin and ignorance of who or what we really are. All three illusions are compounded by the illusion of self or separation, because if we are all one, then ultimately there is no one else to answer to and we are doing all of this to ourselves. At some point in our story, we have to start using a little basic logic around our religious beliefs. We have to find the common ground between science and spirituality, because it just does not square up that if we are one with God we would set ourselves up for failure with unrealistic standards for holiness and perfection and then punish ourselves with and eternity of pain and anguish. Who would do that to themselves? Who indeed!

It is high time we had a better explanation for our being than the fearful, controlling and self-contradictory nonsense we have so far been fed by organised religion. After all, it could not be said in all honesty that Jesus was completely without sin himself. The Bible, however, contrived and tailored towards emphasising the divide between man and the divine, contains accounts of Jesus losing his self-restraint and doing things that would today at the very least put him in a courtroom facing a judge. For example, when he thrashed the temple in Jerusalem, because he didn't agree with it being used as a place of trade for herdsmen and money changers: 'And making a whip of cords, he drove them all out of the temple, with the sheep and oxen. And he poured out the coins of the money-changers and overturned their tables. And he told those who sold the pigeons, "Take these things away; do not make my Father's house a house of trade."' (John 2: 13–16). An understandable sentiment by Jesus, but these people obviously had permission from someone to do what they were doing and just because he didn't agree with it didn't give him the right to attack them, their animals and their property. There are lots of practices and institutions that I don't agree with, but I would be arrested if I did what Jesus did. We have somehow rationalised that when a divine and perfect Jesus or God loses his cool and does something illegal, it is OK. But if us misguided and imperfect humans misbehave, it is not.

There was also the time he expelled some violent 'demons' from two men and redirected them into an unfortunate herd of pigs who just happened to be nearby. The pigs subsequently ran over a cliff and drowned in the water. Aside from the fact that I don't believe in demons and suspect that the two men were probably suffering with a mental disorder that Jesus liberated them from, there are two things to note about Jesus' actions. One, it was entirely unnecessary to do that to innocent animals when I am sure there were other options available to the son of God. Two, the pigs were not his to kill in the first place, and since there is no record of him apologising to or compensating the owner for what would have been a substantial loss, what Jesus did was not just unkind it was unlawful, son of God or not. It is no wonder that the people of the village asked him to leave. 'When he arrived at the other side in the region of the Gadarenes, two demon-possessed men coming from the tombs met him. They were so violent that no one could pass that way. "What do you want with us, son of God?" they shouted. "Have you come here to torture us before the appointed time?" Some distance from them a large herd of pigs was feeding. The demons begged Jesus, "If you drive us out, send us into the herd of pigs." He said to them, "Go!" So they came out and went into the pigs, and the whole herd rushed down the steep bank into the lake and died in the water. Those tending the pigs ran off, went into the town and reported all this, including what had happened to the demon-possessed men. Then the whole town went out to meet Jesus. And when they saw him, they pleaded with him to leave their region.' (Matthew 8: 28–34).

Then there is the story of the fig tree as discussed earlier, where Jesus cursed a fig tree to death because it had no fruit on it and he was feeling a bit hangry. While it is certainly not a crime to release your frustrations on a tree, it is not the most divine thing to do, if we are to believe the literal interpretation of events. 'The next day as they were leaving Bethany, Jesus was hungry. Seeing in the distance a fig tree in leaf, he went to find out if it had any fruit. When he reached it, he found nothing but leaves, because it was not the season for figs. Then he said to the tree, "May no one ever eat fruit from you again." And his disciples heard him say it.' (Mark 11: 12–13). The disciples recorded that the tree Jesus cursed subsequently withered and died. We all get a bit grumpy when we need food, but killing the tree was not the most godly thing to do, especially as it was hardly the fig tree's fault; it wasn't even fig season. Even if Jesus was using symbolism to make a point, its death meant it would never bear fruit for anyone else again. Not exactly in the spirit of love. You would imagine that Jesus could have taken the high road here and done something more godly, such as nurturing the plant to produce fruit miraculously for everyone to eat. That would have benefited everyone and he could have made the point about how love helps us grow and prosper. I am not saying what Jesus did was right or wrong. I am just pointing out that the son of God was human, too, and his actions were not always in keeping with the divine standards we have outlined for ourselves, but still they remained the will of God. Perhaps Jesus was precisely making the point that he was being human and it was OK to be human. And if he had nurtured the fig tree into bearing fruit to show how love helps us flourish, it would not have been a real truth. Life and humanity has shown us that sometimes all the love in world will not guarantee that we will live our best life.

As the Ten Commandments has failed somewhat in its efforts to keep humanity in check over the years, we have had to invent a few extra laws to ensure people are made responsible and accountable for their conduct. In an attempt to placate our ever- increasing existential anxiety, we invented laws to establish an acceptable standard of behaviour, to maintain order, to resolve disputes, and to protect liberties and rights. We created law- keepers to uphold these laws and designated a strategic and workable justice system to determine guilt or innocence and designate a proportionate punishment for the crime committed. Applying boundaries and consequences to individual and social activity gives the impression of control and security in our lives.

It is a comforting system that, in principle, should serve as a deterrent for divergent behaviour, or if not, at least provide the satisfaction of punishment. Sometimes the system appears to work very well and sometimes it doesn't. Sometimes (a lot), even the wrong person becomes the victim of its shortcomings. Its shortcomings being the fact that the entire system is composed of and dependent on the human factor that is innately fallible with its dark side and limitations that manages to infect everything.

Humanity's age-old concept of justice through vengeance, retribution and punishment began centuries ago, and over time we have invented an impressive variety of ways to extract our well-deserved pound of flesh. We have employed the horrors of mutilation, branding, stocks, workhouses and exile, and now prisons, but crime always seems to be one step ahead of us and nothing seems to be as effective as we would like. As crime continues to expand and evolve, we make new laws and revise old ones, trading more and more of our civil liberties in exchange for a false sense of security and harmony. It is a false security because, as science indicates, we cannot control the circumstances of our lives no matter how much we think we can, and nobody is actually responsible for anything because our course is already set and we are simply experiencing life events that we cannot either control or change. Physics tells us that life as it currently stands is a consequence of a stream of deterministic events that began its flow long, long before we were even born. Neurophysiology indicates that the awareness of our actions trails behind the intent by at least half a second. In other words, we appear to be encountering our reality rather than manipulating it. So, if we are just watching a series of events unfold in a determined manner, like a movie, how could we possibly be responsible for our actions? It is like saying that you are responsible for the actions of one of the characters in a movie that you are watching.

At the most fundamental level, criminal law is based around a single Latin phrase: 'Actus non facit reum nisi mens sit rea', which translates to 'an act does not make a person guilty unless the mind is also guilty'. If the mind is so far behind our actions and our awareness is so minimal, how can any of us be guilty of anything, good or bad? In the exactness of our reality, this misalignment of thought and action was not a mistake by God. I believe this gap was a purposeful construct. God could just as easily have calibrated the intent and the act precisely. Instead, he factored in the delay to undermine culpability spirituality while still maintaining the illusion that we are responsible for our lives, as well as give us the clue to eventually figure it out.

I am not saying that sin does not exist, it does, but only the illusion or experience of sin, because if we scratch beneath the surface we find that there is nothing compatible with sin as we know it. Laws and punishments are all part of the human experience, but we cannot secure the safety of our future with laws or punishments because our entire lives have already been secured in a deterministic chain of events where all actions are a result of prior causes arising out of an infinite regress. In such a sequence, there is no ownership or accountability, so if you want to find out who is responsible for what, you have to go back all the way to the beginning to who started it all. Yes, the buck stops only when it reaches the creator himself, God.

Humanity has an understandable need to point the finger of fault at someone or something, but never would we suspect that our loving father in heaven could be the one who is really responsible. Over the course of history many of us have experienced unimaginable horrors, but the question of blame is a complex one and has been the subject of many a philosophical debate over the years. Even on the surface, it could be argued from the perspective that criminals are mentally ill and/or products of their social environment and that they are the true victims. It is certainly a viable argument given the back story of some offenders. At the very least it makes the issue a lot less black and white, and when we dig down to the most fundamental, microscopic level of our existence, the problem of cause or fault disappears completely. For example, in a game of billiards, if you strike the little white cue ball and it smashes into a stationary collection of coloured balls causing them to disperse in different directions, you would very understandably assume that the cue ball 'caused' the breakup and movement of the other balls. However, because the laws of physics place the past and future on an equal footing, all the balls are treated equally. From any given point, these laws run equally well backwards as they do forwards, so technically the reverse could just as well be true, where, the collection of coloured balls 'caused' the little white cue ball to move. The unsettling truth here is that it all boils down to the direction we perceive life to be taking. If we all were to experience life in reverse, like the story of Benjamin Button, we would all think it perfectly normal and natural and fault would present differently. Fault is a perception, not a reality because on a fundamental level there is no culpability.

On a philosophical level, even with free will it is hard to pinpoint the blame. On an atomic level it is impossible. That leaves us with one level left to hold responsible. The spiritual level. God. Yes, God is showing up as the culprit once again. Yes, it is all God's fault for creating the whole thing in the first place. And just in case you need reminding, we are all one with God; separation is an illusion. We are God, infinite love and intelligence, so ultimately we ourselves are the ones who are to blame for creating this reality of experiences and we have done an almighty good job of fooling ourselves with it.

God's natural law requires that all things kill to live, as one cannot live without another dying. This orderly law is abundant in the natural world and has facilitated the progression of life since the beginning of time. A long-established food chain or sequence of events where one organism eats another, and is then eaten by another in turn. Beginning with a primary source, either the sun or chemicals produced by hydrothermal vents deep in the ocean, then an organism uses those sources to make food. This starts the food chain within that plant or animal and continues all the way up to the apex predator, an organism that eats others but is not eaten itself. It is a savagely brutal yet efficient system and that is how God designed it. The lion eats the antelope and that's OK with God and us. God created the natural world billions of years before he created us and the concept of predator and prey, victim and perpetrator, was in full swing long before we arrived. From a place of love God created the brutal nature of our reality. It wasn't the devil that created life on earth and made many of the dinosaurs into huge, fearsome carnivores, it was God. In fact, the entire evolution of life is seemingly based on this brutal struggle in the survival of the fittest. Even in the microscopic world of unicellular organisms there is a constant battle of life and death. Bacteria, viruses and fungi have been waging war on everything since life began and their infinitesimally small size is immaterial as they have been able to take down the biggest and the best life has to offer. If you have ever observed the battle between a pathogen and an immune cell under a microscope you will be amazed at how barbaric it can be. Not unlike taking a seat at the colosseum in Rome to watch two gladiators battle it out in the arena.

Death and destruction seems to be the modus operandi of all life big and small in this realm of experiencing, and God hasn't had a problem with it until we humans came along and decided he did. With the introduction of humans and their belligerent tendencies, God took the experience of life on earth to a whole other level with our lofty ideas about good and evil, right and wrong, consequences and punishment. We drew a line in the sand between the natural world and ourselves and said that, at human level, God was no longer OK with the brutal nature of existence and we would be punished severely for our wrongdoings. Thou shalt not kill only applies to us humans and not to the natural world or even God himself, who engineered the torture and death of his own son when there had to be any number of more advantageous and less gruesome options available to our infinitely creative creator in his desperate attempts to save us from our sins. The whole thing is self-contradictory, not the story itself, just the explanation behind it. Still, we developed a plethora of rights and wrongs based on the subjective opinions of our varied human judgements. We decided it was wrong to kill each other, but OK to inflict misery, torture and death on any other sentient being for the purposes of sport, scientific research or our unnecessary, yet insatiable appetite for dead flesh. We separated ourselves from God's natural law with the reasoning that we are special, we are superior and we have free will, none of which is true. We are neither separate nor special and it certainly doesn't look like we are the ones making the decisions. We occupy a deterministic reality that from the beginning of time and within all its life forms has relied on the struggles between life and death, the agony and the bliss. More recently, with the inclusion of humanity, came the added dimension of the right and the wrong, the saint and the sinner. It might be easy to justify the lion killing the antelope for survival, but what about when the lion kills his own cubs in the herd to force the lioness into oestrus where she will be more receptive to his sexual advances? Lions are not the only animal that exhibit this behaviour; hippos and dolphins have also been observed in the act of infanticide. In addition, dolphins are known to engage in gang rape and recreational killing. Rape and murder would certainly be considered a sin in human terms, but we don't expect that God is angry with these animals for it and that they will be sent to hell as punishment. Nor do the animals seek revenge or justice for their loss and suffering, and not, I expect, because they couldn't or because they do not feel grief or pain, but because the spectre of right and wrong is human baggage and not part of the experience available in other forms of life. Either that or every other species possess a far greater level of spiritual discernment than us mere humans who are burdened with its endless conundrums. In truth, God/we created all the many facets of our existence, the physical and the philosophical, and he has/we have no intention of punishing himself/ourselves for it. The need for justice or revenge is a human concept not obvious in other species and in the presence of infinite oneness and the absence of free will means it could not either be a principle of the divine.

So punishment and revenge have no place in spirit and sin is a very convincing spiritual illusion in this perceptual dimension. Just to be clear, I believe that sin exists not as a spiritual truth, but as something that we came here to experience and I am totally invested in its illusion. I find it just as hard as the next person to comprehend or condone the actions of mankind on his own and other species and even harder to find forgiveness in my heart, especially when I feel personally hard done by.

Despite my enlightened and liberating beliefs about the nature of sin I still struggle with it, definitely not as much as I used to, but I still do. Not because I don't believe my own theories about sin, but because, for now, I am human and I am supposed to.

With all that being said, now it means we have to deal with the uncomfortable contradiction of 'how' and 'why' this universal book of fate is written with so much tragedy. How and why an infinitely loving God could or would orchestrate so much tortuous suffering and misery, with millions of innocent people and animals dying every day from abuse, neglect, starvation, genetic defects, disease, natural disasters, wars, etc, etc. How can we rationalise a 'good God' with this cruel suffering, with murderers, rapists, dictators and all the rest? How can it be that we if we are indeed one with God, why resemble the deity so remotely? Why would we want to hide our sacred connection? And why are we capable of so much that would seem so ungodly?

Well, the 'why' question seems straight forward enough. As discussed earlier, we are all here for the experience. We are here to see and to feel. Yup, that is pretty much it. We did not come here to be happy and safe all the time; that is what we left behind in our infinity. We came here to feel other stuff, uncomfortable, painful and challenging stuff. And we have to remember that this life is not just about the bad and the difficult, it is about the beautiful and the glorious, so much beauty, so much glory. It is about the struggle and the overcoming, the winning and the loosing, the love and the loss, the tragedy and the triumph. It is about realising our similarities despite our differences, it is about learning and growing, etc, etc. I could keep going forever, but you get the message. Everything seems to have an opposing force and the trouble is that in order experience one aspect we have to be exposed to its opposite. We would never be able to appreciate the warmth of the sun unless we knew what it is like to be cold. We came here to experience these polar opposites, yes, even in the extreme. It is the day and the night, the light and dark of existence. Life in this realm was never designed to be easy, it was designed to be experienced, and even though some of us have had really difficult times and low points in our lives, when we look back we can identify at least enough highs to have made it worthwhile.

The question of 'why' therefore seems to be quite a simple one and certainly not the dark, fearful one that religion would have us believe. The reason we have come here to this dimension seems to be nothing more complicated than our desire to be something other than our infinite, all-being selves and feel things other than our true essence of all love and all knowing. We created those opportunities within all the different levels of awareness, different forms, perspectives and challenges, but we left nothing to chance. It is a reality that is as calculated as it is magnificent and it is available to spirit in any timeframe and capacity.

The answer to the question of 'how' we managed to create so much of what appears to be a blatant spiritual contradiction of our true divine and loving nature is a somewhat more complicated, but nevertheless decipherable with a little digging. For a start, God can do whatever he wants to do. And God can be whatever he wants to be. If God wants to create chaos and catastrophe in order to live it and experience it, then that's what he is going to do. Here is a reality check for every Bible enthusiast that likes to give God such a righteous persona: God has never ever claimed to be either good or bad, right or wrong. In fact, when Moses had his conversation with the burning bush high on the mountain slopes of Sinai, God simply explained himself as, 'I Am.' Nothing else. Not being one thing or another, not feeling one way or another, not having one attribute or another. The state of 'I Am' is a highly flexible condition. Being 'I Am,' God has the freedom to be anything, everything and nothing. Being 'I Am' is probably the most objective, unapologetic and liberating statement there is. So God, the Almighty, the all-powerful, all-knowing, all-everything, can be whatever he wants to be. God can be as bad or as good as he so wishes.

Then there is the fact that all our human notions of what is good and bad, right and wrong, are nothing more than our individual interpretation and experiences of life. Life repeatedly demonstrates that what is good for one person is bad for another, what is right for one is wrong for another, what is pleasing to one is repulsive to another. Life is only what we think it is. In reality, nothing is either good or bad, right or wrong, only in our very individual and subjective beliefs, opinions and feelings. Here, in our thoughts, God can be as badass as he likes. Here, God can seem to be anything he wants, unfair, sadistic, unstable, even absent.

Consistent with our fundamental all and nothingness, our story exists as this non dimensional, non-partisan, non-feeling language of mathematics that cradles a blunt biological perspective of corresponding sensory, emotional and intellectual illusions that support it. So, like everything in this bubble of deception, God can present as bad or as wrong as he so wishes, but only in our perception, because in reality, God/we, life, are neither.

There is no doubt that life can be exceptionally difficult at times, but technically, difficult does not mean bad or wrong, especially if there is good reason or divine purpose for it. The Bible tells us that it was God's love and will that his beloved son should die at the tender age of thirty-three under circumstances of unspeakable brutality. The excruciating torture and preordained murder of his own son was an act of love by God. In other words, something so bad and wrong was actually a demonstration of unconditional love and service by God for reasons of the same divine nature. The ultimate paradox. God didn't have to engineer the death of his own son in order to save us from our sins and heal the world. He could just as easily have written the story of Jesus' life where he lived to the ripe old age of ninety-three, performing miracles, healing the sick, saving sinners, preaching the good news and just generally spreading the love. That would have been a much more rational intervention if God really want to help us poor, struggling, sinners. Much more good could have been done, you would think. But God in his eternal wisdom knew different, and instead orchestrated for his son a long and painful death, one normally reserved for the most wretched of criminals. All from a place of unbounded love and service. The devastating betrayal, savage torture and unjust execution of Jesus was not bad or wrong, because it was both the will and the love of God. It was unfathomable love disguised as a most dastardly deed, because it had divine purpose.

So, in the name of love, God can dish up any manner of adversity and hardship for us because, just like Jesus' death, it is not bad or wrong when it has a spiritual motive or objective. God's love, it seems, can be responsible for all sorts of difficulties in our lives. On top of this, I don't believe it was ever God's intention to 'save' humanity by sending his son to die. That would mean that God had made a mistake in his creation of us, a mistake he needed to rectify, but God doesn't make mistakes. It would also mean that God and Jesus have both failed miserably in their mission to rescue mankind from itself, as it clearly hasn't worked. We are no better than we were 2000 years ago; if anything, we are worse. There is no mistake or failure, anywhere, at any time, because God created everything just how he wanted it because God can do whatever he likes. If God really wanted to save the world he would have done it a long, long time ago in spectacular fashion, and I wouldn't be here writing this book now.

Orthodox Christianity is adamant that Jesus came here to free us from our sins and save the world. This, however, is something that we decided and not something that Jesus himself had any aspirations of. While Jesus came to teach us some very profound truths, he also knew that his story would cause division and strife for generations to come.

In the Gnostic Gospel of Thomas, Sayings of Jesus, 16, Jesus is attributed with the quote, 'Perhaps people think that I have come to cast peace upon the world. They do not know that I have come to cast conflicts upon the earth: fire, sword, war.'

I would say, well done, Jesus, mission accomplished. Because, true to his word, this is exactly what has transpired, with lots of fire, swords and wars thrown about since his coming. Let us not sugar-coat this. Jesus' life story has caused as much suffering as it has cured, where countless people, innocent or otherwise, have suffered and died in the name of Christianity and indeed every other religion.

While we would all like to believe that there is a separate entity or evil force that is creating all the difficulties of life there is nothing to say that God isn't doing all this himself. Like it or not, it may be time to face the truth that God might have his own dark side. After all, if we are all one with each other and with God, then God is present within all thought and action in this realm, good and evil. The prophet Jeremiah was wise to this fact a long time ago when he stated in the Old Testament Book of Lamentations that both 'evil and good proceed out of the mouth of the host High'. The Gnostic gospels also make numerous references to this perceived dualism of God. In The Testimony of Truth, there is a strange but beautiful poem that addresses God's bipolar tendencies. Entitled, 'The Thunder, Perfect Mind', it includes the lines:

'For I am the first and the last.
I am the honoured one and the scorned one.
I am the whore and the holy one.
I am the wife and the virgin. . .

I am the barren one,
and many are her sons. . .
I am the silence that is incomprehensible . .
I am the utterance of my name.'

It is understandably hard to imagine how God's love could possibly be responsible for creating the enormous amount of collective and individual suffering throughout the ages. But love is far more cunning than we can appreciate from our hindered human perspective, and, love is infinite. That is its secret weapon. Despite the numerous and varied notions of God offered by many religions, we seem to hold the common conviction that this godhead is the source of infinite love, wisdom and perfection and we are its children. If this is so, then as a product of the divine we, too, are love, wisdom and perfection that stretch to infinity. If we are infinite love, then we cannot be anything other than love. If we are infinite wisdom, then we cannot be anything other than all knowing. If we are infinite perfection and order, then we cannot be anything other than flawless and there is no room for chaos or uncertainty. In other words, being infinite means we cannot be anything else other than what we already are, or we cannot go anywhere else because we are already there. Being infinite means this fact pervades every dimension, realm, world or form we occupy. With nothing else to be and nowhere else to go, the only way to be someone else or go somewhere else is to create the illusion of such. To create an illusion of fallibility, ignorance and disorder, from the illusion of different forms, in an illusion of somewhere else. It is a most elaborate and ingenious deception that allows us to experience a personal journey of limitation and challenge, as well as be of service to a plan much greater than ourselves.

Shakespeare had a deep understanding of the enormous staying power of love and few have been able, before or since, to pen it quite as well as the immortal bard himself in his beautiful

Sonnet 116:
> Let me not to the marriage of true minds
> Admit impediments. Love is not love
> Which alters when it alteration finds,
> Or bends with the remover to remove.
> O no! it is an ever-fixed mark
> That looks on tempests and is never shaken;
> It is the star to every wand'ring bark,
> Whose worth's unknown, although his height be taken.
> Love's not Time's fool, though rosy lips and cheeks
> Within his bending sickle's compass come;
> Love alters not with his brief hours and weeks,
> But bears it out even to the edge of doom.
> If this be error and upon me prov'd,
> I never writ, nor no man ever lov'd.

Here, Shakespeare pays tribute to the limitless and indestructible quality of love which will withstand any circumstance or obstacle and even time itself. Love is a constant, unwavering force that will yield to nothing and nobody. Otherwise it is not nor ever was love. With all respect to Shakespeare's prodigious writing skills, his description of love in this sonnet is incomplete. It discusses love in all the ways we perceive it to be, strong, uplifting, helpful, comforting, etc, but love has another side to it that is often very hard to see, especially when it hurts. The truth is that love can be very uncomfortable and even cruel at times, but can remain love. We just perceive it differently. Love is exceptionally resourceful and has the incredible ability to portray itself as an opposite, even in the extreme. How? Because love is immortal and love is limitless. Therein lies its secret, its paradox, its genius. Its infinite nature allows it to be so much more than all things good and fluffy and nice in this realm of experiencing.

The true nature of our being is that of infinite love, so we can never, ever, ever not be love. That is the deal with infinity, it goes on forever, it has no beginning and it has no end and therefore it is impossible to be outside of it. It is therefore impossible to be anything other love. There is no escaping being love, there is no not being love. While love can never change what it is, can never be anything else except love, what love can do is present itself in many different ways and forms, often giving the impression that it is not love at all. Albeit superficially, love can look exactly like fear, malice and even hate. This is because love possesses an infinite complexity that allows for a whole lot of camouflage, shapeshifting and surprises that affords us the double-edged experience of our lives and our story. Love is a master illusionist, but despite any outward appearance of otherwise, love can only and ever be love.

In order to experience love in all its forms and glory the opposite has to be available to us. In order to experience the opportunity to forgive we must have something to anger us. In order to discover the courage or fortitude within ourselves there must be something to fear or overcome. We would not be able to exercise patience if there was nothing to irritate us. Some of our greatest achievements have been a consequence of our greatest challenges. In the name of love we created a realm that contains all the contrasts and paradoxes to experience our story. From a place of love we provide these gifts for each other, simultaneously where love is so heavily disguised we are completely fooled by its display and it appears totally conflicted with our idea of love.

Most of us have experienced events in our lives that at the time seemed disastrous, but actually ended up evolving into something beautiful. Sometimes the reason for our challenges cannot be deciphered before or even during our trials, only afterwards. With the gift of hindsight we often get to see the blessing and reason for our difficulties. This is love in action, even though it may only become obvious to us outside or after the fact. This is one of the many ways that love likes to present itself. Instead of being blatantly obvious all of the time, love gives us the opportunity to feel, to endure and sometimes to overcome. However, sometimes we do not reap the benefits of the challenges and tortures we go through, sometimes we do not grow and learn from them, sometimes we don't conquer or overcome, we just feel and endure, and sometimes it can be excruciatingly difficult and we never get to see its reason or its blessing.

This does not mean that love is absent or has an opposite, it simply means that its blessing and its service is too far outside or after the fact for us to perceive it within the confines of this temporary physical occupation and journey, i.e., there is a bigger picture. There are many things in this existence that are outside of our ability to see them, but that does not mean they are not there. Sometimes people never get to see the reason and gift of their suffering because it belongs in the service of each other and in the overall plan that is not available to us in this life of limitations that we have created. Our life story is not just personal to us, but also reverberates before us, after us and in every direction around us. It has meaning in the past, the present and the future, but we may not always be afforded the divine or personal 'why' for everything. This can often seem unfair and be more than a little frustrating, but everything has purpose. Being denied the chance to see or appreciate love's rationale or reason in a difficult situation gives the desired impression that it is bad or meaningless. Love is never meaningless, love is never bad, it is just exceptionally good at hiding itself.

Love can often seem ridiculously unfair and horrifyingly brutal, but if it did not show up in this way then we would have very little to experience. We did not invent a mediocre story to partake in, we did not want to be mildly taxed or only slightly stimulated, ergo we wrote a gigantic, epic expedition of extremes so that we could feel deeply and diversely and also be sufficiently duped in its maze of smoke and mirrors. In our love for adventure and our love for one another, love created a countless collection of experiences from a countless number of different platforms and perspectives. This is only possible through what appears as a contrary or an opposite, but it remains that within the emotional depth and intelligence of love. 'Both light and shadow are the dance of love,' says Rumi.

Sometimes love appears to have taken things just a little too far, especially where there is dire physical pain and or mental anguish. At this point in the development of our story there are very few of us who have not observed or experienced man's inhumanity to man and indeed every other species on the planet for reasons of fear, greed or sport. War, torture, mutilation, pain, disease, grief, loss, despair, environmental disaster, if this is love then it is either taking the mickey or has made a terrible mistake. Love does not make mistakes, it can't; it is infinite perfection. In our desire to feel things other than love, joy and eternity, we had to create behaviours and circumstances to accommodate that need. In the very brief expanse of our lives, we get to see and experience so much, but in order to experience the best of it we had to make provision for the worst. It is the paradox of living and experiencing a life. The more deeply we wanted to feel the more extreme we had to go with the plot and the proceedings. This extremism that allows us to experience such deep and different emotions has the added genius of fostering the illusion that love is absent or has an opposite which we call 'evil'. Love cannot be absent when it is infinite, nor can it have an opposing force. It is simply that love is limitless and therefore so are the lengths it can go to show itself.

Love has been so utterly effective in disguising itself for humanity that we have given its perceived absence an identity all of its own. In the Bible, this delusive counterforce in creation, which produces disharmony, disease, separateness and ignorance, is personified as Satan. Satan has a rather disturbing image with a tail and horns and an intriguing story of his own. Once a cherished angel of God, he fell from grace when he became hungry for power and was banished 'below' to a fiery hellhole. Satan and his many friends or demons spend their time trying to recruit human souls to their cause only to torture them for an eternity in an inextinguishable fire. Man, with his penchant for self-destruction, has proven himself to be very weak and susceptible to Satan's charms and is now dragging the entire planet and every other soul in it to oblivion. God, despite all his infinite power and knowing, unconditional love and goodness, appears to be at a complete loss of how to deal with the awful situation.

While the theory of Satan and his ongoing conflict with God is an entertaining one, it is full of so many enormous, gaping holes it's hard to know where to start. To begin with 'dualism' cannot exist in infinity. If God is infinite, then there is no room for someone else. There is no dissident other or opposing force in God's infinity. God is everything and everyone so Satan or any of the rest of us for that matter cannot exist as a separate entity. As God's infinity extends to us then God is the mastermind behind all of our thoughts and actions, the best and the worst in this realm of contrast. Plus, it is quite clear that God is more than capable of committing murder and creating mayhem on his own without the help of any evil force or being.

Separatism is an illusion of epic proportions. As if the oneness of all could ever be separated from itself. This dimension thrives on the illusion of division. We experience separation in many ways, none of them real. By impairing our ability to appreciate fully our oneness we create the illusion of separation. Being separated is a crucial aspect of our reality. By thinking we are separate we can then experience the challenges of both aloneness and companionship in different situations. We come from a place where we know with certainty that we are all of one. In our lifetime we get a brief glimpse of what it is like to be removed from source and each other. This is what we want to experience, even though we can never really be disconnected at any level. Disconnection is an illusion; it is a feeling, not a reality. There is no 'sinful' thought, 'sinful' word or 'sinful' deed that can ever disconnect us from who or what we already are, i.e., the source itself. We are infinitely connected so there is nowhere to disconnect to.

When we conceived the genius of separateness, we wanted to take the concept to deeper levels of detachment by dividing and subdividing it even further. As well as the Illusion of our physical separation, we are set apart by species, gender, social status, race and colour, beliefs, language, location, likes and dislikes, abilities physical and intellectual, the list goes on. We have discriminated against each other and even fought wars over our differences, but we have also united against and overcome our prejudices and fears of them. Anything that makes us different, makes us separate and our many differences give us ample raw material for the story and our experience within a matrix of interdependence and individuality. Separation is an essential component of a reality that relies on contrast for its experience. In the words of the author Khalil Gibran, 'And ever has it been known that love knows not its own depth until the hour of separation.'

Jesus was fully aware of the truth that lay beneath the surface illusion of fear and sin. He stood before his captors and persecutors able to love them and forgive them, because he knew they were doing what God, he and all of us wanted. Jesus knew they had agreed to their limitations and were playing their part in the incredible story of his life and death, a story that has survived the ages and enthralled the millions. It is becoming increasingly obvious through science that we are not what we perceive ourselves or each other to be, that our true nature is a oneness, hidden or disguised by a physical limitation to see it and a spiritual impediment to appreciate it. This of course means that even that person who you dislike the most or the one who has caused you the most pain is really a glorious extension of God's love that adores you beyond measure and has agreed to an often difficult and seemingly soul conflicting role for your mutual benefit and at the same time play a pivotal role in life events as they are designed to unfold. Ouch! That is a tricky one to grapple with in our day-to-day lives.

Judas has always been portrayed as the villain who betrayed Our Lord. But what if Judas' character performed an act of ultimate devotion to Jesus, one that he had agreed upon well in advance from a place where we are not blinkered by a limited perspective? A place where we can see the reason and purpose of it all? Both Jesus and Judas were beings of infinite love and oneness before they entered this physical realm. Both adopted a human form, a certain awareness and a specific purpose. Jesus had an advantage from the start because his knowledge of who he was and why he was there was not at all restricted. Judas, however, purposely agreed to an awareness that was much more deficient for his role in the story. In an act of unlimited, unconditional love and service to Jesus, to the plan and to all of us, Judas consented to his spiritual limitations in order to fulfil his part in the plan, as did Caiaphas and Pilate and everyone else who was instrumental in Jesus' destiny. And if they had no choice but to do God's bidding none of them is to blame for Jesus death and therefore there was no 'sin' committed, at least not in God's eyes. For how could their actions be sinful if they were abiding by God's wishes and doing their part in fulfilling Jesus' destiny? How could God condemn them to hell for doing what he wanted? These were the questions that were never dealt with in religion class, but bothered me no end as a child. For me, it was like my father asking me to do something and then punishing me for doing it. It took a crazy horse and a little science finally to understand that we are not really the diabolical misfits and sinners we have been told we are, and that each role is equally important in a story that was clearly written in advance. Their acts of betrayal and murder were love from inception and love in implementation. The story of Jesus would not have been able to demonstrate the love of God so totally without the existence of what would seem to be the opposite. All roles were equal in service, all roles were conspired from a place of love and all roles had a purpose, a divine purpose. Judas, Pilate, Caiaphas and everyone else in the story was simply following orders and acting according to a prewritten plan and script, a very precise one judging by the maths. As it was God's wish and prognostication that Jesus should die, then everybody who played their part in Jesus' death was doing so from the cleverly disguised and deeper spiritual truth of unconditional love and service. Perhaps, this is why Jesus never had any difficulty with forgiveness. He knew there was nothing to forgive.

Forgiveness can be a difficult pill to swallow. It can be challenging enough in the minor and the petty, let alone in the catastrophic. It is very hard to let go of a well-earned grudge, no matter how much we want the peace and freedom of it. Holding on to anger and resentment can cripple us emotionally and burn us on the inside like acid. It can destroy our quality of life both physically and mentally, even if it is wholly and utterly justifiable. The Bible has much to say about forgiveness, but seems to struggle as much as the rest of us with it, as it can't just get its story straight on the issue. On one hand, the gospels tell a story of the moral perfection of Jesus with his lessons of humility, unconditional love and forgiveness. They also tell a conflicting story of judgement, punishment and eternal damnation. In Mathew 18: 22 when Jesus is asked by Peter how many times he must forgive his brother, he answers, 'I do not say to you seven times, but seventy times seven.' Obviously, we can assume that this was not an instruction to forgive a total of 490 offences before pulling the plug, but instead a recommendation to forgive without limits. However, in Luke's version of the story, Jesus inserts the condition of remorse. That this boundless forgiveness should only be extended 'if there is repentance' (Luke 17: 3). Again, putting conditions on something unconditional doesn't make any sense. Jesus then goes on to tell the parable of an unforgiving servant, who after being released of his financial debts by his master refuses to offer the same mercy to a colleague who in turn owes him money. When the master hears of this, the servant is condemned to prison and torture. We are warned that the same fate awaits us if we do not forgive each other like God forgives us. 'So my heavenly Father will also do to every one of you, if you do not forgive your brother or sister from your heart.' (Matthew 18: 35). So, here the Bible tells us that God expects us imperfect and ignorant humans to forgive unconditionally and endlessly, but he, the divine and perfect father, is not prepared to do the same for us unless we can muster the same level of charity towards each other. The virtue of forgiveness is so important that we are threatened with eternal damnation if we do not possess it. Now there is one hell of a contradiction.

Then there is the sin that God will not forgive under any circumstances: 'Blasphemy against the Holy Spirit' (Matthew 12: 31–32; Mark 3: 29; Luke 12: 10). Wait a minute. Isn't that the thing Jesus was doing all his life, going around proclaiming to be the son of God? Isn't that the thing he was prepared to give up his life for? Wasn't it Jesus who said we are all gods, sons of the most high and all that? And then he says that it is the worst sin in the history of sins and is totally unforgivable by a God who will forgive anything. Oh, the inconsistency of it all!

Perhaps the Bible is referring to the element of blasphemy that relates to a bit of profanity or slandering, in which case God is quite sensitive, takes things quite personally and does not take kindly to attacks on his character. According to the Bible, murder can be forgiven but blasphemy cannot. Really? I would have thought there are worse things going on in the world that would incur the wrath of God than a bit of cursing or name-calling. For offenders of this fairly minor indiscretion (relatively speaking), they will suffer the terrible fate of an eternity of anguish, remorse, pain and misery. A terrifying prospect, weeping and gnashing of teeth are mentioned. The Bible would have us believe that the quickest way to ruin God's day is with a little bit of back talk. We are told by scripture that one of the main reasons for Jesus' coming was the forgiveness of sins and it is the only obligation that is placed on humans in the Lord's Prayer. Jesus was not a hypocrite, so how could he ask us imperfect and ignorant humans to forgive unconditionally and endlessly if God the divine and perfect father was not prepared to do the same for us? That would be a blatant celebration of double standards to say the least. It is fair to say that the concept of sin and hell does not line up with what science is telling us about the objective nature of reality and the oneness of our existence. The truth is, Jesus condemned the sin, not the sinner, as he knew he could not make anyone accountable for a disadvantaged awareness and could not condemn anyone for doing what God wanted them to do. In his death, Jesus demonstrated that truth by forgiving all involved in that ultimate violation of life, murder. For how could he do anything else, because, even if you are to believe the literal take on the story of Jesus, it was God who sent his son to die, not anyone else. God planned the whole thing from start to finish. God orchestrated the extreme torture and brutal death of his own son and made it look like it was all our fault. Sneaky! There is an outrageous number of inconsistencies on the topic of sin and punishment in the Bible and when you pit them against the circumstances of Jesus life and death, they don't make any sense. When you pull up the science that demonstrates the unified nature of our existence, it makes even less sense. Many scholars and theologians who have studied original scripture now argue that eternal damnation was never a part of early Christian thinking, nor was it ever in the words of Jesus. As mentioned earlier, Ancient Greek text used custom symbols which could be easily misinterpreted. An example being the word, "metanoeō," found in the account of John the Baptist preaching in the Judean wilderness "repent for the kingdom of heaven is at hand," (Matthew, 3). The custom symbol 'metanoeō' means a "change" or "transmutation." Applying the word 'repent' in the context of change implies sin where it is not necessarily meant to be and puts a whole other spin on the sentence.

    The early Gnostic Christians had an interpretation of heaven and hell that was much closer to home. Believing that our reality here on earth to be borne out of and made possible through ignorance, both spiritual and physical, that our hell is right here with us rather than being a parallel dimension or underworld. That the true font of suffering is a state of being for those whose mind is attached to the material construct of their reality. Quantum science and Gnosticism seem to be singing from the same hymn sheet on most things, while the concept of heaven and hell in orthodox Christianity screams earthly agenda, something Jesus, whether real man or mythical creature, clearly did not have. The bottom line, I believe, is that struggle with forgiveness is an individual dilemma, and whether or not we can find forgiveness in our hearts in any situation is a personal prerogative where we are wholly correct either way. My point is that on a spiritual level it is a complete non-issue.

It happens all too often that wrongdoers manage to get away with their crimes or misdemeanours. For the devout Catholic, they can at least rely on the fires of hell to serve up the necessary punishment. For all others, there is karma. Karma will catch up with them at some point, if not in this life then surely in their next incarnation. However, the word karma is a Sanskrit word with the syllable 'kri' as a root, means 'action'; it does not mean either punishment or reward. While it has become part of almost all world languages, it is often expanded, interpreted or manipulated beyond its basic meaning in order to satisfy our deep desire for retribution. It has come to be accepted as a kind 'tit for tat'. 'What goes around comes around' sort of cosmic principle. Karma can apparently be active or invisible and can lurk insidiously over individuals, families and communities, following them from one life to the next with an eternal tenacity that is impossible to shake off. But karma really means action and its implied follow-on consequences. Karma is quite possibly the spiritual description of the cause-and-effect nature of existence that we are bound by within the laws of physics. An existence that we bear the brunt of but are *not* responsible for.

Karma is akin to the Christian concept of original sin portrayed by Adam and Eve in the Bible. When Eve succumbed to the temptations of the snake who offered her the forbidden fruit of the apple tree, she broke the connection to heaven and began an ancestral chain of events that continues unabated today. For Eve's indiscretion of consuming the illicit fruit from the tree of the knowledge of good and evil, we must all bear the consequences. As a child in religion class, I could never figure out why Eve's disobedience meant that I would have to suffer the repercussions of her actions. From a science perspective, things now make more sense. The story of Adam and Eve is the symbolic depiction of what began as choice to enter into a realm of consequential cause and effect of the laws of physics. Eve was presented with the option to enter this alternative reality of light and dark, but once accepted she was caught up in the deterministic flow of events that exists as our reality. But as humans we not responsible for this out of control domino or karmic chain reaction. We are not here to shoulder the blame, the guilt and the shame of what Eve did, we are here, just like Eve, out of choice. We are responsible only in spirit for creating this dimension in the first place. Ultimately, there is never any point at which we are truly responsible, since all actions are nothing more than egoless, impersonal, calculated prior causes, irrespective of how it feels to us. Sin is an individual and subjective analysis of a situation. It is the illusion that accompanies the totally unbiased and unfeeling laws of physics that narrates our stories.

The emotional struggle with forgiveness and the deep-rooted need for justice plays a huge part in the human experience. The victim and the perpetrator narrative is embedded into our psyche and our reality. It has been lived at many different levels and in many different ways throughout our lives and history and it has been relived and re-enacted in theatres and books for our edification and entertainment. We have been intrigued and horrified by the true life and fantasy stories that this concept of blame and retribution brings. The sufferings and losses of those who have experienced a true violation of our laws and the stories we have invented have fed our morbid fascination with the most heinous crimes and brilliant detective work. We love the adventure of an unsettling thriller with a difficult puzzle to solve. So does God; that is why he wrote them all.

Not wishing to diminish the very real pain caused by the conditions of crime and punishment, it is love's manifest in this realm in all its shapes and colours that is exactly what we came here to experience. We did not come here to master unconditional love; that is who we are and what we came from. We came here to experience physical love, broken and messy love, complete love, crazy love. We wanted and we created a dimension that supplies generous contrasts of light and dark, good and bad in order to facilitate our experience and also to make it as convincing as possible. To be fooled into believing that love has an opposite or can be absent at times is precisely the point of it all. We have been duped well through the ages by love's clever little ruse and will continue to be for a long time to come. We are all gods who wanted to get out of our comfort zone and be something other than an eternity of love. Our time and difficulties here are not a punishment, a trial or an atonement. It was our choice to be involved in the enormous adventure of feeling everything that we are not, of living a character and a storyline and of serving each other's experience and journey. If we didn't want it, we could just as easy stayed where we were.

Chapter 9: The Illusion of Evolution

'But how could you live and have no story to tell?' - Fyodor Mikhailovich Dostoevsky

Our entire existence is based on the phenomenon of a story. We are living a story, individual and collective. Everybody's life is a story. The evolution of life on our planet is a story. Story is the key to identity and is at the core of our experience as humans. Story is how we explain to ourselves and to others who we are and why we're here. Our stories create our world, our reality, they give us a diverse and colourful history and they give us reason and purpose in the present. Stories connect us to each other and the world we inhabit. We love stories, we write books, watch movies and are constantly communicating in story. We are the character in the story of our own lives and the lives of others. Our individual story and role is an integral part of the evolution of our planet in the past and the present and will reverberate well into the future long after we are gone. Whether we are immortalised in someone's memory or book or are rendered anonymous and forgotten over time, each one of us will have played a unique and crucial role in this mammoth story of life on earth.

The story began some 13.8 billion years ago with what has been labelled the Big Bang. Though it was neither big nor did it bang. This event has been calculated using the known physical laws of nature extrapolated back in time to an initial state of extreme density and temperature. After the initial expansion, there was a cooling off that allowed for the formation of subatomic particles and, later, atoms. The universe was a cold, dark, uneventful place for at least 100 million years. Stars and galaxies were the first born in this new realm as giant clouds of the first elements, hydrogen and helium were drawn together by gravity. The atoms in these collections of matter collided with each other and began to heat up to the point where they fused together. This fusion created the energy for the star to switch on and shine. Soon a cold, dark universe was filled with billions and billions of hot, bright stars that became the key players in the evolution of life.

Glowing lamplights in the blackness, they radiated heat and light from which more life could develop as they fused more and more atoms inside their core to make more and more elements. Once they had reached their capacity, the larger stars exploded, releasing all their elements as the raw materials that now make up the earth and the planets, as well as ourselves. Yes, we really are made from stardust.

The earth was formed around 4.54 billion years ago from a massive swirling cloud of dust and gas that circled the young sun. The dust particles in this disc collided with each other and clumped together to form larger and larger bits of rock, eventually creating the planets of our solar system. Billions of small space rocks never evolved any further and still exist today as comets and asteroids that hold the basic elements of existence and have the potential to initiate life, as well as end it. It is thought that the ice and other materials contained in some of these celestial bodies impacted the earth early on, delivering some of the water and other ingredients that allowed the complex chemistry of life to begin on earth.

Life on planet earth started out very simply indeed, with nothing more complicated than a variety of single-celled organisms. For roughly a billion years these little beings enjoyed a life of relative peace and harmony in an atmosphere that was much more methane than oxygen. Life was good for these untroubled, no-nonsense little creatures until a new breed of organism emerged with a Viking fondness for invading and conquering. The concept of predator versus prey makes its historical debut on the stage of life with these first bad boys known as viruses, which have survived to this day with the same intelligent talent for death and destruction. Around this time there was a suspicious decline in the methane-producing bacteria on the planet and/or an increase in the oxygen-producing ones. Either way, the atmosphere became increasingly oxygenated and toxic to these primitive inhabitants, who found that they had to evolve and adapt to their new conditions or perish, which many did. This became known as the Great Oxidation Event and was the first of many mass extinctions to come, some of greater magnitude than others.

A short time later (some 300 million years), the earth froze over in its first 'Snowball Earth', possibly as a result of a lack of volcanic activity. When the ice eventually melted, it led to more oxygen being released into the atmosphere. The surviving simple cell figured out a way to develop itself further, by engulfing other cells. Once ingested, the engulfed cell morphed into functioning internal cellular structures known as organelles inside the host cell. It was an amicable enough liaison between the two organisms, allowing the simple cell to fashion new and sophisticated internal machinery, such as chloroplasts to extract fuel from sunlight and mitochondria to produce energy.

The first animal-like forms made their appearance when some single-celled creatures came together and formed colonies consisting of many individuals. Over millions of years sponges emerged and thereafter the Placozoa which were thin plate-like creatures about 1mm across, and consisted of only three layers of cells. Things were just starting to get interesting for life and it was making some real progress when disaster struck again and the planet froze over in another 'Snowball Earth'.

After the thaw, the comb jellies arrived with the ancestral beginnings of the worm Acoela, followed closely with the rudimentary constituents of insects, spiders and crabs. About 540 million years ago, the first animals with a backbone made their appearance, or at least a primitive version of it. This is followed by the famous Cambrian explosion where a striking variety of new organisms popped up suddenly with many new body layouts, including the first animals. Their sudden and rapid appearance on the stage of life seems to run contrary to Darwin's theory of evolution that predicts new life forms evolve gradually from old ones in a constantly branching, spreading tree of life. It was a conundrum that troubled even Darwin himself. With the absence of fossil records, these brave new creatures appeared to have no predecessors. He believed they would turn up eventually, but alas they have not.

But life marches on and the trend continues over the next many millions of years with the Great Ordovician Biodiversification Event, which must have been a very exciting time in the evolution of life, producing many weird and wonderful new life forms on land and in the sea. Fast forward a few hundred million years and we have a plethora of glorious little creatures and plants, evolving and better equipping themselves with the wherewithal necessary to meet the challenges and thrive in an ever-changing environment. By this time, the common impetus to compete for food, shelter, territory and a mate was well developed in all species. Life was getting exciting, there was things to do, places to go, others to interact with, lots of feelings to feel.

Complexity continued to build on complexity and before long (millions of years) the seas were heaving with coral reefs, fishes, shellfish, trilobites, plankton, and many other groups. Life on land, too, was getting much more animated and interesting with sabre-toothed gorgonopsian reptiles and their rhinoceros-sized prey. There was also an abundant group of large herbivores called dinocephalians and pareiasaurs. This time is known as the Permian period, but it came to rather a catastrophic end some 251 million years ago when life on earth was almost completely wiped out again with the greatest mass extinction in earth's history. A series of massive volcanic eruptions in Siberia created a greenhouse-gas planet and global warming that decimated complex ecosystems all over the globe and left animals unable to breathe. As temperatures rose and the metabolism of marine animals sped up and because warmer water holds less oxygen, there was not enough oxygen for them to survive. Life on land and sea fought desperately for survival in what must have been an excruciating scramble for food, water and air. Only 5% of species survived the catastrophe and for the next millions of years to come, life had to claw its way back from oblivion and do it all over again, dividing and multiplying, branching and diversifying, to create new life forms and ecosystems.

But claw its way back it did, at least for another little while. The Triassic period saw the ecosystem gradually recover itself in a generally dry continental climate of hot summers and cold winters, no polar ice caps and coastal monsoons. Conifer forests emerged again at higher latitudes, while mosses and ferns survived in coastal regions. The oceans regenerated and repopulated once more and included marine forms with dolphin-shaped bodies and long-toothed snouts. These streamlined predators were air breathers and gave birth to live young. On land, the ancestors of mammals survived as small, nocturnal creatures.

The Triassic period gave rise to an era of reptiles and the beginnings of dinosaurs. Spiders, scorpions, millipedes and centipedes had survived the Permian Extinction, as well as some beetles. In the skies the first pterosaurs made its appearance as a Sharovipteryx, a glider about the size of a modern crow, with wing membranes attached to long hind legs.

But the Triassic period was short lived, only about fifty million years, and ended with the demise of a staggering 76% of all marine and terrestrial species. Theories as to the cause of this dynamic episode range from global warming due to widespread volcanic activity, to the impact of an extra-terrestrial body such as an asteroid or comet or simply a prolonged turnover of species across a considerable amount of time. Whatever the cause, this event, which occurred about 200 million years ago, ranks fourth in severity of the five major extinction episodes that span geologic time. Dinosaurs, pterosaurs, crocodiles, turtles, mammals and fishes were not so much affected by the environmental upheaval at this time and as it turned out it was the key moment that began the Jurassic period where the dinosaurs became the dominant land animals on earth. Around the same time, proto-mammals evolve warm-bloodedness, giving them the ability to maintain their internal temperature, regardless of the external conditions.

Over the next hundred million years, birds develop from a half-feathered, flightless dinosaur called Epidexipteryx, to the famous Archaeopteryx, the 'first bird' to live in Europe. Placental mammals split from their cousins the marsupials and, like the modern kangaroo, gave birth when their young are still very small, but nourish them in a pouch for the first few weeks or months of their lives. Following a period of rapid evolution, the first flowering plants emerged, along with a hugely diverse group of creatures, including all the hoofed mammals, whales, bats, primates, anteaters, armadillos, elephants, aardvarks and others. The Cretaceous dinosaurs reach their peak in size. The giant sauropod Argentinosaurus, believed to be the largest land animal in earth's history, lived around this time. Life then experienced a 'minor' disruption, possibly due to a huge underwater volcanic eruption where the oceans became starved of oxygen and 27% of marine invertebrates were wiped out. Despite this little hiccup, evolution continued to march forward for another thirty million years or so as the ancestors of modern primates diverged to give rise to the ancestors of modern rodents, which proved to be a hugely successful and resourceful bunch of characters. They eventually made up around 40% of modern mammal species. Grasses, too, evolved at this time, though it would be several million years before they developed into vast open grasslands.

After roughly 150 million years of transformation and adaptation, the reign of dinosaurs came to an end with the Cretaceous-Tertiary (K/T) extinction when a meteor the size of about ten kilometres in diameter struck the earth's surface with unimaginable force, smashing into the tropical lagoons of the Gulf of Mexico and gouging out a hole twenty times deeper than the Grand Canyon. This was followed by a series of tidal waves and fires that swept across North and South America, ejecting tonnes of debris into the atmosphere. The sun was blocked out and the planet was blanketed in darkness and cold for months. At least, that is one explanation for what wiped out the dinosaurs sixty-five million years ago, but it is a theory that remains hotly debated. In any event, swathes of species were annihilated, including all the giant reptiles: the dinosaurs, pterosaurs, ichthyosaurs and plesiosaurs. The ammonites, which were predatory molluscs that had eyes, tentacles and spiral shells that resemble the nautilus, were also wiped out.

What was a catastrophic event for some species turned out to be timely and advantageous for others. The loss of the dinosaurs at this time cleared the way for mammals to go on and dominate the planet. Life settled down somewhat and continued to differentiate and expand uninterrupted for another ten million years or so. But mass extinctions are never very far away, and drama arose once more when the ocean floor belched up more than a trillion tonnes of methane gas into the atmosphere, sending temperatures soaring and killing thousands of species in the ocean depths, though sparing species in shallow seas and on land. As devastating as this event was on marine life, it did also trigger an evolutionary explosion among land mammals, including early primates. Without it humans might not be here today. One would be forgiven for thinking it was all part of the plan.

In the last fifty million years, life has continued to evolve into the world as we know it. About six million years ago, humans diverged from their closest relatives, the chimpanzees and bonobos, although this evolutionary theory is well up for discussion. Soon the hominids were walking around on two legs and breeding like rabbits, eventually succeeding to become the most dominant species on the planet. But the addition of humans to the mix added another dimension to this huge story of evolution, adaptation and survival on earth. We appeared to have made a significant and unexplainable leap on the evolutionary ladder. Perhaps a little extra-terrestrial DNA made it to earth wrapped up in one or other of the meteor strikes that impacted the planet over the course of our history or perhaps, like the previous Cambrian explosion, we had no known predecessors. However it happened, we did seem much more complex emotionally and also superior in our physical and intellectual capabilities, which we dutifully put to good use making life more comfortable and stimulating for ourselves.

Here we are, the newest of arrivals on earth, give or take, full of our own self-importance and arrogance, combined with a strong appetite for acrimony and excess. Here we are, thinking the universe was designed and made especially for us, for the purposes of some sort of spiritual evolution or purging, depending on our religious orientation. However, we are by far not the superstars of evolution that we think we are. That crown must surely go to the tardigrades or water bears, strangely adorable microscopic creatures that are capable of withstanding some of the worst that nature can throw at them. Genetically optimised to survive extinction events, they are an ancient species dating back to the pre-Cambrian period. They have survived five mass extinctions and are looking in pretty good shape to handle the upcoming sixth. They can withstand temperatures as low as -458°F and as high as 300°F. They can survive extreme radiation and the vacuum of outer space and even go without food or water for thirty years to rehydrate later, forage and reproduce. Recent research suggest they may also do something rather surprising, snuggle each other for affection. So we may not be as special as we think we are, and the reason for human emergence at this point in the story of life on earth might be a lot simpler than what we have been led to believe by various teachings and religions. It may just be that we are here, like all other life that currently exists and has existed so far, to experience. End of. To experience a story and be a part of a bigger story that we wrote for ourselves.

On the surface, the evolution of life appears to be a natural yet random process that began as a mindless cell and gradually developed into the incredibly sophisticated and talented individuals that we are today. The unbroken chain of being still evident now as we inherit family resemblances, traits and even diseases. But Darwin's theory of a godless creation, that all living things are descended from a common ancestor and the product of a blind, mechanical process that altered them over the course of millions of years, has a few holes in it.

Aside from the lack of supposed predecessors for the Cambrian creatures, fossil records in general provide almost no evidence for the intermediate connecting links in species. Fossil records contain fossils of only complete and fully formed species. There are no fossils of partially evolved organisms to indicate that there was some kind of gradual process of evolution. Also, it is hard to imagine how a partially formed, intermediate being could survive in a harsh environment for any length of time in order to evolve and adapt sufficiently to fend off its competitors. Like a wounded animal, it would be easy fodder in an opportunistic, dog-eat-dog wilderness. With advancements in technology, it has been revealed that genetic and biological similarity between species is not definitive evidence they had the same ancestor. This kind of microscopic information was not obtainable by Darwin and is enough to cast some serious doubt on his theory.

It is clear that natural selection does occur to some degree in nature, but the big question is whether it is really enough to create the level of diversity and sophistication we see in the natural world. As it turns out, probably not. Natural selection can produce variations within a species, but there is no convincing evidence to show it can produce entirely new ones. Proponents of the evolutionary theory believe that new species are formed by the random mutations in the genetic code of the DNA that when combined with natural selection result in a completely different species. However, this theory would require genetic mutations of a magnitude that would most likely be devastating to the organism. Major genetic mutations don't happen very often and it is just as well they don't. Such alterations have been found to result in problems for life, rather than progress, with deformities, weakness and death. Minor genetic mutations, on the other hand, do happen fairly often, but they haven't nearly enough clout needed to transform one species into another.

Even if an organism does somehow manage to affect a genetic mutation that is workable and not problematic or fatal, the new gene must then generate a new protein design to support the organism's new structure and functions. This is one of the most mind boggling, complex processes imaginable. Proteins are highly specific with intricate designs. They twist and fold and flatten in a very particular way, in a very particular place, for a very particular purpose. Distinguished biologist Douglas Axe carried out a series of experiments to estimate the odds of an organism being able to create a stable protein that performs some useful role and subsequently has the power to advance evolution. Axe put them at 1 in 1077, which is as good as saying it is zero. This estimate puts Darwin's hollow, mechanical theory under serious pressure and forces us to, at least, consider some other theories.

There must be more to evolution of life on earth, and indeed the entire cosmos, than just a fortuitous combination of subatomic particles, vibrating forces, random mutations and natural selection. As beautiful and intelligent as Darwin's theory of evolution is, the revolution in biological knowledge over the last half-century has opened the debate for a new understanding of the origin of species. Contenders for a new theory are up and coming. One of the more popular is the theory of intelligent design, the presence of a conscious, creative and purposeful force beneath the surface of life's immense diversity and complexity. Not an easy one to prove and the mere mention of it usually sends every pro-evolutionary biologist into a red rage. But, is it really rational to believe in a design without a designer? It is like believing that the Sistine Chapel randomly evolved out of bricks and mortar without the vision of an architect behind it. After all, Darwin had some reservations about his own theory, which he delayed publishing for twenty years, and there is no reason why natural selection should be the only possible explanation for evolution of life on our planet. To be fair to Darwin, his theory never ruled out the presence of the divine and intelligent design went to great pains to create the appearance of a slow, evolutionary process which Darwin spent most of his professional life uncovering. However, as they say, the devil is in the detail, and it is here that the theory breaks down.

The impossibly low odds for useful genetic mutations, even over millions of years, as well as the need for detailed, precise information to build brand-new, never before organisms that require exceptional accuracy to fit into and survive in their natural surroundings, screams intelligent design. Life and intelligence are in everything, they have to be because we are unified and we are infinite, so they cannot exist in one thing and not in another. It is only human arrogance and human ignorance to believe that life and intelligence can exist in us and nothing else, especially when we are all one. Life is in everything, from the largest scale in the cosmos to the microscopic life that is even more abundant than our own. Decision-making and logic are found at every level of biology. Not the kind of intelligence that most people think of as intelligence, to be sure, but intelligence is a very debatable commodity in this spectacular universe of experience. There are many different kinds of intelligence and there is not a size requirement for it in the seemingly infinite variety of life forms on our planet, some of which lie beyond the boundaries of our observation,

This is exactly the question that is posed by a kind of minute marine protozoa, called the agglutinated foraminifera. These tiny, single-celled, water organisms occupy a rigid shell often less than a millimetre in diameter. One form of this microscopic species that lives in the sediment on the bottom of bodies of water self-builds its own home by using pseudopodia (false feet) carefully to select grains of sand or other materials found in its environment. Construction of the shell does not appear to be some random process; different species are known to be very particular in the construction and composition of their homes which they build in the most regular geometrical symmetry of form. It is a truly astonishing feat for a single cell with no visible differentiation of organs, no nervous system and no brain. This curious creature is designing and building its house with the beauty and complexity of the finest architecture and it doesn't even have a brain to figure it out or coordinate its efforts.

Since its discovery, the 'intelligence' behind this tiny life has baffled those who have studied it. For something with no apparent means, i.e., a brain, to design and execute such an intricate and functional structure, where is the intelligence coming from? Is it God? There doesn't seem to be any other physical explanation for its brainpower and brilliance. If this is the case, it means that the organism has no inherent power of its own, but is being directed by an unseen force, i.e. God or simply operating according to the laws of physics. You might ask how this little creature is so relevant or even interesting. The answer is that if it is the case that this little guy is just mindlessly following a particular set of rules or coordinates in the creation of his life and home, in the name of consistency, such a principle would then have to be applied to all organisms, including us. That just like the foraminifera, we were designed by God or physics, and acting not according to our own will, but to a divine or physical law. That consciousness is operating at the most fundamental level of our being and is in total control of it all. It is clear from the foraminifera that there is something deeper than biology running the show, and what's more, the foraminifera is not the only organism that exhibits an invisible intelligence without the neurological physiology to support it. The virus, the smallest of all microbes, has no brain, but can navigate its way into the core of our biological being and incorporate itself into our genetic material to induce it to replicate its own genome. Now that's clever by any standards, but if it doesn't have a brain to think for itself then it must be following some other instruction, on a physical or divine level.

The foraminifera on its own gives a fairly convincing argument for intelligent design. This of course means that intelligent design exists not only in the formation of new and wonderful forms of life, but also in the challenges they face. That ID created the predator and the prey, the harmony and the discord, the creation as well as the destruction of life, and given the immense intelligence in the form and function of all life forms past and present, it stands to reason that same intelligence has a very intelligent reason to go with it all. Experience. Since consciousness is less about 'doing' and more about 'feeling', intelligent design itself created every form, every perspective and every journey solely for its experience. And here is the next shocker: the experience that consciousness seeks may not only be limited to biological or organic forms.

Other objects such as the sun, moon and stars may also contain consciousness and may have a little more awareness than we have formerly credited them with. Panpsychism is the belief that consciousness is a fundamental property of the physical universe and is infused into all states of matter. Where every single speck of matter contains a kind of proto-consciousness, a basic or lower level of cognisance that when added to and built upon can create more complex structures with increasing levels of awareness. It is a theory that is being tackled more and more by science, but was first introduced by British theoretical physicist Sir Roger Penrose, three decades ago. Penrose is known for linking consciousness with some of the goings-on in quantum mechanics. If consciousness is about experience and this core field of pure energy that runs through the entire universe is consciousness, then there is nothing to say that these basic components of experience and awareness could not be found in all forms of life, human, plant and animal alike, regardless of form or sophistication. I do think that more and more we are coming to realise that consciousness and experience is present in all species on earth, but given the infinite and universal nature of this field of consciousness we cannot rule out the fact that it may exist in non-biological systems such as stars and planets also.

Physicist Gregory Matloff has given this idea some serious food for thought by suggesting there is actual evidence that stars are controlling their own galactic paths by 'the emission of a unidirectional jet,' early on in their creation. Parenago's discontinuity is the observation that cooler stars, like our own sun, revolve around the centre of the Milky Way faster than hotter ones. Matloff believes that this could be an act of its own volition, consciously manipulating itself, in order to gain speed.

Some scientists attribute this activity in stars to interactions with gas clouds, but Matloff argues that if this were the case then it would cause each star to operate in a different manner according to the different chemical makeup of the clouds it comes into contact with. But this is not how it is, as all the stars act in exactly the same way. The presence of consciousness and its role in experience in all existence tells us that each life form is providing a unique point of view, a unique adventure for spirit. The experience of life is made possible through different levels of awareness and being, not just human or animal. In ancient times, when the divide between the natural and the supernatural was far less distinct than in modern thinking, it was common for people to view the sun and moon not as inanimate objects, but rather as living, interactive deities or gods. A view that has lost favour over the years, but perhaps these ancient people weren't too far off the mark. Not that I am advocating sun or moon worship, but rather the acknowledgement of the divine within everything. It is perhaps time we realised that the whole universe is conscious.

Einstein was not a fan of quantum theory because he had difficulty believing that the moon did not exist if it wasn't being observed. But perhaps there is nothing wrong with quantum theory and matter does indeed 'disappear' when focus is removed but the reason that the moon does exists even if no one is looking at it is because it is conscious and aware of its own self. It has its own consciousness and a level of awareness that ensures it is not reliant on us or any other measuring device to bring it into existence. It is our own awareness that brings us into being, we are observing ourselves in the act of living, and if this field of conscious awareness runs through everything then surely it is in the moon as well. I believe the entire universe is alive and awake and experiencing at some level. It was created a very long time ago before any human could bring it into existence by looking at it and it is the utmost arrogance to presume that it is anything we do to keep it here. The universe has its own life and is certainly not dependent on us for its participation. From the earth it is easy to map out a face in the full moon from the craters left by meteor strikes on its surface. As children we were told there was a man in the moon and that was his face. This may not be as ridiculous as it sounds. I still remember my beautiful mother saying something I still repeat today when I look at a full moon. 'I see the moon and the moon see me, God bless the moon and God bless me.'

It is an understandably difficult notion for humans to accept that the universe is not all about us and that we are not the most important, self-aware and intelligent objects in the universe. But who are we to dismiss any level of knowing and feeling that might be contained within another system or species? The only subjective experience that we can be absolutely certain about is our own. Maybe every other form is infinitely more aware of its divine identity and cosmic greatness and we are the only ones who are so grossly spiritually ignorant. From a distance star, humanity must resemble more of a giant, parasitic infestation, feeding on and sucking the life out of its host planet, rather than an intelligent form of life. If you think about it, from the distant perspective of an alien on another planet viewing life on earth through a telescope, parallels could be very easily drawn to humans viewing life under a microscope. We must look like lots of little creatures scurrying about, eating, mating, multiplying and killing each other. And just like life on a Petri dish under the microscope, some organisms are beneficial to life and some are detrimental. En masse and from afar, we would appear to be the nasty sort of organism you would want to avoid at all costs. I bet the all the other planets and their occupants in the solar system are hoping we are not as contagious as we are deadly, but it looks as though we might be, as we have already made our way to the moon and have identified mars as our next destination.

Perhaps the life that exists within a star or a planet is no less than our own; divine infinite beings having a different experience with form and awareness. It is not too hard to imagine if we get over ourselves and open our minds a little. Stars were life's first born and are our true material ancestors, making possible all life in our universe as we know it. Our galaxy continues to give birth to about seven new stars a year in 'star nurseries' that are visible by telescope and are some of the most unbelievably beautiful places in the entire universe. Stars have a very dynamic existence at birth, in growth and in death. They don't just sit idly in the sky, twinkling their life away. They travel in their own separate orbits through the Milky Way galaxy moving along at fantastic speeds, but they are so far away that it takes a long time for their motion to be visible to us. They live very busy and productive lives fusing hydrogen together in their core to make every other elements we know. They have been playing dodge ball with meteoroids and asteroids from the start and all the other planets have the scars to show for it. Small stars can live for several billion years, burning fuel at a slower rate than their larger sisters who like to live fast and die young in a glorious explosion that can outshine all of the other stars in the galaxy.

Stars are born, they live and they die. Same with all life in this realm. We may have very different gestation times and processes but we all emerge from the same fundamental elements. The sun is no different. It is estimated that the sun has about another five to seven billion years left before it runs out of fuel and goes through the process of death, taking the earth with it. It will expand to a hot red giant and vaporise the life it once nourished, us. So the human experience in this world was always going to be a temporary one, but if we don't kill ourselves off first we may have another few billion years of a story yet to experience.

As of now it seems the earth is facing another mass extinction crisis, the sixth large scale great mass extinction event of animal and plant species. Over the course of our very colourful history, humans have pillaged and polluted the world to a dangerous level of global warming, threatening to scorch, starve and suffocate the life out of the planet once more. Soon our petty squabbles about possessions and identity will mean nothing as we scramble for the last morsels of oxygen and food to survive. The fault, it appears, of this latest catastrophe in earth's history lies firmly at the feet of the debatably most intelligent life form to date. Us. With current extinction rates estimated to be up to a thousand times higher than they would be if people weren't in the picture, we are looking very guilty indeed. However, it is abundantly clear from the story of evolution that the earth is altogether capable of creating dramatic climate changes all on its own, without human help and while the surface illusion of human fault is very effective, spirit has been engineering this story from the very beginning. Just like the tiny, agglutinated foraminifera, God is working behind the scenes at every level of existence.

It must also be pointed out that because God is all-knowing, then he knows, and has always known, what was going to happen when he introduced humans to the world and he must be OK with it or else, knowing everything, he would not have created us in the first place. Free will or no free will, God in his eternal wisdom knows everything, including how it all is going to turn out. God knew the fate of his 'son' just as he knows the fate of every living thing that has every lived or will live. He saw it all before it ever happened. It was all his, ours, love's idea. It is important to understand that God is not just watching things unfold in real time like us. He is not bound by time and space like us. He is not sitting on the edge of his seat, biting his nails wondering what is going to happen next, hoping against hope that mankind will wake up and realise his stupidity before it is all too late. God/love exists beyond the limitations of blindness and ignorance in this realm. God knows the position and momentum of every atom in the universe, he put them there, so he can calculate where everything is and what everything will be doing, past, present and future. Also, unlike us, he is not flummoxed by the Heisenberg Uncertainty Principle, because he was the one who came up with it. God has a bird's-eye view of all that has gone before, all that is happening and all that is yet to come. Not, it must be stressed, all the infinite creative possibilities that might occur, because that would mean that he does not know what choices or direction we will take. How foolish of us to think that God does not know how things will turn out. God knows exactly what is going to happen because, one, the future has already happened and, two, God is all-knowing. And God is delighting in the experience of so much feeling within each of us in a story that he, we, infinite love and intelligence wrote. We are one consciousness experiencing itself in its entirety. We are gods who got bored and created their own drama to participate in, where every thought is engineered and every word is scripted.

For now, the world has become a small place for humans who appear to be on a mission of their own demise and that of every other species on the planet. The very qualities that make us human have become the reasons we are so close to extermination. Our restless inquisitiveness and creativity, as well as our many fears and insecurities, have taken their toll on our world and more and more heroic efforts are required to save ourselves and the ecosystem that sustains us. How will this chapter in the story of life on earth unfold? Will we rally just in time to save the planet and stave off a total wipe-out? Are there enough of us willing and able to undo the damage of so many for so long? Will we emerge triumphant from our self-inflicted predicament as new and enlightened beings or will we succumb to the darker side of human nature and force evolution back 100 million years with yet another mass extinction event? Is the human chapter set to close in earth's history just like the dinosaurs, triggering the dawn of another species and form that will take centre stage and hopefully do a better job than we did? Riveting stuff! Someone should write a book or make a movie about it. Oh wait, they already have, lots of them!

Our deep fascination with stories is no coincidence. Stories are everything we are and they also provide us with our education and our entertainment. The circumstances and events of our stories provide us with the emotional experience that we came here for. The very purpose of a story is to feel. When we read a story or watch a movie we want it to be as thrilling as possible. Nobody wants to watch or hear a dull, humdrum tale of nothing particularly interesting. We want the rush of adrenaline, being on the edge of our seat, feeling and identifying with the characters, be they real life or fantasy, hero or villain. We want to be moved, terrified, amused, appalled, amazed and surprised by the adventure. We have retold countless real-life stories and concocted as many more fictional. But the crucial element to the experience of any story is the suspense factor, the not knowing the outcome for our favourite character. If we know the ending it changes the experience of the story entirely. For example, if we watch a movie for the second time, we lose the intensity of emotion that is inherent in the not knowing what will happen next.

It is the same for us. It is the reason we so cleverly hid the future from ourselves. If we knew that everything would turn out well, we would not feel the anxiety or stress of a challenging situation. If we knew something dreadful was going to happen in the future, it would taint all our good experiences in the present.

Our permanent position in the now does not mean that the rest of the story is not written, only that we need to turn the next page. We occupy a reality where every atom from the beginning of time has behaved exactly as it is supposed to. Where not a single manoeuvre, atomic or energetic has been unscheduled or miscalculated. These atoms and their accompanying forces will continue to operate and evolve as per their directive well into the future, at least that is how we will perceive them. The truth is that the story is already written from start to finish but in order to experience it fully, just like any book or a movie, we will encounter it individually, word by word, moment by moment, frame by frame.

Life is a journey that is fuelled by the not knowing. It is a reality where we are following a course in which each challenge and outcome has already been figured out for everybody's best interest, irrespective of how it seems. However, if we knew this for certain then there would be no need for fear and worry. If there was no fear then we would have nothing to experience except love and joy. Without fear or insecurity there would be no frustration, anger, hate, jealousy or any other of its disguises. With nothing other than love or joy to experience, this reality would be pointless and redundant because it would be the same as where we came from. Therefore, fear and uncertainty are necessary illusions in creating our reality. If we all had no fear because we were aware of a prearranged outcome and its place in the bigger picture, then our reality as we know it would dissolve in an instant. Not knowing what lies ahead provides for all the uncertainty in life that makes it seem as though there is none and therefore something to fear.

We are living in a story of our own creation. But the story of life is not just about earth and us, it is a story of a universe. Our quantum oneness runs through all creation, in all forms, at all times, observing and feeling in different ways and at different levels. Before we arrived and long after we are gone the entire story of the universe exists as a playground for spirit. Consciousness is not confined to the human experience or even biological organisms. It has been present from the start and will it not die with us. We are just one small segment of a story that extends all around us in time and in space. There are many ways to be born into existence, there are many forms and times to be born into. There are many stories contained within each form, all contributing to the one gigantic evolutionary story. Being human is just one aspect of an experiential, deterministic reality that spirit has to choose from. The diversity of form and experience that the story of earth provides for spirit is immeasurable all of which are up for grabs at any time, past, present and future. Time is not real, there is only now and the feelings and awareness that accompany it. If we are to be the cause of the next great wipe-out, I wonder what new and exciting creatures will emerge in our wake. New forms, new intelligence and new experiences for spirit to revel in. There is at least another seven billion or so years left for earth and I expect Intelligent Design has a few more weird and wonderful forms, characters, plots and surprises up its sleeve after we humans have exited the story. We are not as special as we think we are. 'We are like butterflies who flutter for a day and think it is forever,' said Carl Sagan, astrophysicist and astrobiologist. Experience is what everything in life in this dimension is about. From the energy and dynamism of a star to the simplicity of a single cell, all the way to the physical sophistication and emotional complexities of the human experience, there is much to choose from for an imaginative and curious spirit who wants to get out of its comfort zone and live a little, or a lot.

Chapter 10: The Illusion of Everything

'This place is a dream. Only a sleeper considers it real. Then death comes like dawn, and you wake up laughing at what you thought was your grief.' – Rumi

If quantum physics has taught us anything it is that nothing in this reality is as it seems. By demonstrating the absence of definite quantities at the heart of reality it has highlighted the huge divide between what we see and what really is, which is in effect nothing, at least nothing in terms of life as we perceive it.

Our entire existence in this realm is generated by illusions of the physical, the emotional and the intellectual. It is these illusions that facilitate our life's journey and experience where we are incarcerated in a calculated perceptual reality that has no more actual substance than a dream. We are God having a dream, at times a nightmare, and we will only wake up when we die.

In the previous chapters I have detailed my hypothesis for the nature of reality. In effect, I believe that our entire existence in this realm is merely an experience, perception or illusion which is predetermined by the uncompromising laws of physics. I would now like to put forward a scientific theory to support my hypothesis, but first let us examine one of the more well-known theories and the role of observation and consciousness.

The double slit experiment demonstrates that the true nature of our reality is energy, but the act of observation or measurement turns that energy into the particles that we perceive as matter. Observation or measurement is fundamental to the nature of reality. In an attempt to reconcile the matter and no matter aspects of our reality, science has put forward a few different theories. One of the most famous ones is the many worlds theory. In an effort to locate matter in quanta, physicists use maths to map out the probability of where a particle of matter might be on the quantum spectrum. The Schrödinger equation is a lengthy, brain ache of a formula that gives us all of the probabilities of all the probable places where it could probably be. The many worlds theory postulates that all the possible outcomes of a measurement are equally real. That there are different worlds, all of them real and in each of them the particle that we are looking for is in a different position. However, the solution to the Schrödinger equation only gives us probabilities. It does not tell us that there is an actual particle there. According to the maths, a particle could be on Mars or it could be on the earth, but when we observe the particle it is only ever in one place and one place only. Ultimately, the Schrödinger equation predicts unambiguously that there will fail to be facts about anything.

The many worlds theory suggests that there are other worlds, with other near infinite versions of ourselves superimposed in the same physical space all evolving independently with different events and outcomes. It is a popular theory because it fits with our everyday assumption that the future does not yet exist and there are infinite possibilities available to choose from. The many worlds theory was first proposed by the young physicist Hugh Everett III in his 1957 doctoral thesis at Princeton. The problem with the theory was that if it is the observer and the observation that brings the particle or matter into being and we are not aware of or observing these other 'realities', how can they exist? Not only that, but if this theory is true of our future then it must also be true of our past, so when all the possibilities of our past converge to bring matter into existence by our act of observation in the present moment, we would have an infinite amount of memories about all of our experiences in our past. Not to mention the fact that, upon observation, all of these possibilities, paths and outcomes in our past ultimately brought us to the exact same position and circumstance in the present moment. In order for this theory to be viable, God or the universe or whatever would have had to erase all other memories in the past in favour of one line of events, and if that is what is going on in the past it means it also applies to the future, which brings us right back around to determinism.

Everett got around these problems by doing away with the measurement problem in wave function collapse altogether and suggesting that none of the alternative states vanishes at all, except to our perception. In other words, it is a perception problem rather than a measurement problem. In Everett's view, reality begins as a combination, or superposition, of all possible states of its constituent particles. As it evolves, some of these superpositions break down, making certain realities distinct and isolated from one another. The other realities fall away and we are left with the one we are perceiving. While Everett's theory is certainly plausible, for some reason it just doesn't provide that full, satisfied feeling or eureka moment that you would expect from a successful explanation of problem of this magnitude. Also, I don't believe we can disregard such a fundamental observational aspect of our reality just because it doesn't fit with our idea of how the universe operates. It is like saying that gravity does not apply to our experience of life, in which case, we would all be floating around like helium balloons. The many worlds theory is different from the multiverse theory. M Theory proposes multi universes rather than multiple worlds, with M standing for mystery or mother of all theories.

The measurement problem is a problem because in the double slit experiment we have not been able to define a measurement. A measurement is defined as an interaction between the system you're measuring and the measuring device. The measuring device used in the double slit experiment was equipment with the technology to detect particles on a microscopic scale. Some physicists who have investigated the concept of panpsychism, such as Eugene Wigner and Roger Penrose, have toyed with the idea that it is the consciousness of the observer that causes the collapse of the waveform and creates the impenetrable divide between life and the quantum abyss of infinite possibilities that is our true nature.

The question of where or what consciousness originates from is a difficult one for obvious reasons. Does it, one, arise out of matter, that is, neurological activity in the brain? Or is it, two, separate entirely from the body as a soul or spirit? Or is it, three, everywhere, in everything, living and non-living? It is easy to rationalise that humans contain consciousness and could therefore be causing the collapse of their own wave function to bring ourselves into existence. But what about everything else in reality? Does a snail, for example, have enough consciousness to keep it in existence, and what about a rock?

What keeps a rock in existence? Surely a rock cannot be conscious. Let's take a look. Everything in existence is composed of the same fundamental particles that we can perceive in our reality and the invisible forces that hold them together. These particles are simply arranged in different states and configurations to make up all the different features of our reality. Everything in the universe is made of the exact same stuff, visible and invisible. Nothing is truly separate, so if consciousness exists in us humans then it must exist everywhere and in everything, just at different levels of awareness. This is the important difference to consider when talking about consciousness and awareness and it is the crucial point of existence. Consciousness is not intellect or thought, nor is it feeling or sensation. Thought and feeling is what being conscious in this life is all about, but it is not what consciousness is. Feelings and thought are generated through our awareness. For example, an inanimate object such as a rock, which consists of all the same particles and forces as humans and everything else in the universe, could well contain consciousness but have minimal awareness of itself or its surroundings. It is not thinking about itself or feeling anything, emotional or physical, sort of like consciousness in a coma.

Our fundamental oneness of being indicates that consciousness is most likely omnipresent, in all matter and energy through all of space and all of time. In the equation of life, consciousness is the constant and awareness is the variable. Awareness can be focused on a particular coordinate in the block universe correlating to the experience and it can vary according to the physical specifications of its viewing platform, i.e. its form, but consciousness remains constant throughout form or location holding everything in place from beginning to end. So yes, the snail and the rock have the exact same consciousness running through them as us humans; we are just more aware of ourselves and our surroundings and feeling things a little differently than they are. Just because the rock is not seeing or feeling does not mean it does not contain the consciousness to hold itself in existence.

Max Planck, the theoretical physicist who originated quantum theory, which won him the Nobel Prize in Physics, knew this back in 1918 when he said, 'I regard consciousness as fundamental. I regard matter as derivative from consciousness. We cannot get behind consciousness. Everything that we talk about, everything that we regard as existing, postulates consciousness.'

All this of course indicates that every single instance of time that makes up our lives still exists in consciousness, but we are only aware of the present moment we occupy.

There are a few different theories circulating about quantum theory that attempt finally to find that elusive Unified Theory of Everything. Some crazier than others. Of late, this area of interest has been somewhat set aside by science, except for a handful of great physicists who continue unabated to ask questions and provide theories and keep the candle burning on this important issue. All scientific evidence so far indicates that we are one on at fundamental energetic level, so it stands to reason that there is a unified theory that makes sense of everything, even the perplexing riddle of the double slit experiment. At this stage, it really is something that should be available to us, as, while we might not understand everything about this reality, we have uncovered all the particles of the Standard Model of how the universe operates and the nature of the fundamental forces that mediate them. In other words, we have all the pieces of the puzzle, we just need to put them in their right places.

In my theory of everything, I will be hoping to find the following:

1. An explanation of how all of the illusions of life are generated.
2. The metaphorical light and dark aspects of our reality and how the duality of life can arise out of one.
3. That essential element that separates us from the quantum world of everything and nothing that might possibly account for the mysteries of the double slit experiment.

Let's have a go. First, let's strip everything back to the different aspects of our existence and put the individual pieces into their appropriate box. I am a bit of a neat freak. Generally, I don't care if there is a bit of dust around my house, but I do like to have things in their place. So we are going to tidy up the basic components of this perplexing reality into boxes and start from there. If mathematics is the language of the universe, it gives us some very interesting numbers.

In the first box we will put the Higgs field. Nobel prize-winning scientist Professor Peter Higgs was one of six physicists, who in 1964 proposed the mechanism that suggested the existence of a theoretical field that permeates space, giving mass to all elementary subatomic particles that interact with it. It took thirty years and cost €4.6 million to build the Large Hadron Collider in Switzerland that, in 2012 began smashing protons together at high speed, which sent bits of shrapnel flying off in different directions. In images that looked like a bunch of strings tied at the centre, they showed the paths that could represent the actual quantum thread unit and seemed to confirm the presence of the Higgs field, a field of energy that holds us all together and gives us mass. A veritable framework or scaffolding without which all that we are and all that is around us would disperse like dust in the breeze. All of our atoms, particles and sub particles are suspended in a Higgs network that we cannot see. The quantum particle associated with the Higgs field is called the Higgs boson, often referred to as the God particle. This Higgs field seems to have a single universal function, so we will put that in the first box on its own.

Into the second box we will put the three fundamental forces that can be identified on a quantum level. The electromagnetic, the strong nuclear force and the weak nuclear force. Gravity doesn't belong here because it cannot be found at this level, but don't worry, we will find a box for it in a moment. Again, just like the Higgs field, these three forces have associated quantum particles that mediate them and collectively they are called gauge bosons. The electromagnetic force is mediated by the particle that carries light, the photon. The strong nuclear force is mediated by the gluon particle, which is the glue that holds the tiniest particles of matter together. The weak nuclear force is mediated by three particles called Z, W+ and W-.

Into the third box we will put all the elementary particles of our perceivable world of matter in the atomic nucleus. Atoms are not elementary particles in themselves but contain smaller particles in the nucleus, called protons and neutrons, which in turn contain even smaller particles called quarks. There are six of these that are identified with the least scientific names you could possibly think of, they are called up, charm, top, down, strange and bottom. Each of these particles has its own antimatter counterpart with an opposite charge, making a total of twelve quarks. These particles of matter are held together by the, already boxed, strong force and its gluons.

In the fourth box we will put the remaining fundamental particles of energy that surround the atom, the leptons. As with the quarks, there are six of these, just with better names. They are the electron and its neutrino, the muon and its neutrino, and the tau and its neutrino. And again, as with the quarks, each of these particles has its own antimatter counterpart with an opposite charge, making a total of twelve leptons. These leptons are held together by the, already boxed, weak nuclear force and its W and Z particles.

In the fifth box we will put all of the illusions or experiences that life in this dimension affords us:

1. The three physical illusions associated with our physical reality: gravity, motion and space.
2. Time, thought (ideas and opinions, etc) and emotion (joy, despair, etc).
3. The five sensations of taste, smell, sight, touch and hearing.

All of these sensations provide us with the individual and subjective experiences of living. There are eleven in total.

In the sixth and final box we will put the six dimensions of possibility as outlined by string theory. They are:

1. The first is a whole other world, slightly different from our own that would allow us see all the similarities and differences between our world and this new one. It would exist in the same position as our own and have the same beginning, i.e. the Big Bang.
2. The next dimension is an entire plane of new worlds that would contain all the other possible futures, presents and pasts, and again have the same beginning as our own universe.
3. Going deeper, the next dimension contains the possibility of other universes with different laws of nature and gravity and light. These other universes would also have a different beginning from ours.

4. Getting even deeper, this dimension is a plane of all the possible pasts and futures for each of the new universes. These stretch to infinity.
5. In this next dimension, all the universal laws of physics and the conditions of each individual universe exist.
6. At its deepest level, in this dimension anything is possible. There are all futures, all pasts, all beginnings and all ends, anything you can imagine in an infinite expanse of everything. Everything comes together.

So we have six separate boxes:

Box 1: One Higgs field.
Box 2: Three fundamental forces.
Box 3: Six elementary particles of perceivable matter, plus six antimatter. Total twelve.
Box 4: Six elementary particles of energy, plus six antimatter. Total twelve.
Box 5: Eleven illusions.
Box 6: Six possibilities.

Now that we have everything packed away neatly into six separate boxes we can start to put things together and have some fun with numbers. Don't worry, it is just some simple maths, nothing more complicated than splitting the bill at a restaurant. And before anyone hops on their maths and physics high horse, I would like to point out that I am not declaring any scientific fact, just making some observations and drawing some parallels with my Theory of Everything. After all, isn't that what theories are all about? And if everyone else can do it, then so can I.

At first glance there seems to be some obvious multiples of three going on. That is, except for our eleven illusions, which would fit in nicely with all the other numbers if it there were twelve aspects to it. There seems to be something missing. Perhaps we can find it. Let's examine things a bit closer. Our reality can be separated into three parts:

1. Matter with twelve quarks.
2. Energy with twelve leptons.

2. Energy with twelve leptons.
3. Light, electromagnetic spectrum or one photon.

We are going to take a closer look at light. Visible light or colour is just one portion of the electromagnetic spectrum, which has other frequencies and wavelengths. The messenger particle for light is the photon. In fact, the photon is the messenger particle for the entire electromagnetic spectrum. The electromagnetic force is responsible for keeping a magnet stuck to the refrigerator and also keeps electrons bound in orbitals around the nucleus of the atom, keeping matter together. So the particle that allows our eyes to see the world is the same particle that holds it all in place. This is a very important fact about the nature of our reality and you will need to keep it in mind. We are going to refer to the whole electromagnetic spectrum as light, as all of it is mediated by the photon.

As we can see can from our boxes, matter has twelve quarks and energy has twelve leptons. Light only has one aspect to it, the electromagnetic spectrum. In the name of consistency, we would expect that light should have twelve components to it, too. Maybe it does. Let's dig a bit deeper and see if we can find the missing pieces of the puzzle. The photon is the quantum particle of the electromagnetic field that 'carries' its force and can be thought of as both particle and wave. A photon does not experience the electromagnetic force itself, but it is thought that the effects of electromagnetism are produced by the energy and momentum it carries. So it appears as though it is the activity of the photon that creates the electromagnetic force. If we examine the electromagnetic spectrum we find that it can be divided into eleven different wavelengths and frequencies. They are as follows:

1. Long-wave radio
2. Short-wave radio
3. Microwave
4. Far infrared
5. Thermal infrared
6. Near infrared

7. Visible (Colour)
8. Ultraviolet
9. Vacuum UV (EUV)
10. X-rays
11. g-rays

So, our light puzzle consists of one unified electromagnetic field arranged into eleven segments. Hold that thought. Next let us take a look in the box of quarks. Quarks, you will remember, are the most fundamental particles of perceivable matter contained in the nucleus of the atom. There are six quarks and six antiquarks. These particles are the basic components of a three-dimensional reality, height width and depth. Within these three dimensions, we experience the illusions of gravity, motion and space. As it happens, quarks also carry on them three 'colours' (not in the literal meaning of colour, but charge). These three colours or charges are called ±red, ±green and ±blue. The quarks are held together by the strong nuclear force that is mediated by the gluon. The gluon also carries colour charges, eight of them, eight out of nine possible combinations of colour and anti-colour. Since there are actually nine possible colour-anti-colour combinations, we might expect nine different gluon charges, but the mathematics works out such that there are only eight combinations with no intuitive explanation for this result.

Region	Wavelength range (approx.)	Frequency range (approx.)
Long-wave radio	>10m	<3×10^7 hz
Short-wave radio	10cm - 10m	3×10^7 - 3×10^9
Microwave	1mm - 10cm	3×10^9 - 3×10^{11}
Far infrared	30mm - 1mm	3×10^{11} - 3×10^{13}
Thermal infrared	3mm - 30mm	10^{13} - 10^{14}
Near infrared	700nm - 3mm	10^{14} - 4×10^{14}
Visible	400nm - 700mm (1.7 - 3eV)	4×10^{14} - 7×10^{14}
Ultraviolet	200nm - 400mm (3 - 6eV)	7×10^{14} - 1.5×10^{15}
Vacuum UV (EUV)	10nm - 200mm (6 - 120eV)	1.5×10^{15} - 3×10^{16}
X-rays	120eV - 100keV	3×10^{16} - 3×10^{19}
g-rays	100keV	3×10^{19}

Accordingly, as it happens, there are eight remaining illusions: time, thought, emotion, sight, touch, hearing, taste, smell. Could our eight colours on the gluon and three colours on the quarks have something to do with our eleven illusions? It is my theory that they do and I will explain why.

The interesting thing about these colour charges is that they are analogous to the electromagnetic charge, except they come in different types rather than one, which results in a different type of force, with different rules of behaviour. Light, as we perceive it, travels in a straight line through space at a speed of 3×10^8 m/s but is refracted or bent as it passes through one substance or another, affecting its speed. This is easily visible if you observe a spoon in a glass of water, it appears distorted, like an optical illusion. It is my theory that, in the same way as visible light is altered as it travels through a glass of water, the entire electromagnetic spectrum is transformed through its interplay with the colour charges that are associated with the quarks and gluons. The eleven colour charges distort the light by interacting with the different wavelengths and frequencies to alter its behaviour and characteristics and in doing so creates all of the illusions of our reality.

The eleven colour charges that exist actually have more in common with the electromagnetic spectrum than with the quarks and gluons on which they appear to sit. For this reason, I am going to deduce that they are indeed components of the electromagnetic spectrum and therefore make up the missing pieces to our light puzzle. Light now has its full complement of twelve parts; one electromagnetic spectrum and the eleven colour charges that facilitate the distortion of light. So now we can see that all three aspects of our reality have twelve components to them. Matter has six quarks and six antiquarks. Energy has six leptons and six antileptons. Light has one electromagnetic spectrum and eleven colour charges.

Now recall that the photon is the particle that allows our eyes to see the world and is the same particle that appears holds it all in place. Here is my point. Everything is in the electromagnetic spectrum. Matter and everything else that we perceive in our world are nothing more than illusions created within the light spectrum. Everything is an experience created by light's distortion facilitated by the colour charges that only appear to be a part of the quarks and gluons, but in actual fact it is the colour charges that create the illusion of matter and indeed every other experience of our reality. Our hard and fast material world is nothing more than a trick of the light.

It is hardly a coincidence that there are eleven different colour charges identified with the quarks and gluons, eleven frequency bands on the electromagnetic spectrum and eleven illusions that accommodate our reality. Everything we experience in life, its visual and sensory illusions, is generated by light's different guises as it is modified or transmuted by its colour charges that effectively generate all the illusions of life, material, emotional and intellectual.

When we consider how thought and information is processed in the brain electrically, things make more sense. Electricity is everywhere in the human body. Our cells are specialised to conduct electrical currents. Electricity is required for the nervous system to send signals throughout the body and to the brain, making it possible for us to move, think and feel. All brain and nervous system activity relies on electricity. We are electromagnetic beings. Everything is happening within the electromagnetic spectrum. The colour charges are manipulating the electromagnetic spectrum creating the perception of everything, physical and non-physical. If we examine basic atomic structure we see that the electrons surround the atom emitting waves of light in circles. Here is the bombshell. The electromagnetic spectrum does not just hold everything together, it is also creating the atom, or at least the creating the illusion of the atom. The illusion of all reality, all form and all feeling, exists within the electromagnetic spectrum and its eleven colour charges. There is no actual matter, there is no actual space, there is no actual motion, etc., we are just interpreting the light as form and sensation with these colour charges.

Think about it: the only thing you are seeing with your eyes is colour, the innumerable different shades within the seven bands of colour on the visible portion of the electromagnetic spectrum. In every instance of time, it is just like looking at a 2D painting in front of you. The other bands on the spectrum are where the physical, emotional and intellectual experiences are created that bring the colours to life. The sensations of time, space, motion and gravity, as well as the five senses and emotion and intellect, convert a 2D colour image in front of our eyes into a 3D material experience. Life is a collection of experiences. We sense motion; it is not real. We sense space, it is not real. We sense gravity; it is not real. We sense touch, taste, smell, sight and sound, we feel emotion and experience thought. Everything is a sensation, not a reality, and if the sense of sight is situated within the electromagnetic spectrum then it stands to reason that all the other sensations must be there also. Every experience and every thought you ever had is manufactured by alterations to the wavelength and frequency of light at different points on the electromagnetic spectrum. Yes, matter is an illusion, all we are perceiving with our eyes are the different colours of the rainbow that have been tweezed out of a band of white light with electrical charges which affect its speed to facilitate all of the sensations of living. All the other sensations that accommodate our reality are manipulated on the other bands of the spectrum with these same colour charges. Everything really is just energy, and lights illusion. There is no actual 3D atom, there is no exterior, material world, there is only the illusion of a material world, which is generated by lights trickery within the electromagnetic spectrum and its eleven colour charges.

    Light creates the illusion of matter where all of this make-believe material and its pretend atoms abide by the undercurrent of the strict laws of physics creating all of the illusions of our life's story written in numbers. All form and feeling is generated as light energy is transformed into a different force with different rules of behaviour, but remains the light. All existence as we know it belongs in the illusions of light. Everything we see and feel in this life is created by the light. This means that the different forms, colours and textures of our outer being are all made possible by the distortion of light energy by the colour charges on the electromagnetic spectrum resulting in the subsequent corresponding illusions. In essence, the chair that you are sitting on is no more solid than the thought in your head or the feeling in your heart.

The term 'colour charge' was coined simply because of the loose analogy to the primary colours. Theoretical physicist Richard Feynman referred to his colleagues as 'idiot physicists' for choosing the labels, as they had nothing to do with colour. I happen to think it may have been a fortunate folly if these colours are indeed the illusions or 'colours' of our reality. These eleven illusions are what provide all the joy and all the agony of life, physically and emotionally. They provide the perspective of form and space, the sensation of movement and position, the delights and the horrors of the senses, and the spiritual dilemmas of right and wrong. Firmly embedded, in this cold, hard mathematical object of our reality, reside the eleven illusions that bring it to life and make it pop. It is these illusions that afford us the journey and experience of life in an otherwise calculated, sterile and stationary construct of a numerical existence in the block universe. Within the mathematical formula of reality, it is a trick of the light that tells us that we are not divine, that we are people and not animals or plants, a trick of the light that tells us that we are different from or better or worse than each other. A trick of the light that gives us physical feelings as well as emotional rights and wrongs, and then tells us that we are moving, doing and ageing. Everything is in the light and its illusions and it is absolute genius.

There are some other properties to light that cannot be ignored here. In the reference frame of light, there is no space and time. In the Theory of Relativity, Einstein established that the closer you get to the speed of light, the less time you experience and the shorter your distance becomes. For photons of light, which exist at the speed of light, time stops and space shrinks to nothing, so the photon itself has no space or time. Also, the photon has no mass. If a particle has no mass and is at rest, then the total energy is zero. But an object with zero energy and zero mass is nothing at all. Therefore, if an object with no mass is to exist physically, it can never be at rest. Such is the case with light. But if there is no space or time for the photon then it has nowhere to go because it is everywhere so it cannot be moving. If everything is light and light is everywhere then it is possible that it is awareness that is moving through the light and not the other way around, where the speed of light is the outer limit of our perception of motion and indeed all reality as we know it.

Scientists claim that because of the finite speed of light, 299,792km/s, if an alien sixty-five million light years away were to view earth through a powerful telescope, it would see dinosaurs still roaming the earth. If this so, then the age of the dinosaurs is not gone but still exists within the light. And because we cannot separate the past from the present and the future, then everything else must exist in the light. Moreover, if time and motion are an experience, not a reality, then light is not travelling anywhere, instead it is our awareness that has shifted from then to now.

The rearrangement of Einstein's equation $E = mc^2$ tells us that $m = E/c^2$, or mass is created by the division of energy and light. For me, this equation raises three simple issues.

1. That 'solid' matter is created out of two forces that contain nothing solid.
2. The speed of light is crucial to the formation of our material experience.
3. Something must be causing the divide between energy and light to create matter.

The answer, I believe, lies in the colour charges. Awareness is the colour charges that are altering the light at different points on the electromagnetic spectrum. We are the colour charges, travelling at breakneck speed within the light, navigating a well- defined path and creating all the illusionary sensations along the way. We are the awareness that is travelling a 360°, pre-programmed route within the light. We are the electricity of life; we are the colour charges experiencing the light and all of its illusions. Without awareness or colour charges there is nothing to see or feel in the light, it is just the wavelengths and frequencies of the electromagnetic spectrum. The true nature of light is energy, the illusions of light only exist when there is someone or something to be deceived. This is where the act of observation is fundamental to reality. Matter, motion and everything else are the illusions or experiences of life that are created by us, awareness, we are the eleven colour charges within the electromagnetic spectrum. We, the colour charges, are creating the great divide between the quantum world and what we perceive as our reality.

The colour charges exist in a 3 and 8 combo, three on the quarks and eight on the gluons. I believe that the three charges on the quarks provide the basic proto-consciousness that is omnipresent. The remaining eight colour charges facilitate the increased awareness for spirit by creating a very sophisticated nervous system to act as a conduit for the electricity of life. In this way we can be aware of, sense and experience so much more.

Then there is string theory. Without going into its mind-bending details, suffice to say that there are five different interpretations which seemed to be consolidated in the eleven dimensional multiverse M theory, which Stephen Hawking thought was our best bet for a Theory of Everything. Especially, since the oscillation of one the strings could be mathematically interpreted as a graviton, a quantum mechanical particle that carries gravitational force. Could our eleven illusions or the eleven colour charges on our quarks and gluons have something to do with the eleven strings of M theory? I believe so. Currently, science identifies the eleven discernible strings of string theory a little differently. They are defined as time, height, width, depth and the six possibilities of existence, with gravity in there somewhere. While I believe time and gravity do belong in this interpretation, I also believe science is making a mistake in its labelling of the other strings. I believe what science has mathematically identified as the eleven strings of M theory are the eleven illusions of life and living in this reality, especially since the particle corresponding to gravity has been located in the oscillation of one of the strings. If gravity is one of the illusions of our reality and it has been located on one of the strings, then it is highly likely that the other strings are the remaining illusions that bring our block theory of existence to life.

Science is also a little unsure on whether the multiverse theory has ten dimensions or eleven, but it cannot have more than eleven dimensions because of self-consistency, where it becomes unstable and collapses back down to ten or eleven. One of the aspects found on the M-theory interpretation corresponds to the idea that M-theory should be viewed as an eleven-dimensional theory that looks ten-dimensional at some points in its space of parameters.

Let's go back to our eleven illusions. All life is experiencing much the same sensations irrespective of the form it takes. However, it may be that there is one or other of life's illusions that is absent in some forms. For instance, the ethical conundrums imposed on human thinking appear to be unique to us. They are not present in the natural world where there are no such dilemmas of right and wrong. I imagine that other life forms are not continually struggling with a voice in their head that insists on analysing every aspect of their existence. The intellectual dimension of the human experience is possibly not consistent throughout all forms of life, biological or non- biological. Perhaps this is the reason M theory wavers between ten and eleven strings.

Proponents of string theory believe that the ten or eleven strings or dimensions are united as a unified field or superstring and it is from this superstring that all creation emerges. This superstring undergoes a metamorphosis or internal transformation (several of them) in the process of creating creation, where the structure of the superstring gives rise to the universe. I believe science is making a mistake here. Nothing wrong with the modifications or calculations, but what is there to create? If the block universe theory is correct then everything already exists. Everything that has happened, is happening and will happen stands independently and objectively and there is no creating to be done. Nothing can be removed or added to the block, (the block being the architecture of existence, numbers, laws of physics). So the eleven strings of the superstring are not the source of creation but instead, I believe, are all of the feelings and illusions that make an objective reality, subjective. The elements of sensation that elevate an otherwise dispassionate, unbiased existence to a personal and individual experience. Another peculiarity of the superstring is that in the final stage of transformation the string has a 192-fold vibrational structure; 192 tones or sounds is the field reverberating within itself, where the sum of the root digits is 12, (1 + 9 + 2 = 12). Coincidence? Probably not.

To sum up so far, there are three aspects of our illusionary existence, matter, energy and light, each having twelve components.

1. Matter has twelve quarks.
2. Energy has twelve leptons.

3. Light has twelve elements to it (one electromagnetic spectrum plus eleven colour charges).

Actually, it is a three for the price of one deal, as everything is created by and held within the light.

Now let us examine our two nuclear forces of strong and weak that dwell within the light. While these two forces, as well as the electromagnetic spectrum itself, can be identified separately, it is possible that all three are simply different manifestations of the same force. This is because their differences are more to do with their range than their strength. At short distances the strong force is weak and at long distances it is strong, and the weak interaction of the weak force has intrinsically the same strength as the electromagnetic force. All things considered, we could deduce that it is one unified force behaving in three different ways.

Then there are our numbers. Deeply hidden within all the material and energetic illusions created by light, at the most fundamental level, numbers are the architecture of existence, the block universe. They are the infallibly accurate and objective language of our story that exists forever in consciousness. Yes, they are the intelligent and unwavering laws of physics. We know that the number is the most fundamental element of existence. The totally impersonal and dispassionate mathematics of the universe that is the language of its evolution or the word equivalent of a story. Just like the words in a story book, the maths on its own has no life or feeling, it only comes to life when we read it, interpret it and experience the story as it unfolds. The words of a story in themselves do not contain all the colours and shapes and movements and feelings that they describe; that is for the individual readers to conjure up in their own mind and everyone will interpret it in their own way.

So who is reading our book? In essence, our reality consists of numbers at the infinite core of existence, which are in turn surrounded by all of the illusions of the light spectrum. All of the numbers and all of their illusions are all wrapped up in one single, unifying and participatory force that infuses all aspects of our reality, the Higgs field, which appears to be present throughout and holding it all together. Could this be the fundamental consciousness from which all awareness arises, the movie screen onto which all our visual images are projected, or the canvas on which God painted the universe and all its forms? Could this be who is enjoying all of our stories across space and time, form and feeling? I expect it is. I also expect that it is only a matter of time before science identifies a common correspondence between all four forces, the strong nuclear, weak nuclear, electromagnetic and Higgs to prove that it is one observational and experiential entity that lies beneath all of the surface illusions. In other words and most importantly, the innumerable and variety of robes we wear as different species are nothing more than an assortment of different colours that disguise our fundamental singularity. What differentiates a human from an animal and from a plant is an illusion of colour and experience.

In keeping with our numbers pattern of twelve and its multiples, in October 2003, a team including French cosmologists, Jean-Pierre Luminet of the Observatoire de Paris and Jeffrey Weeks, a freelance mathematician and recipient of a MacArthur Fellowship or 'genius award,' used data collected by NASA on cosmic background radiation to develop a model for the shape of the universe. The study analysed a variety of different models for the universe, including finite versus infinite, flat, saddle-shaped, spherical and cylindrical. The study revealed that the maths adds up to the universe being finite and shaped like a dodecahedron, a twelve-faced polyhedron with thirty edges and twenty vertices. As it turns out, Plato and a few of his Greek philosopher buddies had hypothesised over this more than 2000 years ago. While it is as yet an unproven theory, it is a promising one, and if the maths makes sense that is usually a very good sign.

So far it is quite obvious that the number twelve is of great significance to our reality. The number twelve governs matter, light and energy and possibly the dodecahedron shape of the universe. Twelve is a superior highly composite number, the smallest number with exactly six divisors, its divisors being 1, 2, 3, 4, 6 and 12, all of which play a crucial role in our reality, which we will examine shortly. And there is yet another number twelve to consider. The most fundamental element of our existence is not the atom but the number. Deeper than the atom or the quark or the leptons, our entire universe can be reduced to a mathematical object. The Ramanujan Summation is a calculation named after a famous Indian mathematician named Srinivasa Ramanujan and states that if you add all the natural numbers, that is 1, 2, 3, 4, and so on, all the way to infinity, you will find that it is equal to -1/12.

$$\zeta(-1) = 1 + 2 + 3 + 4 + \ldots\ldots = \frac{-1}{12}$$

Sounds ridiculous, I know, that the sum of the all the numbers all the way to infinity should amount to a fraction, and a minus one at that. As mathematical problems go, it is not a difficult one to work out; it is actually quite fun. But while it has some mathematicians banging their fists with the illegitimacy of it all, the fact remains that no real mathematical rules were broken in its calculations and minus a twelfth is not such a crazy value when you are talking about physics. As counterintuitive as it seems, it is a value that has proved its worth in the calculations of physical observables, such as the Casimir energy and bosonic string theory. It is also interesting that when -1/12 is expressed as a decimal it is 0.083.

In case you haven't noticed the recurring pattern of the numbers three and eight by now, I will lay it out for you.

1. The weak and strong nuclear forces have three and eight gauge bosons respectively. (W+, W-, Z and 8 gluons.)
2. The colour charges have three on the quarks and eight on the gluons.
3. The speed of light travels at 3×10^8 m/s.
4. The fraction 1/12 when expressed as a decimal is 0.083.

I think it is appropriate that the sum of the all of the numbers to infinity should come to a minus fraction, -1/12. This numerical value represents a fraction of a material reality that is not really there and where the other eleven pieces of the whole are to be found in our eleven illusions generated by light's elaborate ruse.

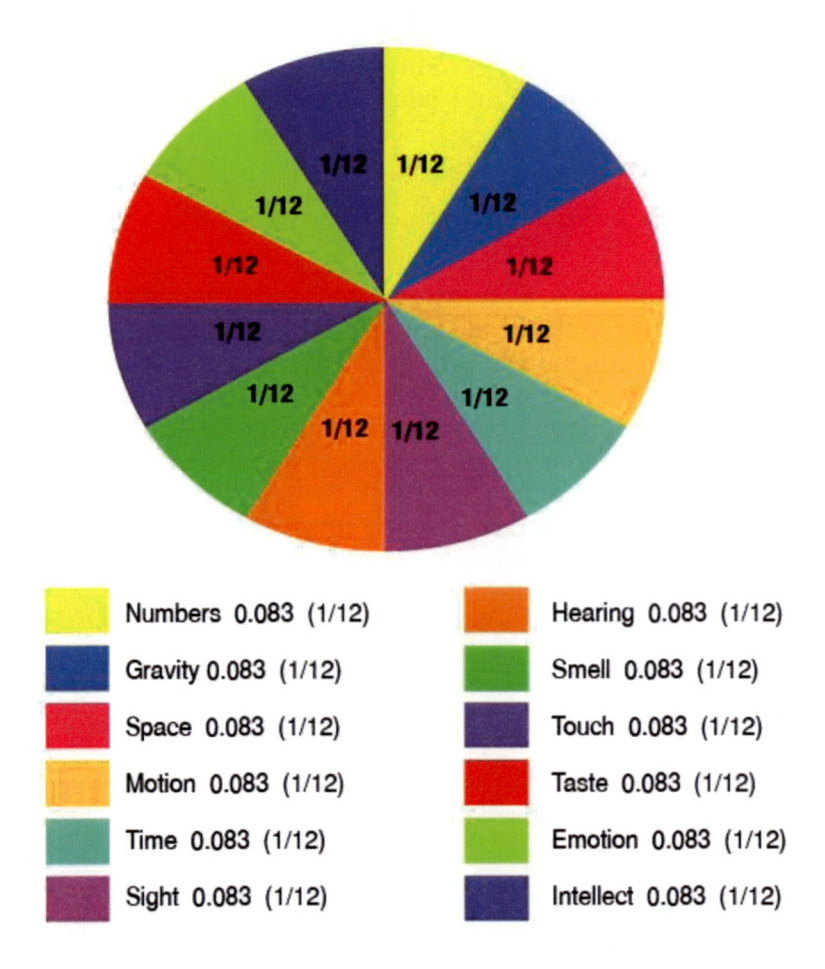

■	Numbers 0.083 (1/12)	■	Hearing 0.083 (1/12)
■	Gravity 0.083 (1/12)	■	Smell 0.083 (1/12)
■	Space 0.083 (1/12)	■	Touch 0.083 (1/12)
■	Motion 0.083 (1/12)	■	Taste 0.083 (1/12)
■	Time 0.083 (1/12)	■	Emotion 0.083 (1/12)
■	Sight 0.083 (1/12)	■	Intellect 0.083 (1/12)

So now that we have a theory about how the illusions of life are engineered, let us now see if we can find the metaphorical light and dark aspects of our existence. For this, we are going to look in the box of energy with its twelve leptons and the box with our three fundamental forces. Leptons are mediated by the three particles of the weak force, W+, W- and Z, this force interacts with all of the quarks and all of the leptons to facilitate the energy of life. The W bosons interacts through the electromagnetic force as they carry charge. The Z bosons interact with themselves as they carry mass.

The photons however, cannot interact through this force as they do not have mass, neither do they have charge or colour charge. So the photon cannot mix with the gluon either. The photon is the carrier particle of light, it is essential for existence, yet it is not mixing or exchanging with anything. Doesn't that seem a bit odd to you? I believe this is because it is the colour charges that are interacting and playing with the light to create all of the other elements of our reality. These elements are the 'darkness' or the experiences of life. They are only possible because of the colour charges, which is awareness, which is us.

This is the divide of light and dark. The light does not mix with the darkness or illusions of our reality yet darkness is not possible unless there is light. We are creating it. The divide of light and dark is both a physical phenomenon and metaphorical explanation. Darkness is the confined, deterministic, imaginary, illusionary, pretend, material world that we occupy in this realm that is made possible because of the light and the colour charges that interfere with it.

Now that we have the science of reality all figured out, we will next go in search of a little mysticism and a little magic. We will examine a few spiritual insights that correspond to our scientific explanation and while I understand that science and spirit have not been on the best of terms for a long time, I will make no apologies for some of the profound parallels that can be observed between the two disciplines.

In the Bible, we can find some solid comparisons between our light Theory of Everything and Genesis' depiction of the nature of existence in its explanation of creation.

'In the beginning God created the heavens and the earth. The earth was without form, and void; and darkness was on the face of the deep. And the Spirit of God was hovering over the face of the waters.' (Genesis 1: 1–2).

This is where the story exists in numbers, it is lifeless and 'without form'. God can look over it and read it, but cannot live in it and experience it.

On day one, the illusion begins: 'Then God said, "Let there be light" and there was light. And God saw the light, that it was good; and God divided the light from the darkness.' (Genesis 1: 3).

Here, the light that Bible is referring to is *not* the sun. According to Genesis, the sun is a separate creation that does not come about until the *fourth* day of creation week. This is a biblical detail about the creation of the universe that has confused all good Christians and theologians alike for the longest time. What is this light if it is not the sun? This light, I believe, is the electromagnetic spectrum and its corresponding illusions of matter, form and experience that bring the whole story of the universe to life. The sun that we bathe in each day is made up of the illusionary matter that is manufactured by the electromagnetic spectrum and is therefore actually part of the metaphorical darkness that God is referring to. With the creation of light came the formation of this illusionary matter as God 'divided the light from the darkness'. Time is another one of the illusions that began with the creation of 'light' as it is listed as occurring on day one. Time does not exist in the beginning when everything was 'without form' and in 'darkness'. Time only starts with the creation of light/illusion. 'And God called the light Day, and the darkness he called Night. And the evening and the morning were the first day.'

On day two, God created the firmament and the atmosphere: 'Then God said, "Let there be a firmament in the midst of the waters, and let it divide the waters from the waters." Thus God made the firmament, and divided the waters which were under the firmament from the waters which were above the firmament; and it was so. And God called the firmament Heaven.' (Genesis 1: 6-8.)

There is much scientific debate on whether or not the universe is finite or not. The dodecahedron theory suggests that as vast and as limitless as it appears to us, it quite likely may be that it is encapsulated somewhere beyond our human perceptions and capabilities to reach its illusionary outer limits. In the Bible, the firmament is described by God as that which separates our reality from that of the divine. Possibly, where the numerical story and its corresponding illusions were contained and separated from its infinite nature and source. In biblical cosmology, the firmament is interpreted as a vast solid dome, created by God on the second day to divide the primal sea (called tehom) into upper and lower portions. This dome-shaped firmament was believed to be located in the sky. Bear in mind that this was a time when the general consensus was that the world was flat and a dome shape would be the obvious assumption. Now that we know the earth is spherical in its illusionary shape, it might be time to rethink the shape of the firmament. A twelve-faced dodecahedron springs to mind.

On day two also, we are told that atmosphere began to form as the illusionary atoms of hydrogen and helium begin colliding and fusing together. The rest, as they say, is history. And as you can see from the progress of creation thereafter, it is not far off science's explanation of the Big Bang and follow on events.

Day three: Dry ground and plants.
Day four: Sun, moon and stars.
Day five: Birds and sea animals.
Day six: Land animals and humans.
Day seven: The Sabbath day of rest.

Relating to good and bad, enlightenment and ignorance, the light and dark aspects of existence have been metaphored to death by various religious teachings, not just Christianity. A pervasive theme of light can be found in the Kabbalah, Dead Sea Scrolls and the Mandaean texts. Jesus himself was certainly not shy about using the language of light symbolism. However, Jesus often refers to himself literally as 'the light', both in the New Testament and the Gnostic gospels.

In the Gospel of Thomas, Jesus says, 'I am the Light that is over all things. I am all: from Me all came forth, and to Me all attained. Split a piece of wood; I am there. Lift up the stone, and you will find Me there.'

Also in the Gospel of Thomas, Jesus says, 'If they ask you, "Where have you come from?" say to them, "We have come from the Light, from the place where the Light came into being by itself, established [itself], and appeared in their image." If they say to you, "Is it you?", say, "We are its children, and we are the chosen of the Living Father."'

So Jesus is saying that he is the light, but so are we all and so is everything else, even a piece of wood. That is because everything in our perceivable lives is made from the illusions of light. Every colour, shape, sensation, emotion and thought that ever existed has been created within the light. Our entire reality, good or bad, is the darkness or illusions created by the light.

In the Gnostic gospels, Acts of John, Jesus acknowledges the light and dark aspects of existence in a beautiful hymn he sang in secret to his apostles the night before he ascended the mount. Entitled the Hymn of the Lord, some lines include:

> I would be saved, and I would save. Amen.
> I would be loosed, and I would loose. Amen.
> I would be wounded, and I would wound. Amen.
> I would be born, and I would bear. Amen.
> I would eat, and I would be eaten. Amen.
> I would hear, and I would be heard. Amen.
> I would be thought, being wholly thought. Amen.
> I would be washed, and I would wash. Amen.
> Grace danceth. I would pipe; dance ye all. Amen.

Jesus understood quite well the perceived dualistic yet unified nature of life and did not have the same issues with the good and the bad that we have encumbered ourselves with. Jesus, whether he is referring to himself or God, admits that he is who 'would be wounded,' and he is who 'would wound'. Jesus also indicates that he or God is the one playing the tune that we all dance to, clearly meaning he is the one in control of all this perceived duality in life. 'I would pipe; dance ye all. Amen.'

Within a unified existence there can be no 'other'. There is no separate evil, there is no Satan or devil to tempt us into a life of self-gratification and debauchery. If there was another powerful entity that was capable of outdoing or outsmarting God, then we could not very well call God the 'Almighty', because he would not then be all mighty. Both science and Jesus have attested to the unified nature of existence and that oneness is the source of both the light and the dark. Denied to most of us is the knowledge that we are one, on both a perceived physical and a fundamental energetic level, but in truth, we are all one in the light.

Leaving the light behind us for a bit, we are now going to delve into the mystical relationship between numbers and their coinciding events and circumstances of life and living. Many dismiss numerology as nonsense, but numbers are the cradle of creation and we cannot get through the day without using them at some point. If our most fundamental reality is built on numbers, then there must be some merit to its postulating. Perhaps where it falters may be not on its existence but rather in its interpretation. There follows my personal interpretation of numbers and their significance in relation to science and spirituality.

Since the number twelve is of such consequence in our scientific theory we will start there. Each of our three states of perceivable reality matter, energy and light, all have twelve components to them and it is possible that the shape of our universe is a twelve-faced dodecahedron. Jesus was a little obsessed with the number twelve and it stands out as one of the most prominent numbers throughout the old and New Testament. In the aforementioned Acts of John, Gnostic gospels, Hymn of the Lord, the number twelve is described as the 'whole on high'. It reads:

'The number Twelve danceth on high. Amen.
The Whole on high hath part in our dancing. Amen'.

It is not difficult to connect the dots here where the number twelve governs this reality and is taking part in all the experiences of life.

In addition to the twelve dancing on high, Jesus had twelve apostles and mentioned the 'twelve legions of angels' at his disposal. Jesus spoke for the first time in the temple with religious leaders at the age of twelve when he and his family had travelled to Jerusalem for Passover. The Old Testament Book of Genesis states there were twelve sons of Jacob and those twelve sons formed the twelve tribes of Israel. In Genesis 6: 3, God even puts the number of years that man should live at 120, when he says man's 'days should be 120 years.' The number twelve can be found a staggering 187 times in the Bible, indicating it is not arbitrarily placed in text. Christianity is not the only religion with an affinity for the number twelve. For the ancient Greeks, the number twelve was considered holy and sacred. There are twelve main gods in Greek mythology. Additionally, Odin had twelve sons in Norse mythology, and there is twelve Imams in the Islam religion. Religiously, the number twelve represents the creation of the universe and the division or fractionating of unity into twelve individual distinct vibrations or tones.

In more practical terms, the number twelve seems to reside over and organise our lives in a very precise manner. There are conventionally considered to be twelve pairs of cranial nerves that emerge directly from the brain. The number twelve also governs our time here. There are twelve months in the year and the twelve-hour clock is a time convention in which the twenty-four hours of the day are divided into two periods where both night and day are composed of twelve hours each. In astrology there are twelve signs in the zodiac.

Moving on and counting backwards, the number eleven appears to hold as much significance to life as the number twelve, but in a different context, namely, in the eleven illusions of life that fool us and give us some of the greatest and the worst experiences in this reality. In Germany, the number eleven is known as the fool's number. The word 'elf' means either eleven or a pixie, and the origin of elf means 'one more than ten,' so it is a clumsy addition to a perfect number. Because of this, eleven is considered the 'fool's number'. This fool's number is celebrated every year in carnival spirit on the eleventh day of the eleventh month, beginning at 11 am. The number eleven, in numerology, has been associated with some fairly momentous occasions, good and bad, in human history.

Apollo 11 was the first manned spacecraft from which astronauts landed on the moon.

On 11 November 1918, the eleventh hour of the eleventh day of the eleventh month, the armistice that ended the fighting in Western Europe during the First World War took effect at 11am Paris time.

Nelson Mandela became the eleventh president of South Africa in 1994.

Israel was accepted as member of the United Nations on 11 May 1949.

On 11 September 2001, the first plane to crash into the World Trade Center complex in Lower Manhattan was American Airlines Flight 11. Both 110-storey towers collapsed.

Ground was broken on the first day of construction for the United States Pentagon building on 11 September 1941. Exactly sixty years later on 11 September 2001, a hijacked American Airlines Flight was crashed into its western side.

On 11 March 2011, there was a major earthquake and tsunami in Japan off the Pacific coast of Tōhoku.

In the Bible, there is a convincing affiliation between number eleven and the illusions of chaos and disorder in life. In Genesis 11, man rebelled against God and built the tower of Babel. They were subsequently punished by God who muddled their language, resulting in absolute mayhem. Jehoiakim, one of the last kings to rule over Judah, was in situ for eleven years, 609 to 598 BC. There were eleven promises mentioned in the Gospel of John, and in the Book of Revelation we are told that the apostle John had a vision of eleven things that were connected with the final judgement.

Whether you believe in numerology or not, the abundance of these events seem to defy chance or coincidence and it is hardly an accident that the eleven illusions of existence are responsible for affording us all of the opposing poles of the physical, emotional and intellectual experiences of our time in this dimension. In line with our illusion theory, a typical human eye will respond to wavelengths from about 380 to 740 nanometres. Both root digits have a sum total of eleven. Just saying.

Continuing down in our numerical regression we have the number ten. The number ten stirs a sense of completeness or singularity in us. In the Bible, Jesus used the number ten often in his parables to denote entirety or the full number of something.

'What man among you with a hundred sheep, on losing one of them, will not leave the ninety-nine behind in the wilderness and go after the lost one until he finds it?' (Luke 15: 4).

'Then the Kingdom of the heavens may be likened to ten virgins who took their lamps and went out to meet the bridegroom.' (Mathew 25: 1).

I imagine that the relevance of number ten is fairly self-explanatory, being the same as one and denoting the fundamental unity of existence. Simple as that.

Moving along we arrive at the very magical number nine. While all numbers can display some interesting mathematical patterns and characteristics, the number nine has a little more ammo in its belt than the others.

To begin with, the sum of all digits including and excluding 9 reduces to 9: 1 + 2 + 3 + 4 + 5 + 6 + 7 + 8 = 36 and 1 + 2 + 3 + 4 + 5 + 6 + 7 + 8 + 9 = 45.

In addition, if any natural number is multiplied by 9, and the digits of the answer are repeatedly added until it is just one digit, the sum will be nine: 6 × 9 = 54 (5 + 4 = 9).

Also, if you take the number nine and add any number to it what you will observe is, the sum of the digits of the number added to 9 is always equal to the sum of the digits of the result. For example, 9 + 146 = 155 where 1 + 4 + 6 = 11, the answer will also equal 11, 1 + 5 + 5 = 11, both root digits equal eleven. So nine plus any digit, or number of digits, will return the same digit. When adding the root digits on both sides of the equals sign, nine is the number that exists but does not exist. Hold that thought, because this is the particular characteristic of number nine that I am most interested in here.

Let us see if we can find that same magic disappearing act in our material world. We are going to count our fundamental particles. Counting fundamental particles is a dodgy business, because there are detectable particles and theoretical particles and some come in more than one type and some names correspond to more than one particle. So the answer will depend on what is included and what is left out. However, I am not interested in counting them all, the only particles I am concerned with here are the ones related to our hard and fast material world, the quarks. The quarks are the most fundamental constituent of perceivable matter and as we can recall from our box of quarks, there are six types of quarks, called, up, charm and top, and down, strange and bottom. These six quarks come in three colours or charges which, as you will see from the chart, gives us eighteen unique quarks. You can probably guess by now where I am going with this. The six quarks of our material experience and their three colours ultimately return our mysterious number nine (3 x 6 = 18, 1 + 8 = 9), the number that exists but does not exist. Where our perceivable world of matter does not really exist but does exist for the observer.

18 quarks

red up quark	red charm quark	red top quark
green up quark	green charm quark	green top quark
blue up quark	blue charm quark	blue top quark
red down quark	red strange quark	red bottom quark
green down quark	green strange quark	green bottom quark
blue down quark	blue strange quark	blue bottom quark

The great inventor Nikola Tesla was obsessed with the numbers three, six and nine, and believed these numbers to somehow hold the key to unlocking the secrets of the universe. This has led many to be convinced that these numbers possess nothing short of supernatural powers that we should be able to access if we could just figure out how to harness their magic. This idea has been further encouraged by intense interest in what is called vortex mathematics. Discovered by a guy named Marco Rodin, it is a process of doubling numbers arranged in a circle from one to nine, which creates a pretty pattern, but where the numbers three, six and nine manage to dodge the entire sequence to infinity. While some believe vortex maths to be the key to understanding all of maths, all of physics, all of metaphysics, all of medicine and everything in between, I think they might be getting a bit ahead of themselves, as frankly no one has been able to apply its supposed powers to anything practical as of yet. That being said, I don't think it is entirely without significance. I believe three, six and nine to be of great importance to the nature of reality, where our three colour charges create the illusion of a 3D, 360°, material world with our six quarks that give rise to eighteen particles, which is the magical number nine of our tangible, yet illusionary existence. The following diagram is just a visual representation of these numbers and how they correspond to the organisation of our reality.

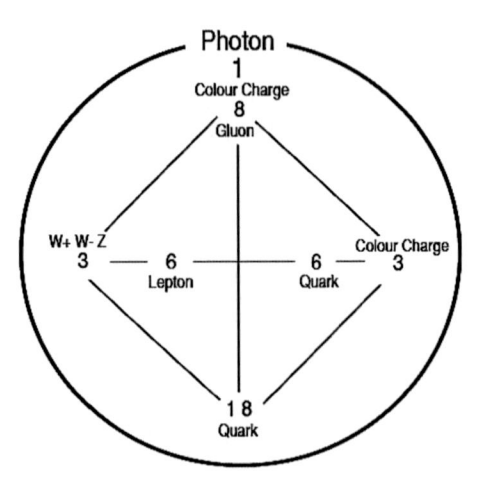

Photon
1
Colour Charge
8
Gluon

W+ W- Z   Colour Charge
3   6 — 6   3
Lepton   Quark

1 8
Quark

And there's more... By dividing 18 by 2 we get 9 and when we add the root digits 1 + 8 we also get 9. The pivotal aspect of our existence is contrast. Our reality is split in two, good and evil, chaos and order, ignorance and wisdom, hot and cold, etc. This dual nature is reflected in the genius of our eighteen fundamental particles of matter where the two poles of our experiences can originate from one, 18 divided in 2 equals 9, and 1 plus 8 equals 9. It looks as though Jeremiah was correct when he called it out, thousands of years ago, in the Old Testament book of lamentations when he said that, 'Evil and good proceed out of the mouth of the host High.'

Not forgetting our two-faced biblical menace in our numbers theory. Satan, too has a magical number: 666, where 6 + 6 + 6 = 18 and 1 + 8 = 9. Here again is our mysterious number nine that exists but doesn't exist. Just like the horned devil himself. There is no devil; again, he only exists in our human ignorance.

Also, in the Old Testament there are nine groups or individuals who are called out for practising sorcery. By all accounts, witchcraft and wizardry is frowned upon and discouraged in the Bible where it is has been interpreted as an abomination to God. I don't believe that God is at all offended by our attempts to do magic or predict the future. I believe that the reason it is condemned by the Bible is simply because it is a fruitless endeavour, as God has the magical illusions of this life all figured out and under control. It is foolish to think we can outdo the greatest magician of them all.

According to Chinese culture, the number nine is strongly associated with the Chinese dragon, a symbol of magic and power.

The dragon consists of nine forms, described in terms of attributes, and it has nine children. The dragon has 117 scales – 81 yang (masculine, heavenly) and 36 yin (feminine, earthly). All three numbers are multiples of 9 ($9 \times 13 = 117$, $9 \times 9 = 81$, $9 \times 4 = 36$), as well as having the same digital root of 9.

The circle is a very significant shape in our universe. Circular objects are to be found at every scale we can scan. From the enormous planets and stars to the microscopic protons and neutrons of the atom. We perceive all that life has to offer on a 360° rotation. At quantum level, electrons emit waves of light in circles. In the Gnostic gospels Acts of John, the Hymn of the Lord is often referred to as the round dance because Jesus instructed the apostles to make a circle and hold each other's hands. Jesus himself stood in the middle and told the apostles to respond with the word, Amen. Two of the lines are as follows:

"To the universe belongs the dancer."

"Amen."

"He who does not dance does not know what happens."

"Amen."

Life as we know it must be lived in the round. Life is a celebration for spirit; it is the round dance of light and dark where nothing happens without the dancer. It is where the act of observation is fundamental to our reality, where nothing exists without the observer. This is what I believe Jesus is referring to in these words.

If our awareness is indeed the colour charges on the electromagnetic spectrum, I expect this is the reason electricity travels in closed circuits, the word 'circuit' coming from the word 'circle'. And of course the root digits of our ubiquitous circle of life provide us with the magic of nine in droves. Not only is $3 + 6 = 9$, but when we bisect a circle the resulting angle always reduces to nine.

Also if we refer back to our dodecahedron, which may be the shape of our illusionary universe, we can see that a dodecahedron has twelve faces, twelve five-sided pentagons that are just bursting with the magic of number nine. Each interior angle of a regular pentagon = 108°, $1 + 8 = 9$. Each exterior angle of a regular pentagon = 72°, $7 + 2 = 9$. The sum of the interior angles of regular pentagon = 540°, $5 + 4 = 9$. The pentagon also has a rotational symmetry of order 5 (through 72°, 144°, 216° and 288°), all root digits add up to nine.

Next, let us take a look at the possible significance of the number eight. Jesus appeared to be partial to a bit of numerology and I have a feeling that he knew a lot more about quantum science than he was letting on.

In the Hymn of the Lord, the number eight is mentioned when Jesus says:

'The number Eight singeth praise with us. Amen'.

By any standards this is a very random statement to make and can't have made a lot of sense at the time. However, with a bit of can't have made a lot of sense at the time. However, with a bit of quantum understanding it doesn't seem so ridiculous. I believe it is a reference to the eight illusions created by the eight colours of the gluon in the weak nuclear force. Outside of the three dimensions of a fundamental physical reality, we experience the eight illusions of emotion, intellect, ageing and the five senses. It is in these eight experiences that God really gets to feel alive. They are what life in this dimension is all about. Whether they are good or bad, right or wrong, it is these eight feelings that God made this reality for.

Identifying a scientific and spiritual correlation for the number seven is a little harder and the best I can come up with is its association to the sense of sight as we perceive the seven colours of the rainbow on the band of visible light on the electromagnetic spectrum. It is the illusion of our form or species, animal, human and plant, that is nothing more than an assortment of colours and shapes in front of our eyes. It is God's artwork and it took him seven days to complete all that we see before us in this universe. Actually, he painted it all in six days and rested on the seventh. It is believed that when Isaac Newton first used a prism to separate light into all the colours of the rainbow that he initially only identified six colours but later added indigo because he was following an age-old pattern of sevens: the seven days of the week, the seven main planets in our solar system. Whether true or not, the week is certainly synonymous with creation and we are told that when he was finished, that God was indeed very pleased with his art. And so he should be, because he, we, did an absolutely outstanding job.

Additionally, in yoga, there are seven main chakras which align the spine and continue to the crown of the head. First mentioned in the ancient, sacred texts of spiritual knowledge, the Vedas, dating from 1500 to 1000 BC, they are described as spinning wheels of energy that correspond to bundles of nerves, major organs and, of course, the colours of the rainbow. Each of these seven main chakras has their own number, name, colour, location and health focus that are believed to affect all aspects of our physical and emotional wellbeing. It would seem that the colours of the light spectrum not only provide the form we take, but also have significance at a much deeper level of awareness.

Next, down the line, we have the number six. As already discussed in association with the number nine, the numbers six, three and nine have a very close relationship. For me, scientifically, the number six represents matter at its most fundamental, the quarks and leptons. Our perception of matter as the nature of reality is our deepest darkest ignorance. Our attachment to a false physical self and material possessions remove us from our true divine and infinite nature. It is the dark side of the light and I have no doubt that it is the reason we have given this darkness the devil's number six repeated three times, 666. Our spiritual ignorance is threefold, physical, emotional and intellectual. Jesus told us that if we walk with him we will not walk in darkness. Jesus rejected all the materialism of life and living because he knew they were nothing but illusions borne out of the blindness and ignorance of existence in this realm.

Next, we have the number five. If you have any interest in new age metaphysical theories, you will be familiar with the concept of the 'fifth dimension'. In short, it is a belief that human consciousness in general is experiencing a shift or awakening to its higher, more enlightened self and that this transition will ultimately be what saves mankind from the slippery slope of self-destruction that it is currently on. Sounds promising. Unfortunately, it seems to be a very slow and gradual process of learning and evolving that has not reached nearly enough individuals as of yet to affect the kind of global transformation that is necessary to halt or reverse the next great mass extinction that we are hurtling towards. But we live in hope. I am not saying there isn't a fifth dimension, I am just saying that its intelligence or its intention might not be the elevation of consciousness or the outcome that we are hoping for. I believe the fifth dimension to be that place of transformed consciousness within. The Kingdom of Heaven inside each of us that Jesus tried to direct us to. A state of enlightenment where we are not confined by the illusions of materialism and chaos that cloud our judgement in this reality. It is a mental state of realisation and understanding that there is nothing but love and perfection in this dimension that we have created. It is that state we seek so often in meditation or in mind altering drugs and it is the reason why they can be so addictive in a difficult existence.

I believe there are four fundamental forces in operation at the core of existence. As gravity is part of the illusion theses forces are, the strong force, the weak force, the electromagnetic force and the Higgs field. These four forces are responsible for providing the backdrop for all of the experiences of our reality. The fifth dimension therefore lies beyond all these illusions but is accessible on a mental level when we alter our state of awareness or just change our perception of life.

Next, we have the number four. This, I believe, represents these four fundamental energy fields or forces at a quantum level. I firmly believe all four forces are one and the same thing. Not because I want to believe it, but because based on theory and high energy lab experiments, electromagnetism, the weak force and the strong force all come together and it becomes impossible to tell them apart. All three forces morph into something else altogether, where particle interaction and the laws of physics become indecipherable.

If this is the case for these three forces, I expect their unifying connection to the Higgs is highly likely, too. Science has tried very hard to find a grand Unified Theory of Everything that provides evidence that these four forces and gravity make up the five fundamental forces that govern our reality. I do not believe this will ever be possible, as gravity is not present at quantum level and gravity is part of the illusions of life, not the reality. There are only four fundamental forces, electromagnetic, strong, weak and Higgs. These four forces are our fundamental divide. Our oneness quartered at its core, but only in appearances. Materialism is not the true state of being, energy is. These four forces, which are really one, are the real reality where our energetic unity is behaving in different ways and pretending to be something different entirely.

On 18 July 2016, Polish physicists from the University of Warsaw, published a paper in *Nature Photonics*, having created the first ever hologram of a single light particle by observing the interference of two intersecting light beams.

Believed to be an important insight into the fundamental quantum nature of light, it is a beautiful image that appears to show light divided into four equal parts.

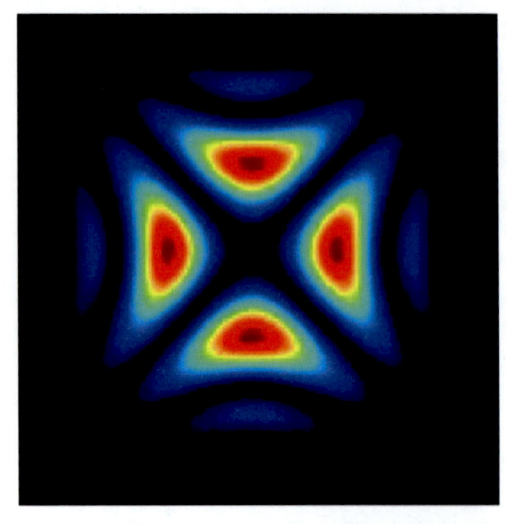

Hologram of a single photon: reconstructed from theoretical predictions.
Source: FUW

It is significant, I believe, that the Photon is divided by four to reflect the four fundamental forces. And of course, our number interpretations would mean nothing without a little religious mysticism, so here goes... Most obviously for me, in the image of the Photon is the cross of darkness in the light. In our reality, where every detail has profound significance, this is why Jesus died by crucifixion. Jesus said he was the light who perished on the darkness of a cross. According to the Book of Revelation, the Bible speaks of the earth having four corners where four winds are held in check by four angels. In the Old Testament, Book of Jeremiah, these four winds are from the four quarters in heaven. Both these books seem to be in agreement on the destructive nature of these forces. Also, in the Book of Revelation, God divides humanity fourfold, people, language, tribe, and nation. Possibly my favourite reference to the number four in the Bible is the division of Jesus' clothes after his death on the cross at Calvary where four Roman soldiers came forth and tore his clothes into four parts, each soldier taking one part. Jesus, the quintessential me, I would say that the number four represents both division and completion. It is the reality of our wholeness masquerading in the divide. However, our true divine oneness cannot ever be separated, nor can it stay hidden forever; science is on its case.

In all of our numbers and calculations there is one number that stands out the most. The root number three. It is clear from our numerology chart of twelve, that three is an important number. We occupy a 3D space with three aspects of time, past, present and future. Conventionally there are three states of matter, solid, liquid and gas. Science is studied within three main disciplines, physics, chemistry and biology. Crucial to our reality, the speed of light is 3×10^8m/s. We view life on a 360° rotation and just as pi is defined as the ratio of the circumference of a circle to its diameter, so the speed of light can be defined as the square root of the ratio of the energy of an object to its mass. In addition, Ohm's Law is one of the most fundamental and important laws governing electrical and electronic circuits. It relates three values, current, voltage and resistance. If our awareness in this reality is the colour charges or electricity of life, then the number three is foundational in the both the construction and experiences of life. The number three is also the square root of our magic number nine.

Pi Day is an annual celebration of the famous mathematical constant, pi. It is observed on 14 March to coincide with the value 3.14. I doubt it was by chance that Einstein was born on 14 March and Stephen Hawking died on 14 March. The number three can be dug out of just about everything to do with our perceivable reality. In similar fashion, the number three appears in the Bible symbolically hundreds of times. Jesus was resurrected after three days, the Ark of the Covenant contained three sacred objects, there were three wise men, and on and on it goes. Biblically, the number three is the number of the mysterious holy trinity, of three in one, the Father, Son and Holy Spirit. Yes, the mysterious holy trinity of three being one that my good Catholic education taught me I must just accept because it was too complex for the inferior human mind to comprehend. Perhaps it is not that complicated after all. If we deduce that the four forces are really one, we can assume this one force is God the Father. Jesus said he was the son of God and that he was also the light. Jesus was God, experiencing himself as awareness created by the colour charges within the light. God, perceiving himself as matter and human, travelling on a very calculated, predetermined path through the light, or the Holy Spirit. All three being one. We are all this same awareness making our way through the light. Just like Jesus, we are all God, divine and perfect, experiencing a journey of limitations and challenges as we are presented with the alterations in the speed of light to create all the illusions of our well mapped out life. Additionally, I believe the holy trinity is very obviously expressed in Einstein's beautiful equation $m = E/c^2$, the father, son and holy spirit all of which are equal and interchangeable.

To round up our numerology theory, the number two must surely be the obvious representation of the double- edged, bipolar experience of life. Male, female, hot, cold, good, bad, right, wrong, love, hate, up, down, left, right, over, under, light, dark, etc, etc. So what of our box of six possibilities as outlined in string theory? These represent all of the other possibilities for the story of our lives that God could have written for us but did not. Out of all the infinite possibilities God chose one story, one deterministic chain of events for every particle of matter in our universe, held together in a three-dimensional perception mediated by three fundamental forces, housed in and arising out of one universal Higgs field, which could be interpreted as a twelve-faced dodecahedron. In the same way as any author will write a book out of all the different possibilities, he/she will choose one story line that connects all the different characters and circumstances and then bind it together as one, narratively and materially. Bound in this block universe or book of consciousness, we are totally removed from the true nature of our being and we will experience our character and our story just as it was written by its author, love. We are God and we are inside the book that we wrote. That is not to say that there is no other possible realities and stories. I imagine there are many more books in God's library, residing in all the different possibilities. Different realities, different universes, different forms, different, stories, available to experience for the adventurous spirit with an eternity to occupy itself. British cosmologist and astrophysicist Martin Rees has suggested that the laws of physics aren't absolute and universal and it is possible that they are localised bylaws that vary from place to place on a vast cosmic stage. It is possible these realities could accommodate many different realities and stories. As Jesus said in John 14: 2, 'My Father's house has many rooms.' For now, though, we are stuck in this room, in this reality, in this story, walled in by our twelve perceptual particles of matter, energy and light.

Our entire life experience is made possible by the divide, both on the surface and at a fundamental level. We are one to infinity, yet divided in every conceivable way. One consciousness divided by space, time, species, race, culture, language, beliefs, abilities, circumstance and journey. The ultimate divide being the difference between what is going on at quantum level and our experience of the world, which is the difference between who we really are and the character we have adopted. With no evidence that we can oscillate between universes, realities or possibilities, whether they exist or not, we are stuck in a deterministic chain of events that is played out in front of our eyes. It is a reality that combines the conventional view of physics where the world exists objectively and independently of how we perceive it and where the act of observation at a quantum level is fundamental to the nature of reality. But our observation and awareness of our world does not create it, only gives us the experience of it and holds us in it. Everything, past, present and future already exists in consciousness, but we are only ever are aware of and experience a single instance in time on our journey from life to death. Even in death, consciousness remains in the very dust we return to as our awareness undergoes the homecoming and restoration of its oneness. But we came here for the divide, it is what we gladly signed up for.

Chapter 11: Conclusion

'Finally I am coming to the conclusion that my highest ambition is to be what I already am.' - Thomas Merton.

In every moment of our lives, we are exactly what we are meant to be. We can be no more or no less than we have been created, crafted by our own divine perfection, wisdom and love. In every moment in the past, we were precisely what we were required to be, doing exactly what we were meant to be doing, at exactly the right time we were supposed to be doing it. And in every moment in the future we will be and do exactly who and what we are intended to because it is impossible not to, in a story that was composed and constructed in advance of our arrival.

God doesn't deal in imperfections; he can't, because it is impossible to make something flawed out of something that is flawless. We cannot be inaccurate or imprecise unless it is a pretence. That is why our story was written in numbers. Numbers don't lie. This means that we are nothing but perfect in every moment of our being, in whatever capacity or place or time. We are perfection personified and we cannot deviate from that. Everything we are and everything we are not, everything we did or did not do is perfection. Every tiny detail of the evolution of our universe from the Big Bang to its eventual end was dreamed up and meticulously organised by the greatest mathematician and magician of all. Us. We are perfect in our illusionary imperfections, our limitations and our ignorance, experiencing the joys and challenges of an individual yet interdependent journey.

In a nutshell, we are immersed in a simulated reality created by the distortion of light where nothing is real except the experience. Matter, space, motion, gravity, time, senses, emotion and thought are all experiences generated by alterations in the light spectrum. All of life is an illusion, a meticulously calculated individual illusionary experience that we are incarcerated in for the duration of our story. We are watching and feeling everything but in control of nothing.

Let's get one thing straight: everything we perceive as real is not. The kaleidoscope of sights and sensations that we intuitively accept as reality at every moment has no more substance than a politician's promise. Actual reality exists beyond the atom, at quantum level, in the energy of everything and nothing, that is who and what we really are. But we are stuck in this alternative existence in a very determined chain of events for a very determined length of time. Access to all of the infinite possibilities and probabilities that is our true nature are totally denied to us by awareness and any notions to the contrary are nothing more than woolly headed, wishful thinking.

In the block universe theory, everything that has ever happened or will happen already exists, fixed and determined by the equations of the universe where our experience of life is a specific location of awareness in this block, one frame at a time. What we consider the 'present' is a collection of experiences and a matter of perspective of where we are located on this static timeline. Moving through the block we gather memories of a past but cannot see what lies ahead. Memories are important because, in order for us to make sense of where we are in the now, we need to know where we have been. Our passage from one moment to the next seems fluid thanks to our sensory limitations and the illusions that accommodate them, but our position in the block and our awareness of where we are and what we are doing do not line up exactly. Our perception is slightly behind our position by at least half a second, but we do not notice the delay so we think we are in control and responsible for our actions and circumstances. The block universe is nothing more than a completely impersonal and objective mathematical object that resides within the electromagnetic spectrum. We are awareness, we are the electricity of life, which follows the numbers precisely, interacting with the light at each location and frame of reference allowing us all of the illusions that facilitate each experience in each instance. However, each instance goes by so fast it is gone the moment we think we are in it. Our lives are quite literally flashing before us in a series of images but, each individual snapshot of life comes with its own infusion of sights, tastes, smells, sounds and feelings (physical and emotional).

As our awareness shifts from one position to the next in the block, we also get the sensation of motion, space, time and gravity. In truth, there is no time and we cannot move up, down or sideways because we are infinitely timeless and we are everywhere all of the time. Change is only an appearance within a block universe. Change, ageing and entropy appear to occur as the collage of colours that creates the image in front of us rearranges itself in each instance of time as we commute from one frame to the next. But as change is impossible for the immutable divine, God cannot change and therefore neither can reality. The illusion of change is simply the different arrangement of atoms at each location on the block. And because beginnings and endings are also impossible for an eternal being, the illusion of birth and death is created as our awareness enters and leaves at a very exact location. But this mathematically precise block universe has existed forever and will continue in consciousness with our individual stories written long before we were born and will remain long after we are gone in the mind and heart of God, or in the Higgs field if you are atheist.

We are not creating the story as we go and nothing has been left to chance. We are an infinite, omnipresent, all-knowing, all-loving force that divided itself up in countless ways to be everything that it is not. We are already infinite creation, so nothing more can come into existence or go out of existence, except the illusion of creating. Within this physical deception we can experience creating as a slow process that requires patience and work, but the work is already done in advance, we just feel as though we are doing it in real time. This in turn affords us the experience of learning and growing.

But God cannot learn something new. In spirit we already know everything there is to know. We are infinite wisdom. Can't get any wiser than that. It must, however, be a bit boring knowing everything. Nothing new to discover and be surprised by. We came from a dimension that has no beginning or ending and where everything is known, so we came here not to learn anything, but only to experience the process of growth and discovery. To experience learning from the very beginning of a life to its timely end. We invented a reality where there is always something new to learn, something new to be amazed by and fall in love with and also something to loose and to grieve for. On a spiritual level we do not have any lessons to learn, nor do we have any evolving to do, there is nothing to create, nothing wrong to make right, and we certainly do not have anything to atone for, there is only the experience of it all.

God is timeless, but the illusion of time pervades and governs all aspects of our lives. This misconception is such that events and encounters appear random, coincidental or deliberately chosen. We are all here, not on our own earthly schedule but on God's cosmic clock, which is infinitely more accurate and administrative than any quartz timepiece. God is always on time, he is never late, early or a no-show and therefore the same follows for all of us. Nothing is accidental, least of all our birth or our death. So no matter how it may appear, our arrival was neither premature nor overdue and we will depart right on schedule. In this life, the natural order of things would indicate that we live happy productive lives where we reach full potential then grow old and die long before our children. Anything short of this is considered improper and untimely and the loss of a loved one at a young age, especially a child, can bring indescribable pain. However, the timing of our entry and our exit is neither by chance nor poorly timed, but instead meticulously calculated for its purpose and precisely orchestrated for its experience.

We have never been delayed in traffic or been diverted from our route. We have never been late for an appointment or been in the wrong place at the wrong time. We have never been too quick or too slow to do something and we have never been ahead or behind anyone else. We have never made and error of judgement, never had a near miss or an unfortunate mishap because just like God and because we are God, we have been right on time, every time.

We have never said the wrong thing or felt the wrong feeling. The whole idea that our thoughts are creating our future or our life's circumstance has no place in the block universe theory, because we are not creating our life, we are experiencing it. Of course it would be wonderful if we could all go about our day with only nice, happy, uplifting, thoughts and intentions, but even with our utmost efforts this is not always doable and is an impossible task for anyone suffering the anguish of mental illness. Such a concept implies that it is wrong or potentially destructive to feel anything other than unbounded bliss and that our emotional state is largely a matter of choice. Try telling someone with depression that it is their own fault and they just need to choose happy thoughts instead. It is barbaric; nobody would choose to be depressed if there were other options available to them. But I think we are slowly learning that it is OK not to be OK. The thing is, we came to this existence precisely to experience other emotional states other than what we really are. Our true spiritual state is that of immeasurable joy and love. We purposely left that state and awareness in order to participate in other conditions of being and all of these different feelings and emotions are an integral part of our life, journey, story and purpose. We are infinite perfection, everything has divine purpose, even our most difficult moments or our darkest times. It is not bad or wrong or limiting to be unhappy. Being unhappy will not thwart or hinder our progress or deny us our destiny. For some, the struggle with deep depression is their journey, it is their story, it is their destiny, it is their service to this magnificent chronicle of life on earth.

One of our greatest dissatisfactions in life stems from the idea that we want something different for our lives. We judge and measure our worth in relation to others' abilities, appearances and acquisitions. Life coaches and life in general love to tell us what we are doing wrong and what we should be doing to get it right. That we need to take control and change our thinking and change our actions in order to change our lives. However, we have no control and we have nothing to change in the block universe story of life and happiness does not always correspond to circumstance, life goals or achievements. Happiness is a fragile thing if we pin it on our successes or our possessions. True contentment lies in the radical self-compassion and acceptance for our essential self just as we are and also for our life as it is, rather than what we think it should be.

All things are orchestrated for a reason and a higher purpose and it is to that higher purpose that our souls are sworn. It is to that plan we will always be faithful regardless of what else we might think we want. In the end, it is consciousness that is the coordinator and driving force of our journey even in this physicality where we are seemingly unaware of it. The plan will unfold exactly as it is supposed to. To fulfil our role in this plan is what we want at the deepest level of our being. There are no 'what ifs', 'could've' or 'would'ves' in this realm. It may often appear that we are not getting what we want or indeed what we deserve in life. We are absolutely getting what we want, but maybe not what we think we want at the time and whether or not we deserve it has nothing at all to do with it. There are so many people deserving of more or better but do not get it despite all their good deeds and happy thoughts. Likewise, there are those who have committed some of the worst crimes imaginable and go on to live long and prosper. The truth is we are getting and providing everything that our soul has wanted in this existence exactly when and how we had planned it.

True contentment is to be found in ultimate surrender to the laws of physics or God where everything about our life and living is exactly what it was designed to be. Acceptance in life does not mean we will be allowed to just do nothing. Acceptance is in the understanding that we are at all times doing what we are supposed to be doing, whether we are an activist or a pacifist, God's will resides in the fight as much as it does in the allowing. We will do and be all that we are meant to.

In his life of absolute submission and dependence upon the father's will, Jesus found perfect peace, freedom and joy. He lost nothing by giving all to God. In the words of Sam Harris, neuroscientist, author and philosopher, 'A puppet is free as long as he loves his strings.' Adopting such an outlook does not always guarantee favourable conditions or outcomes, but it can make for a much smoother ride in life.

Unfortunately for most of us, we did not come here for a smooth ride and we are not all born with the presence of mind that Jesus had. That is a luxury afforded to few and unless we want to forego our modern civilised stresses for a life in the Himalayas with the Buddhist monks, we will be forced through the ups and downs of the emotional roller coaster of existence. A journey that can often seem desperately chaotic and painfully unfair. On the surface, everything about life on earth seems unjust and unbalanced, especially for those born into disability, abuse or poverty. But it is only unfair if we did not choose our life's experience, and since we designed this reality for ourselves, there is nothing unfair about it. We wrote unfairness and misery into the story in order to live it. We were not forced into this reality; we chose to be here. Let's get real: nobody forces God to do something he doesn't want to do. Neither is God unfair, so the only way that this crazy existence makes any sense is that we chose it for ourselves. Granted, it is hard to imagine how we would willingly choose some roles, how we would choose to be a starving or abused child, how we would choose mental or physical illness, grief, loss, injustice, loneliness or torture. But this is not a choice we made from the tainted lens and restricted thinking of human experience. The choice to participate in this reality was made from a whole other perspective, a tireless and unlimited one. Assuming a difficult role is an option that is examined and decided upon from a place of unlimited compassion, understanding, service and curiosity and then, knowing everything that would happen to us in advance and ready to forget, we jumped in, eager to participate, eager to serve, eager to experience. What we go through in life may not always correspond with what we think we want but it will totally comply with our deepest spiritual will and want.

According to the Gnostic description of the Passion of Christ, Jesus is depicted as delighting in his own execution, not as a physical being, obviously, but as a spiritual onlooker. One Gnostic text from Nag Hammadi, the Apocalypse of Peter, reads, 'I saw him apparently being seized by them. And I said, "What am I seeing, O Lord? Is it really you whom they take? And are you holding on to me? And are they hammering the feet and hands of another? Who is this one above the cross, who is glad and laughing?" The Saviour said to me, "He whom you saw being glad and laughing above the cross is the Living Jesus. But he into whose hands and feet they are driving the nails is his fleshly part, which is the substitute."' It would seem, that although the physical presence of Jesus is suffering indescribable torture and pain, the spirit of Jesus is overjoyed at his part and participation in fulfilling the will of his father. Or if you want to read it from a science perspective, Jesus' quantum self was very pleased with how the laws of physics had evolved in time. I imagine it is no different for any of us, our spirits delight in our role and experience, just as Jesus did. In the Acts of John, we are told that during the crucifixion Jesus appeared to John, who was at the time sat in a cave grieving. Jesus explains to John the paradox of the agony and the ecstasy whereby the divine soul transcends the suffering of the mortal being. We are also told, 'Learn how to suffer and you shall be able not to suffer.' While understanding that our mental and physical challenges are part of our journey, I am not sure that such wisdom can reduce the actual pains of life to any great degree but just like Jesus, an appreciation of their divine purpose may give us the grace to endure them.

In quanta and in spirit, we are one. Being one means that no one life is more superior or than another. Being one means that we are all equal and on par with each other, in this dimension and any other. Better or worse is an impossibility for an infinite oneness as there is no 'other' to compete with. The existence of free will in this dimension would mean that some of us are better than others because some of us make better choices than others, some achieve more and are more valuable to society than others. This is not possible in oneness. Being one means that nobody can be better than anyone else no matter what we do or don't do in life. We are all just playing our roles. We often elevate others on a false pedestal of saintly or celebrity status for their life choices and actions. But a hero cannot be a hero without a villain or a cause to conquer. It is the Jesus/Judas paradox. One is dependent on the other. At a spirit level, there is no shame, blame or guilt. God is not ashamed of the story he wrote and we are not to blame for the determined sequence of events that has played out since the beginning of time, so there is nothing to feel guilty about. Neither is God worried about what is going to happen next; he has that all figured out already.

As you have probably guessed by now, I do believe that there is a God, but I also believe in science. In the beginning, science and religion were inseparable and it was difficult to distinguish between the two disciplines. Slowly, a great chasm developed between the two when science became concerned only with the tangible, and the quantifiable while religion refused to relinquish the mysterious and invisible forces that appear to influence our lives. Both became entrenched in their opposing positions and it became harder and harder to find a middle ground. There is irony here for both. Science has uncovered the fundamental oneness of being that Jesus was referring to and religion called it correctly on its teachings about the light.

In early Christianity, the orthodox and Gnostics debated fiercely about whether Jesus was a physical being or a spiritual entity. Actually, both were correct. Jesus was spirit having an imaginary physical experience of flesh and blood. Just as it is for all of us, where we are all one, divine, equal and perfect, living in an illusionary alternative and determined reality where, just like Jesus, our experience of matter is nothing more than an interpretation of the light.

The great divide between orthodox Christian beliefs and the Gnostic interpretations of life mimics the divide between the material and quantum state of existence. The gospels of the Bible serve the surface ideology of the saint and the sinner while the Gnostic gospels relate to the deeper truths of reality. In the birth of Christianity, man did not have the conceptual resources to handle the esoteric depths of the Gnostic gospels and they became obsolete. Now, that they have been dug out of the abyss of time and with our quantum understanding, these profound truths can be appreciated much more. As for the stubborn wedge that sits between science and spirituality, at some point science will have to concede that it is awareness that is causing the collapse of the waveform in the double slit experiment and religion will have to surrender to the oneness of our being and let go of all of the guilt and shame that contradicts it. Many spiritual individuals and disciplines such as Jesus, Buddha, Sri Sankara and Sri Goudpada have declared non-dual truth centuries ago, but we require validation of this truth with science. At least then we can understand that the experience of life, death and the world are mere illusions created out of spirit and that we are here not necessarily to conquer this duality but to experience it.

The core messages that Jesus lived and preached were parity and humility. He recognised the divinity in all and took no credit for his good deeds or apportioned blame or judgement for the misgivings of others. Jesus knew the true identity of each person, each a soulmate, a peer, fulfilling his or her role according to divine intention. Jesus could not have made it to the cross without Judas. By the same token, our good deeds or our outstanding accomplishments do not mean we are better or more evolved than anyone else, nor do our weaknesses or wrong doings make us any worse, only in appearance. The oneness and equality of all that Jesus tried so hard to make us understand is not exclusive to humanity, but runs through all creation, all forms, all beings. Every time you see another species, plant or animal, remind yourself that all you are seeing is colours and shapes, but it is the exact same divine force that runs through us all. Animals and plants contain no less of spirit than any human form. What differentiates one from the other is nothing more than a trick of the light, a totally subjective visual and intellectual perspective, none of which is real. The same divine hand that painted the intricate beauty of every form is equally enchanted by them all.

For those who argue the case that the life and story of Jesus is only the stuff of mere myth and legend, news flash, we are all just mythical creatures existing in the very intelligent and imaginative mind of God. 'They are not of the world, even as I am not of it.' (John 17: 16.) We are God having a dream of being something else, seeing other sights and feeling other feelings. The evolution of the universe is a smorgasbord of experience for a god who has absolutely no evolving to do but, just wanted the individual and overall adventure of it all. An adventure where our divine identities are cleverly hidden beneath the enormous diversity of our earthly and cosmic costumes, but we are all still equal, eternal, connected and acting out of nothing other than pure love.

In the Gospel of Thomas, Jesus warns us that self-discovery and enlightenment will involve inner turmoil when he says, 'Those who seek should not stop seeking until they find. When they find, they will be disturbed. When they are disturbed, they will marvel, and will rule over all.' This statement by Jesus probably describes most accurately my experience of writing this book. As I explored the science behind our reality, I was initially deeply upset that none it was as real I thought it to be, nor did I have the control over my life that I had originally assumed I had. That I am not who I think I am and, most of all, that it is actually God, us, that is responsible for so much suffering in the world. Slowly I began to see the magic, the genius, the reason of it all. From here, I was relieved that I would not be going to hell for stealing a pack of sweets at my local shop when I was eight or indeed any other later transgressions that are nobody's business but my own. I began to see my worth, my place and my purpose and understand completely that my value is no less than anyone else's, human, animal or plant. And from there I found a peace that I had not known before, that, everything is perfect even when it does not appear to be.

It is this inner calm that Jesus is referring to when he says will allow us to 'rule over all'. Not that it makes anyone superior to anyone else, only that it brings the gift of knowing that nothing has ever gone wrong or will go wrong, that all the challenges and hardships that we endure in this life are designed by our own spiritual will. This is the secret that allowed Jesus to transcend the dark and chaotic illusions of the life he was thrust into. This is the kingdom of heaven within.

In the gospels of John, 14:6, there is a quote attributed to Jesus which reads, "I am the way and the truth and the life. No one comes to the Father except through me." This has often been taken to mean that anyone who does not follow Jesus is doomed to never being granted entry into gods holy kingdom in the afterlife. If taken literally, Jesus alienates from god vast amounts of people throughout time who have no knowledge or access to Jesus or his teaching through no fault of their own, meaning that Jesus was a very short sighted, egotistical and uninformed individual that had no business preaching love and unity as prolifically as he did. Jesus was not that person and therefore we must find what he really meant in those words. Jesus knew just how easily words are misunderstood and this is the reason he purposely spoke in parables. Actions are rarely misinterpreted and that is why we must examine Jesus behaviour rather than his words. The two most defining qualities of Jesus was his humility and his acceptance of gods will. Therein lies the secret of the kingdom of god, the internal paradise that is attainable by understanding that we are all equal and one with the father and the acceptance of our circumstances as being the perfect and loving will of god/us even in its most difficult times. This is what Jesus meant when he said these words, that by adopting that same spirit of humility and acceptance that he had we can all know the heavenly peace and joy it brings.

Jesus had no desire to be worshiped or considered superior because he understood the oneness and therefore the equality of all. The truth is that any one of us could have worn the sandals of Jesus and walked his path and perhaps we already have.

In the oneness of our divinity, there is no form spiritually more valuable than another. That would be like saying that a leg is more valuable than an arm. Many indigenous peoples, in particular the Plains Indians of North America, view all elements of creation sacred and consider all life forms, including the earth itself, to be their relatives who must be cherished and protected. The expression to 'walk the red road' means to live a life of equality with all other living things in the understanding that to be human does not mean to be superior. All creation, including the rock, the mountain and the tree, is considered to house a spirit with the same right to life in this world. Life is life, regardless of the robe it wears and the principles by which these indigenous people live are quite possibly the only way we will save ourselves and this illusionary planet of ours.

At a fundamental level, there is no differentiation of life or species, where the form we take, is nothing more than a trick of the light. I can only imagine what it might be like to participate in the story of life on earth from other platforms and perspectives of experience. Such as a tree in a forest, emerging from the darkness of a seed womb, reaching upwards and downwards to behold a whole new world of chemical and mechanical stimuli. Taking that first breath of carbon dioxide and exhaling oxygen to help sustain other life in this beautiful place. Receiving nurture and nutrients from a mother tree, as well as the support and assistance from other species. Extending and expanding in search of food, water, community and companionship. Feeling change and growth as new and exciting possibilities. Enjoying the activity and warmth that is afforded by the sunlight and the rest and the stillness offered by the night. All the time growing stronger and wiser in the fight against the elements and predators. Proudly displaying a splendid floral arrangement in spring and summer and gifting the world with a follow-on harvest of fruit. Maturing to give birth to the new and support other trees, as well as other plant and animal life, with food, shelter and shade. Watching birds busily make their nests and lovingly raise their offspring. Fostering the diversity of insect life that come and go, and who return the favour by organising sex with the neighbour. Sharing in the lives and stories of an entire ecosystem and then taking a well-earned rest in the winter. Yes, I happen to think it would be quite an adventure to live the life of a tree and I also suspect that what I have outlined is but the tip of the iceberg in botanical life, which is much more advanced than we, as yet, understand.

In the words of Hubert Reeves, Canadian-French astrophysicist, 'Man is the most insane species. He worships an invisible God and destroys a visible nature. Unaware that the nature he's destroying is this God he's worshipping.'

This is but one life experience we are having in the here and now. Try to imagine how many possible incarnations, forms and perspectives we could explore in this timeframe and dimension alone. Not counting all those available in the history or the future of this wonderful story of life on a planet called earth. After we leave this dimension, I expect we have the choice whether or not we want to remain in spirit or engage ourselves in another life of drama and experience. That there are many, many other such lives and stories in different realms that we can play in when we wake up from this one. After all, we do have all of infinity to play in and with.

There is very convincing evidence to support the belief in reincarnation, in particular some detailed recollections from children. I imagine there are lots and lots of options for spirit to consider and choose from, including life on other planets that offer a different take on time, space, gravity, form, sensations and intelligence. According to James Green, NASA Director of Planetary Physics, it is highly likely that Mars, being the planet most like earth, previously sustained life: 'Mars was a very different planet, it had an extensive atmosphere, and in fact it had what we believe was a huge ocean, perhaps as large as two thirds the Northern Hemisphere. And that ocean may have been as much as a mile deep. So Mars indeed three billion years ago had extensive water resources. But something happened. Mars suffered a major climate change and lost its surface water.' Dr John Brandenburg, PhD, a plasma physicist, believes that this 'something' that happened, was a nuclear war. From his evaluation of the colour and composition of Martian soil, Dr Brandenburg believes that life on Mars was eradicated by the nuclear fallout after a series of 'mixed-fission explosions'. Not unlike something that could potentially happen on earth. Perhaps Mars was once a fertile and thriving landscape, heaving with intelligent and civilised beings who, like us could not get past their differences and blew each other up.

Space exploration is currently high on the agenda of human endeavour. What began as simple curiosity has gained exponential momentum in recent years as technology and machinery become more sophisticated and capable. Deep space is accessible. Of course, the reality is that there is no deep space, only the experience of it, the very real, very exciting and very seductive experience of it all. Because, for a God that is infinite, there is no 'space', so he created the very clever illusion of the vastness of space and we will explore it with the same dumbass, self-centred, egocentric drive that has all but destroyed the beautiful home that we currently occupy. Exactly as it is supposed to be.

For now, we are here on earth, fulfilling our destiny as surely as the sun rises in the east and sets in the west. We cannot escape it, we cannot change it, we cannot know it. For me, I never would have known that mine would include a crazy horse, Jesus and the laws of physics. In a book that began as a diary of a horse, mysteriously transformed into one about the eleven illusions of life, destiny and the contrasts of the light and dark aspects of our reality. As it happens, I was born in the eleven month, under the
star sign of Sagittarius, half human, half horse, and an annular solar eclipse, like an astrological fate sealed from birth and reflected in the heavenly bodies of the universe. Síon made her way into my life because she had no aptitude for the show jumping career she was supposedly born for and because of the financial circumstances of her breeder. Everything that made her imperfect for that life made her perfect for mine and I am eternally grateful

to this big grey, pain in the ass, pigeon-toed horse that has shared it with me. She was born in a stable just like Jesus and she is no less divine than he. No less divine than any of us or any other life or form in this existence. We dwell in an illusion of form and feeling. The only things that are actually real in this physical adventure are the perspectives and the experiences. Of these there are many and the human vista and role is of no more value or service than any other life form.

As previously discussed, Einstein's Theory of Relativity is based on the principle of perspective, where the perspective of one reference frame is relative to another. Where two observers in relative motion experience the world in different ways, both correct. This framework of relativity that Einstein identified is not exclusive to the world of physics, but is something we experience on many different levels. Everything about our lives is evaluated according to something or someone else. We consider ourselves better or worse compared to someone else. The colour of our skin is light or dark compared to someone else. We have more or fewer possessions relative to someone else. We are more or less successful than others depending on who we measure ourselves against. Our psychological world is every bit as relative as our physical one. However, just as with motion, which is a relative concept with no absolutes, so, too, is our measure of life. Life is neither good nor bad, right nor wrong, more or less, better nor worse. Life is just life with a different individual experience for each of us where truth is subjective and relative to the perspective of the person observing it. In other words, we are all that we are only because there are others who are different from us and each of us is entirely correct within the experience of our own reality.

There is no truth, there is only perception. This book has been, as for any author, a personal journey and is a personal perspective that is a personal truth and a personal prerogative. So in a world where there is no value to determine absolute, objective truth, you will have to decide for yourself whether my interpretation of life in this realm is a truth, or whether I am just as crazy as my horse.

About the Author

Deirdre was born in Limerick, Ireland but grew up in Wexford, the south east of the country. After marrying a Galway man whom she met on a charity cycle in North America, she returned to the west and now has two grown up daughters, a crazy horse, and the rest is history!

Deirdre's passion for health and well-being has been a central theme throughout the course of her life. From nursing to nutrition, for the past twenty-five years, Deirdre has made a point to keep abreast of all things beneficial or detrimental to this topic. In October 2016, she joined the speaker list at the British Society of Anti-Ageing Medicine for their annual conference in London, speaking on the Applications of Redox Biochemistry in health and ageing.

This keen interest has evidently been transferred to her writing, although despite never expecting to become an author, her experience of penning *The Illusion of Everything* was a catalytic one and has led to more ideas and excitement around a new book.